FOURTH EDITION

GATEWAYS TO READABLE BOOKS

An Annotated Graded List of Books in Many Fields
for Adolescents Who Find Reading Difficult

By

RUTH STRANG

Professor of Education and Director of the Reading Development Center
University of Arizona, Tucson

ETHLYNE PHELPS

Director of Reading Program, Normandy Senior High School, St. Louis

DOROTHY WITHROW

Reading Clinic Supervisor, Philadelphia Public Schools

NEW YORK • THE H. W. WILSON COMPANY • 1966

GATEWAYS TO
READABLE BOOKS

PREFACE

GATEWAYS TO READABLE BOOKS is a guide to the selection of reading material of special interest to the adolescent retarded reader.

This bibliography has several notable features:

1. More than one thousand titles are included, to provide for the wide range of interests found among adolescent boys and girls. These references are classified according to subject so that an individual may quickly make connection between his interest and a book which will cater to that interest.

2. As the bibliography is intended primarily for pupils whose reading ability falls below the level expected of them in their high school grade, the estimated grade *level of difficulty* of each book is indicated by the symbol (rd) after each title. Although the majority of books included are of fifth-, sixth-, and seventh-grade *level of difficulty*, more books at fourth-grade level or lower, and yet of interest to adolescents, are now available and are included in this edition. These books can be read without frustration by teen-age boys and girls who, for one reason or another, have never learned to read better than children in the lower elementary school grades.

3. The brief annotations have two purposes: to indicate the nature of the books and to arouse interest in them. The annotations are written simply enough to be read by the pupils as they browse through the bibliography to find books they might like to read.

Because reprints of books go out of print so rapidly, it was decided, except in the case of classics simplified specifically for retarded readers, to list the edition that is most attractive or inexpensive and to mention the original edition. The prices given have been checked. Nevertheless, because of the frequency of price changes, current publishers' catalogs should be consulted before books are ordered.

NOTABLE FEATURES OF THE 1966 EDITION

A large number of recent books and series are included; 75 per cent of the titles are new in this edition. Several new categories have been added.

More characters with whom pupils of different racial and national backgrounds and from disadvantaged homes could identify and more themes in which they might find solutions to some of their problems are included in these more recent books.

Annotations are detailed enough to give clues to interests and motives for reading.

Estimates of reading difficulty are based on averages of formulas and expert opinion.

All the information that might be needed about each book is given, including the price. Although prices change, the price quoted gives a good general idea of the cost of the book.

ACKNOWLEDGMENTS

This bibliography is truly a cooperative enterprise. It has progressed through the steps outlined in the Introduction (see pages 9-21, below) and with the assistance of many persons. The three persons named on the title page assumed responsibility for the final content and form of the bibliography. Christine Gilbert and Margaret Scoggin, two of the authors of the first edition, and others who assisted in the preparation of previous editions, still exert their beneficial influence through the titles retained in the present edition.

The authors also gratefully acknowledge the assistance of Louise Bates, Rights and Permissions Editor, Scholastic Book Services; Opal C. Eagle, Coordinator of Young Adult Services, St. Louis Public Library, and President, 1965, of the Young Adult Services Division of the American Library Association; Ann Hall, Secretary, Reading Development Center, University of Arizona; Margaret Huehner, Supervisor of Elementary Student Teachers, Hunter College, New York; Rosalie B. Klein, volunteer teacher, the Reading Clinic, Philadelphia Public Schools; Dorothy Reinbold, Librarian, Huntingdon Valley Library, Bethayres, Pennsylvania, and her assistant, Catherine Ulrich; and Edna and John Withrow.

R. S.
D. W.

January 1966

CONTENTS

INTRODUCTION

More than twenty years ago a short bibliography for retarded readers of high school age, prepared primarily for Dr. Strang's classes in the improvement of reading, was so favorably received that the need for a more extensive and carefully prepared bibliography of similar nature became evident. In response to this need, the first edition of GATEWAYS TO READABLE BOOKS was published in 1944. Many new books published since then have made a second, a third, and now a fourth, edition desirable and necessary. The proportion of new material in the present edition is shown by the following figures:

	New	Old	Totals
Trade books	645	191	836
Paperbacks	150	0	150
Reading texts, etc.	13	40	53
Books in series	63	30	93
Adapted or simplified editions	1	7	8
Magazines and newspapers	7	37	44
Simplified dictionaries	0	9	9
	879	314	1193

The increase in books published is paralleled by public awareness of the extent of illiteracy in the world today and its personal and social significance. It has been estimated that there are 10 million outright and "functional" illiterates in the United States and 700 million in the world. The illiterate half of the world are hungry and angry. The role of literacy in "promoting individual welfare, social progress, and international understanding" is being clearly recognized. "At no previous period in history has interest in reading been so universal and intense as it is today." [1] Practically every nation is helping children and adults acquire initial reading ability or even greater competence in reaching personal and social goals through reading.

In our country, many of our problems of premature school leaving, delinquency, mental illness, dependency, and unemployment are related to inefficiency in reading. The undereducated youths are often the unemployable. Practically all jobs require ability to read and write. A good basic education is essential today for even minimum

---

[1] William S. Gray, *The Teaching of Reading: An International View* (The Burton Lecture, 1956) Cambridge, Mass., Harvard University Press, 1957, p. 1. See also Irwin Isenberg, *The Drive Against Illiteracy* (*The Reference Shelf*, Vol. 36, No. 5) New York, The H. W. Wilson Company, 1964.

success in any field. Illiterates also find it difficult to protect themselves from malicious propaganda; they are prey for swindlers. Critical reading is needed in an age permeated by propaganda. On a higher intellectual level, reading is important in the understanding of different civilizations, new concepts of energy, and space travel. Sound values, we hope, are built through reading. Literacy also makes possible the enjoyment of newspapers, books, and magazines, and contributes to self-respect and dignity.

A variety of measures are now being taken by governmental and educational agencies to combat illiteracy. Preparation for the teaching of reading is part of Peace Corps and Job Corps training. Recognizing that many young people are unemployed for lack of training and that they cannot get the training they need because of their lack of reading ability, employment and rehabilitation agencies are providing instruction in reading. New York City's Labor Department in a program called "Volunteers for Learning" applied the "each one teach one" principle. It enlisted volunteers to encourage friends or neighbors to join basic adult education classes, go to the library, read books and magazines, and accept help with their educational problems. This program stated that "reading is the key." Welfare directors have organized classes to teach recipients to read and write better.

Educational television is a valuable aid. Memphis, Dallas, New Orleans, Philadelphia, and other cities bring television literacy education to the illiterates in their area. This educating of the parents also has a favorable effect on the children's attitude and interest in school.

These special programs, however, are not a substitute for an effective public school developmental reading program. Such a program extends from preschool into adult life. At every stage of the child's life there are developmental reading tasks to be accomplished. His educational progress depends on his successful accomplishment of each of these tasks year by year.

Suitable reading material at each step of the way makes progress possible. In the junior and senior high schools, and in the seventh and eighth grades of elementary schools, there are many pupils whose reading ability, according to standardized tests, ranges from first to sixth grade—considerably below the average for the grade in which they are placed. A pupil's confusion and sense of failure with respect to reading are increased by the difficulty of the books he is required to read. Some retarded readers are reading as well as can be expected, considering their mental ability; others would improve if they had proper instruction and guidance and suitable reading materials. The latter have adequate mental ability to do the work in their grade, but for one reason or another have not learned to read efficiently. Selection of books from this bibliography would encourage wide reading that would increase fluency, build vocabulary, and contribute to personal development through the content of the books listed.

WHAT MAKES A BOOK EASY TO READ

For all these readers the most generally approved recommendation is to provide easy, interesting reading materials. High-school students' opinions as to what makes a book easy or difficult agree closely with those of librarians, publishers, and teachers. Adolescents say a book is easy to read when it is interesting, "suspenseful," alive with action and adventure, colorful, concrete, and has realistic detail and humor. They like books about science and space travel, about sports and cars, about people of their own age or a little older—such as the popular career books and books about teen-age problems. Increased interest in history and science may have been activated by television. If the book is too slow in getting started, they lose interest. If the book is too fanciful or foreign in its setting, or otherwise too remote from their experience, it is usually not popular with this group of readers.

In reference to style, adolescents mention an easy, simple vocabulary as the first requisite. They prefer conversation to narrative, and narrative to exposition. They dislike long-drawn-out descriptions but welcome sufficient description to make the scenes and characters real. Whatever qualities of style add to the clarity of the text make a book easier to read. Short, simple sentences, naturalness of expression, avoidance of dialect or foreign language, and short paragraphs all seem to give the adolescent a favorable first impression of a book, as do also medium-size print and illustrations having color and action with explanatory captions that supplement the text and clarify its meaning. Retarded readers, having an initial sense of inferiority, usually reject books that appear similar to those used for a much younger age group.

Certain other factors also make a book easy to read. Among these are fast-moving action, a not-too-detailed or complicated plot, a limited number of characters, careful building up to a climax, and short chapters. Relationships within chapters and among chapters should be obvious; the central theme should be clear and always evident, developed in a straightforward, direct way.

These characteristics of suitable books for retarded readers were kept in mind in selecting the titles. The teacher will also find these criteria useful in helping pupils select books from the library resources available to them. He will be alert to indications of interest and ease of reading as pupils read in his class. By noting when the pupils' expressions become animated and eager, when vocabulary difficulties seem to be at a minimum, when pupils are eager to discuss the material and want "another book like it," the teacher will obtain clues to the kinds of books which are most interesting and easily read by his pupils. In general, he will find that books which are short, simple, direct, modern, and concrete will be most likely to meet their immediate needs.

VALUES OF WIDE READING

The recommendation for retarded readers to read much easy, interesting material is sound. In this way they become familiar with the thousand or more words they meet most frequently in any reading they may do. If they read in different fields—sports, animal life and adventure, science fiction, biography, and others—they will get a good start on the vocabularies of special fields. Moreover, being able to read this kind of material fluently helps them to form good habits of eye movement and also builds confidence in their ability to read rapidly and efficiently.

Personal development also takes place through wide reading. The reader meets characters with whom he can identify. He feels with them. He sees how they solve personal and social problems similar to his own. He may get insight into why he behaves as he does and what motives lie beneath the surface of other people's behavior. This understanding may help him work out his own problems and meet his daily life situations with greater courage and acumen.

USE OF THE BIBLIOGRAPHY WITH INDIVIDUALS

A bibliography of this kind is useful not only to classroom and remedial reading teachers, but also to clinic teachers, librarians, and counselors. A list of easy, interesting books can be used by them with individuals and with groups. With individuals it is important to capitalize on their firsthand experiences: part-time work they have done, recreation they enjoy, movies they have attended. This information may be readily obtained by asking pupils what they did from the time they left school one day to the time they came back to school the next day. One girl, for example, mentioned the following activities:

Cooked supper
Looked at the funny pictures in the local paper
Read *True Confessions* story
Watched television, mystery story
Read song sheets
Read second-grade book to little cousin
Went to rollerskating club . . . etc.

In this way and through observation and casual conversation, the teacher may learn about an individual's interests, reading habits, and the amount of free time at his disposal. Still more important is the individual's self-image, the picture of the kind of person he is and wants to be. Books that contribute to his self-development are inherently satisfying. Reading thus becomes not only an expression, but likewise an enhancement, of individuality.

From the list of suggested books the pupil may choose the ones which appeal to him most in the areas of his keenest interest. The bibliography will also help a counselor recommend to individual boys and girls the books that will help them to understand people better and to clarify their personal relationships—for example, stories of family life for adolescents whose families are becoming a problem to them, and "career" books for young people who are trying to find their vocations. One counselor writes, "It has been my experience that, if an adolescent's interest is once aroused, he will seek increasingly difficult books on the subject." For example, a girl might gain an initial interest in nursing by reading a book in which nursing is presented mostly through pictures. She might then go on to other books that tell the story of nursing as a vocation in a narrative way—for example, the Sue Barton stories. Often the girl's interest is sufficiently stimulated by these books to read parts of more technical books on nursing, such as Elting's *First Book of Nurses*. If a student chooses a book, reads it, knows what it is about, and enjoys it, the book can be assumed to be suitable for him. Obviously, some of the books mentioned will be popular with certain individuals but not with others.

The clinic teacher, who works almost entirely with individuals, is concerned with finding material suitable for the most severely retarded readers—those who cannot read beyond the third-grade level of difficulty and who, indeed, must work with preprimer, primer, and first-grade materials despite their normal intelligence. The teacher of these seriously handicapped adolescents will find an annotated list such as this one an invaluable aid in the selection of books to use in clinic instruction.

The librarian can use this bibliography as a guide in buying books. From it he may gain suggestions for books to recommend to the retarded readers who wander aimlessly from shelf to shelf, seeking reading material they can comprehend. He can also use the bibliography to encourage teachers of retarded readers to let pupils select books from the bibliography rather than to require them to read books beyond their level of comprehension. The latter will only convince them that "all 'good' reading is utterly dull and a waste of time." In his contacts with parents, the librarian will find the bibliography useful in suggesting books that will interest individual children in reading or that will be suitable for Christmas or birthday presents.

USE OF THE BIBLIOGRAPHY WITH GROUPS

With groups of pupils the bibliography will be found useful in many ways. For example, one group of ninth-grade students whose average reading grade was 5.2 featured free reading of easy, interesting books as an important part of its program. About 220 books were displayed from which they could choose in accord with their interests and level of reading ability. A simple form of reading record was kept in order to give the pupils a sense of progress as well as to check their comprehension of the books and articles read. Frequently pupils preferred to talk about the books they had read and let the teacher write the record from their oral discussion.

A procedure that has been more formally developed is well known as "individualized reading." The teacher's conferences with individual pupils, held while the rest of the students are reading books of their choice, are invaluable. In these conferences the teacher can help the student with his reading difficulties, encourage him, show him how to appraise and appreciate more deeply the books he has selected, and suggest other books that would broaden his interests and gradually increase his reading efficiency.

One teacher read to the group exciting or humorous bits from selected books to encourage the pupils to finish reading the books in their leisure time. Occasionally some or all of the pupils went to a movie, took a trip, or had some other experience which built a background for certain books. If the book lent itself particularly well to dramatization, the teacher assisted some of the pupils in giving an informal performance for the rest of the class. For example, many of the stories in *Teen-Age Tales* were chosen for dramatized reading by committees, each member reading the part of one character and the best reader taking responsibility for the narrative part. Enough copies of plays or radio scripts, such as those published in *Scholastic* magazines, were also obtained so that selected pupils could read their parts after a small amount of preparation.

In another situation, high-school boys became interested in devising puppet shows based on some of the books and gave performances of their plays to groups of younger children.

If the book is one which the pupils recognize as being read in the lower grades, or if its pictures and format give these older pupils the impression that it is for young children, their first impulse is to reject it. They would feel embarrassed to be seen reading a "baby" book. It would be a threat to their self-esteem and to their self-ideal. For this reason, we should make every effort to find books on their adolescent level of interest but easy enough for them to read independently with enjoyment. However, for the most severely retarded readers, such books, though increasing in number, are still difficult to find.

These readers may be interested in reading some of the less sophisticated books that have other qualities and values for them. The way in which these books are introduced is very important. Retarded readers need to be reassured that large print and picture-book format are not "childish," that many adults enjoy reading books of this kind. Specific instruction in how to read a particular book often makes the difference between acceptance and rejection of it.

Realizing that a new book often has to be introduced to boys and girls, many teachers and librarians use various methods of arousing interest: posting a short list or, better still, the colorful jackets of new books on an attractive and accessible bulletin board; printing titles of selected books and brief annotations written by popular boys and girls in the school or class newspaper under the column "Books We Recommend"; putting recommended books in a prominent position on a special shelf; and distributing to pupils mimeographed sheets giving the title, a short description, and a quotation from one of the exciting scenes of each book. An attractive and comfortable reading room or browsing corner is a general invitation to read. Having a chart with spaces for each pupil's name and the titles of books he has read not only makes the individual more aware of his progress but also may arouse the interest of other pupils in books their classmates have read.

The teacher's first step in using this bibliography would be to select those titles which would be suitable for his class. He would then find out whether the books selected were available in the school and public library. If the library did not have them, he would ask the librarian to order as many of the books as possible, obtaining first the ones most readable and desired by the pupils and those representing all fields of interest. In ways already suggested, he would bring these books to the pupils' attention. He would listen to their comments, read the books himself, and talk about the books he had read. Personal recommendation of a book by a person who knows the individual's interests and needs is particularly effective. Ideally, a committee of pupils would assist the teacher, or even take primary responsibility for all these steps.

Teachers of each subject can turn to GATEWAYS TO READABLE BOOKS to find the books that will help them attack the reading problems in their classes. For example, science teachers might turn to the science section for suggestions of books to bridge the gap between certain pupils' interests and reading ability and the required reading.

The principal or supervisor could discuss this bibliography and its usefulness with his teachers. He would welcome their suggestions as to the best books to purchase and would try to obtain the necessary funds to make enough suitable books and magazines available to all the pupils. He might use this introduction to the bibliography to reinforce a point of view toward reading problems in the high school. Some teachers still tend to put the blame for poor reading in high school entirely on the elementary school, or are not aware that reading is a responsibility of every teacher, not just the English teacher.

Both teachers and librarians may use the reading difficulty (rd) estimates to mark inconspicuously the books in their library or classroom so that books of different levels of difficulty may be quickly located. One librarian, for example, used small circles of various colors to indicate grade level of difficulty.

Because of the individual differences among adolescents, it is impossible to designate a certain book as suitable specifically for junior high school or for senior high school students. However, humor has a strong appeal to junior high school boys and girls. Action has a strong appeal to boys. Certain books about family life, pioneer days, animals, and folk tales are more likely to appeal to junior high school pupils, whereas books on modern romance resembling adult novels appeal to high school girls. Current adventure and science fact and fiction usually are popular with senior high school students. If a book belongs definitely in one or the other group, a statement to that effect is made in the annotation.

Certain books in the bibliography are on subjects of transitory interest, such as Blake's *101 Elephant Jokes,* McGovern's *Summer Daze,* Morrison's *Yours Till Niagara Falls,* and other collections of jokes, cartoons, and riddles. A few of these are included, and the teacher will try to have on hand books of this kind which meet immediate needs and have a high interest value momentarily.

This bibliography will be useful also for retarded readers in the upper elementary school. Many of these children are more sophisticated than those of a generation ago. The books recommended here on low levels of difficulty may appeal to them and increase their self-esteem through the social prestige of reading books recommended for adolescents.

Book lists should be used with flexibility. They offer suggestions, but the teacher must find out what his own pupils *can read, are reading,* and *should read.* The first recommendation of a book to a retarded reader is most important because if the book is too difficult or dull for him, his previous attitude toward reading will be confirmed. On the other hand, if the book is one which meets a real need in his life and is easy enough for him to comprehend and to interpret accurately, he will have an experience with reading which is functional and satisfying, perhaps the first such experience in his life.

CRITERIA USED IN SELECTING BOOKS TO BE INCLUDED

The titles in this bibliography were selected with the idea that a book should be highly interesting to adolescent boys and girls, should keep them reading through the sheer pull of its intrinsic interest, and should give them the feeling that reading is rewarding. Some of the specific interest factors in content are:

1. Stories about teen-agers like themselves with whom they can identify; characters from different socio-economic backgrounds and from other racial and national groups
2. Realistic experiences related to pupils' own lives
3. Suspense
4. Action and adventure; exciting episodes of courage and skill
5. Genuine emotion, giving insight into how people feel when they behave in certain ways and into what motivates them
6. Humor
7. Significance—content that helps young people to understand their world and their life today
8. Information about something they can do or can become
9. Character- and personality-building qualities

Only books below tenth-grade level of difficulty were included, and a special effort was made to find as many books as possible on the lowest levels of difficulty to meet the needs of the large number of retarded readers in our secondary schools today.

Some of the interest factors in style are:

1. A quick, dramatic beginning
2. Much conversation; few long descriptive passages, but sufficient description to make the scene and characters real
3. Logical organization, not complex and confusing
4. Simple, straightforward, clear sentences
5. Few difficult, unfamiliar words—words often explained by the context
6. Style natural and somewhat colloquial, not stilted and artificial
7. Illustrations that clarify the text; pictures, diagrams, maps, and charts inserted close to the text and helping to interpret it
8. Literary merit—unity, coherence, and emphasis; colorful and vigorous style

The physical make-up desired involves:

1. Size—adult in appearance, but short enough to prevent pupils' being discouraged by length
2. Print—deep black, clear letters, easy to read

PROCEDURES USED IN BUILDING THIS BIBLIOGRAPHY

1. Bibliographies compiled for retarded readers of adolescent age were collected and examined for titles that met the criteria of this bibliography. This initial source of references was used on the assumption that these lists represented the judgment of teachers of English, librarians, special teachers of reading, and the pupils themselves regarding suitable books for retarded readers. All these points of view should be taken into consideration. Studies have shown that neither the estimates of different formulas nor the opinions of experts agree among themselves. However, the average of librarians' estimates and the average of readability formulas agree within one grade.[2] Accordingly, the *rd* average obtained from different evaluated sources should be the best estimate available. The recommended lists of books for retarded readers printed at the end of this Introduction represent some of the most recent and useful for this purpose.

2. The composite list obtained from these sources was appraised and supplemented by observation of reluctant, retarded, and limited readers in clinics and in classrooms.

3. Since many of the old favorites are already familiar to teachers and librarians, and since pupils want to read up-to-date material, we made a special effort to find, read, and appraise the new books constantly coming out.

4. From the large number of titles thus obtained, we selected those that best met the criteria for inclusion in this bibliography. The titles were then classified according to interest categories which would be most useful to teachers and pupils.

5. The grade figure given in each reference (rd) represented a composite judgment of *level of difficulty* derived from estimates given by various catalogs and books; from calculation of a reading index representing the structural difficulty of a limited number of titles, according to readability formulas; and from the judgments of experienced persons who worked on the list. This figure does *not* indicate the grade in which the book is to be used, but only the estimated grade level of *reading difficulty*. Books below first grade level of reading ability were indicated as follows: rdPP (pre-primer)—books with a few simple familiar words that could be read by beginners; rdP (primer)—books that could be read by children who had reached the primer stage in the basal reader series. Many books for young people are published in series, such as the Horizon Caravel Books, the Sailor Jack Series, the Deep-Sea

---

[2] George D. Spache, *Good Reading for Poor Readers*, rev. ed. Champaign, Ill., Garrard Publishing Company, 1964, p. 23.

Adventure Series, Signal Books, and First Books. These appear in a separate section, Books in Series, with a general annotation for each series. Individual titles which appear in the series and are also listed and annotated in the main text are marked with an asterisk.

The single figure of grade difficulty should be considered as a central tendency having a possible range of difficulty above and below the level indicated. For example, (rd5) would indicate that a book which is interesting to boys in the tenth grade could be read by pupils in that grade who have approximately a fourth- to sixth-grade level of reading ability.

All the books have some elements that would interest adolescents. The ideal book for the seriously retarded reader of adolescent age is one that has content interesting to him and is not difficult enough to be frustrating.

Any school or library that will buy, display, and promote the reading of carefully selected books from this list of titles of high interest and low difficulty should have little trouble in catching and holding the interest of adolescents who have previously found reading difficult or unrewarding.

Lists of Recommended Books for Retarded Readers

American Library Association. *Aids in Selecting Books for Slow Readers.* Chicago: The Association, 1959.

Eakin, Mary K. *Library Materials for Remedial Reading*, Bibliography No. 3. Cedar Falls, Iowa: Instructional Materials Bulletin, Iowa State Teachers College Library, June 1959.

Hill, Margaret Keyser (compiler). *A Bibliography of Reading Lists for Retarded Readers.* Iowa City: State University of Iowa Extension Bulletin, College of Education Series No. 37, Bulletin No. 681, April 1, 1953.

Kress, Roy A. *A Place to Start: A Graded Bibliography for Children With Reading Difficulties.* Syracuse, New York: Syracuse University Press, 1963.

Mahar, Mary Helen. *A Bibliography of Book Lists for Retarded Readers.* Washington, D.C.: Library Services Branch, Office of Education, United States Department of Health, Education, and Welfare, 1957.

Spache, George D. *Good Reading for Poor Readers* (revised edition). Champaign, Illinois: Garrard Publishing Company, 1964.

SULLIVAN, HELEN BLAIR, and TOLMAN, LORRAINE E. *High Interest— Low Vocabulary Reading Materials.* Reprinted from *Journal of Education,* Vol. 139, No. 2, December 1956. Boston: School of Education, Boston University.

WAKEVAINEN, ALDEN (editor). *Reading for the Reluctant Reader.* Harrisburg: Pennsylvania State Library, September 1963.

ZION, MARY JO. *A Bibliography of Reading Lists for Retarded Readers* (revised). Iowa City: State University of Iowa Extension Bulletin, College of Education Series No. 38, May 1, 1960.

In addition to these special lists for retarded readers, book reviews in the New York *Times Book Review* section and the *Saturday Review* were examined for recent appropriate titles. Also helpful were additional book lists and publications of various associations:

AMERICAN LIBRARY ASSOCIATION. *The Booklist & Subscription Books Bulletin.* Chicago: The Association. Published semimonthly. (See also other publications of the American Library Association.)

BAKER, AUGUSTA. *Books About Negro Life for Children.* New York: New York Public Library, 1961.

BENTZ, DONALD N. "Sports Books, Grade Seven Up," *Junior Libraries,* Vol. 6, November 1959, pp. 11-13.

BOOKS FOR THE TEEN AGE. New York: New York Public Library.

BULLETIN OF THE CENTER FOR CHILDREN'S BOOKS. Chicago: University of Chicago Press. Published monthly by the Graduate Library School.

CANADIAN LIBRARY ASSOCIATION. The Winds of Change. Ottawa: The Association, 1961.

THE CHILDREN'S BOOK COUNCIL, Inc. 50 West 53d Street, New York 10019.

CHILDREN'S CATALOG. 10th edition, 1961, and annual supplements, 1962-1965. New York: H. W. Wilson Company.

THE COMBINED BOOK EXHIBIT. *Book Ways to the World.* 1962, 1963, 1964. Briarcliff Manor, New York: Combined Book Exhibit.

CROSBY, MURIEL (editor). *Reading Ladders for Human Relations* (4th edition). Washington, D.C.: American Council on Education, 1963.

CUMULATIVE BOOK INDEX. 1961-1962 and 1963-1964. New York: H. W. Wilson Company.

DAVIS, E. LOUISE. *Recommended Children's Books of 1960-61.* New York: R. R. Bowker Company.

DeBoer, John J. (editor). *Reading for Living: An Index to Reading Materials for Use in Human Relations Programs in Secondary Schools.* Springfield, Illinois: Superintendent of Public Instruction, Bulletin 18, 1953.

Elementary English and The English Journal. Champaign, Illinois: National Council of Teachers of English. Articles and book reviews.

Haebich, Kathryn A. *Vocations in Biography and Fiction: An Annotated List of Books for Young People.* Chicago: American Library Association, 1962.

The Horn Book Magazine. Boston.

Huck, Charlotte S., and Young, Doris A. *Children's Literature in the Elementary School.* New York: Holt, Rinehart and Winston, 1961.

Huus, Helen. *Children's Books to Enrich the Social Studies.* Washington, D.C.: National Council for the Social Studies, 1961.

Lee, Norman R. *Paperbacks for High School—A Guide for School Bookstores and Classroom Libraries.* Syracuse, New York: Reading Center, Syracuse University, 1962.

Library Journal. *Best Books for Children.* New York: R. R. Bowker Company, 1962.

Logasa, Hannah. *An Index to One-Act Plays.* Boston: Faxon, 1958.

Mersand, Joseph, and others. *Guide to Play Selection.* Champaign, Illinois: National Council of Teachers of English, 1958.

National Council of Teachers of English. *Books for You, Your Reading.* Champaign, Illinois: The Council.

Philadelphia Public Library. Adult and Young Adult Catalog, Children's Catalog. Philadelphia, 1964.

Philadelphia Public Schools. Curriculum Office. Annotated List: Secondary Schools and Adults; Elementary Schools. Philadelphia: The Curriculum Office, 1964.

Publishers' Catalogs

The Reading Teacher. Newark, Delaware: International Reading Association. Articles and book reviews.

Roos, Jean Carolyn. *Patterns in Reading: An Annotated Book List for Young People.* Chicago: American Library Association, 1962.

Saturday Review. New York. Articles and book reviews.

Scholastic Book Services Catalog. New York: Scholastic Magazines, Inc.

SCHOOL LIBRARY JOURNAL. New York: R. R. Bowker Company.

SMILANANICH, HELEN, and PECOT, WILSON (compilers). *Bibliotherapy: Stories With a Purpose*. Bridge Street School, Los Angeles School District, California, 1963 (mimeographed).

STANDARD CATALOG FOR HIGH SCHOOL LIBRARIES. 8th edition, 1962 and annual supplements, 1963-1965. New York: H. W. Wilson Company.

STRANG, RUTH. *Helping Your Child Improve His Reading*. New York: E. P. Dutton and Company, 1962.

WALKER, ELINOR. *Book Bait*. Chicago: American Library Association, 1957.

WILSON LIBRARY BULLETIN. New York: H. W. Wilson Company. Monthly except July and August.

LIST OF READABLE BOOKS

ADVENTURE: Historical

ANDREWS, MARY EVANS. Hostage to Alexander. (rd7) McKay, c1961. 244p. $3.75

A good adventure story of a great fourth-century B.C. man who not only built a vast empire but put into practice his concept of one world, told through the eyes of Damon, a young hostage to Alexander.

ASHLEY, ROBERT P. The Stolen Train: A Story of the Andrews Raiders. (rd6) Scholastic Book Services (Winston, c1953). 160p. Paper, 35c

A little-known episode of the Civil War, when twenty Union soldiers made off with a famous express locomotive and destroyed the southern railway between Atlanta and Chattanooga, lifeline of the Confederate troops. (Winston Adventure Books)

BAKER, BETTY. Killer-of-Death. (rd5) Harper, c1963. 142p. $2.95

A poignant story, told in first person by Killer-of-Death, an Apache boy of the nineteenth century. The young Apache tells of the conflict with the white settlers during the bloody days just before Arizona achieved statehood.

BARTOS-HÖPPNER, B. The Cossacks. (rd7) Walck, c1963. 304p. $4

An adventure story of the sixteenth-century Cossack hero, Yermak, and his daring campaign to wrest Siberia from the Tartars for the glory of Russia. Detailed descriptions of Cossack life and battle scenes.

BAUMANN, HANS. I Marched With Hannibal. (rd7) Walck, c1962. 232p. $3.75

The story of a small boy who became an elephant boy and traveled with Hannibal across the Alps. Vivid descriptions of the marches and battle scenes. Includes maps and a chronological table of the Punic wars.

BERRY, ERICK. Stars in My Pocket. (rd6) Day, c1960. 184p. $3.50

Older readers will enjoy this fictionalized story of Maria Mitchell's experiences as a teacher and librarian on Nantucket Island, where she clashed with the religious Society of Friends over the worldliness of her pursuits.

BEYER, AUDREY WHITE. The Sapphire Pendant. (rd7) Knopf, c1961. 178p. $2.95

A young woman becomes involved in strange intrigue during the Napoleonic War between France and England. This is an exciting adventure with an unusual and vivid background.

The symbol "rd" accompanied by the figure, in parentheses, following the title in each entry, indicates the estimated grade level of reading difficulty (see p. 18-19).

BLACK, IRMA SIMONTON. Castle, Abbey, and Town: How People Lived in the Middle Ages. (rd5) Holiday, c1963. 101p. $3.25

A colorful, realistic story of a nobleman back from the Crusades, of a serf who goes to a walled town to learn a trade and earn his freedom, and of a copyist in a monastery. Through their lives the reader sees the typical people and scenes of feudal times. Many fine illustrations make the stories more vivid.

BRICK, JOHN. Yankees on the Run. (rd6) Meredith, c1961. 149p. $2.95

A good Civil War story. Matt and Eben from Vermont are captured and imprisoned at Andersonville but escape to Sherman's headquarters by posing as smallpox victims. The behavior and attitude of the average soldier is described realistically.

BULLA, CLYDE ROBERT. The Sword in the Tree. (rd3) Crowell, c1956. 113p. $3.50

A story of the days of King Arthur, this is the adventure of young Shan who fights to regain his father's castle. Similar in style and difficulty are *Down the Mississippi* (c1954) and *White Sails to China* (c1955).

BURCHARD, PETER. North by Night. (rd7) Coward, c1962. 192p. $3.50

A good Civil War adventure story in which two Union soldiers are captured and imprisoned. In effecting an escape they have a hazardous trek through the Carolinas before meeting a Yankee regiment. The book is filled with feeling for both the North and the South.

BURTON, HESTER. Castors Away. (rd6) World, c1963. 254p. $3

In 1805, just before Lord Nelson's victory at Trafalgar, a Suffolk doctor and three children revive a nearly drowned sailor. Later, one of the boys fights in the great naval battle along with the same sailor. All of the young people have their ideas of war and of humanity shaped by the way their sailor is treated.

CAVANNA, BETTY. A Touch of Magic. (rd7) Westminster, c1961. 189p. $2.95

A Quaker girl in occupied Philadelphia during the Revolutionary War notes the gay lives the Shippen girls lead in contrast to the suffering American army at Valley Forge. A Revolutionary War romance.

DALGLIESH, ALICE. Adam and the Golden Cock. (rd4) Scribner, c1959. 164p. $2.75

War often brings conflict in friendship and loyalties. Adam dreams about the weather vane on the church steeple and seeks advice about his friend whose father is a Tory in the days of the American Revolution.

The symbol "rd" accompanied by the figure, in parentheses, following the title in each entry, indicates the estimated grade level of reading difficulty (see p. 18-19).

DE LEEUW, CATEAU. Determined to Be Free. (rd5) Nelson, c1963.
176p. $2.95
An exciting story of a young man who helps the patriot cause in the
American Revolutionary War by taking part in the capture of the British
fort at Stony Point on the Hudson.

ELSTON, ALLAN VAUGHAN. Sagebrush Serenade. (rd7) Lippincott,
c1960. 224p. $2.95
A New York tenderfoot goes to Wyoming in 1887 with a plot for wrong-
doing in mind, but he changes his mind and fights for law and order
instead.

FORBES, ESTHER. Johnny Tremain. (rd7) Houghton, c1943. 256p.
$3.50. (Textbook ed., $2.36; paper, $1.32)
A young silversmith apprentice becomes a messenger for the Boston citizens
who planned the famous Tea Party in the exciting days before the
Revolution.

FRANKLIN, GEORGE CORY. Indian Uprising. (rd5) Houghton, c1962.
117p. $2.75
This story of Indians who rebelled against the domination of white men is
an exciting adventure of special interest to older boys.

FRAZEE, STEVE. Year of the Big Snow; John Charles Frémont's
Fourth Expedition. (rd6) Holt, c1962. 180p. $3.50
In 1848 Ted McNabb, a fourteen-year-old boy, travels by mule with
Colonel Frémont along the 38th parallel to find a railroad route across the
Rockies. Vivid descriptions of the bitter cold and the encounters with
Indians and buffaloes. (Winston Adventure Books)

GIBBS, ALONZO. The Fields Breathe Sweet. (rd6) Lothrop, c1963.
184p. $3
A pioneer story of the Harmensens, a late seventeenth-century family of
Dutch homesteaders on the Hempstead plains of Long Island. Young Gretje
is torn between her desire to marry and her loyalty to her hard-pressed family.

GRAY, ELIZABETH JANET. Adam of the Road. (rd4) Viking, c1950.
317p. $4
The adventures of a young minstrel boy in the days of Old England.

GRAY, ERNEST A. The Dog That Marched to Moscow. (rd7) Barnes,
c1960. 222p. $2.75
A story of Napoleon's ill-fated invasion of Russia, as seen by a young French
surgeon attached to the 47th Regiment. Includes the story of a French poodle,
mascot of the regiment.

HAIG-BROWN, R. L. The Whale People. (rd7) Morrow, c1963. 256p.
$3.25
A young boy in pre-Columbian times is trained as the tribe's chief hunter of
whales in order to take his father's place.

HORN, MADELINE DAGGETT. The New Home. (rd4) Scribner, c1962. 128p. $2.95
Life on the prairie holds surprise and danger for the seven Barrows when they move to Illinois. Even young Andrew, called Runt by his big brother, gets a chance to prove he can do a man's job in this story of pioneer days.

HUNT, IRENE. Across Five Aprils. (rd6) Follett, c1964. 223p. $3.95
An unforgettable story of the Civil War, seen through the eyes of a young boy, Jethro Creighton, who gave up childish play to do a man's work at the age of ten, when the men went off to fight. The book traces the child's struggle to understand and reconcile the sadness of the era, the horror of war itself, and the sorrow of pitting brother against brother.

HURLEY, WILLIAM J. Dan Frontier. (rdPP) Benefic, c1959. 48p. $1.80
_____Dan Frontier Goes Hunting. (rdP) Benefic, c1959. 64p. $1.96
_____Dan Frontier and the Wagon Train. (rd2) Benefic, c1959. 128p. $2.32
_____Dan Frontier Goes to Congress. (rd4) Benefic, c1964. 160p. $2.40
The exciting adventures of a young pioneer man who faces frontier life with courage. (Dan Frontier Series)

KIRTLAND, G. B. One Day in Aztec Mexico. (rd6) Harcourt, c1963. 40p. $2.50
The story of a single day in the life of a family who lived in Aztec times in Mexico. The interesting style of writing and the information about details of living will appeal to older readers.

KRASILOVSKY, PHYLLIS. Benny's Flag. (rd3) World, c1960. 40p. $2.50
An Indian boy's love of his homeland inspires him to design the flag that becomes the official flag of Alaska. This true story shows the people and industry of the northernmost state.

LEVY, MIMI COOPER. Whaleboat Warriors. (rd6) Viking, c1963. 189p. $3.50
A story of patriot resistance during the American Revolution. Fourteen-year-old Robbie Tyler helps the whaleboat men of besieged Long Island to reach colonist-held Connecticut by courageously carrying messages for them.

McGIFFIN, LEE. Ten Tall Texans. (rd6) Lothrop, c1956. 220p. $3
Tales of the first Texas Rangers who fought to protect their homes, their families, and the land they loved. To those who needed their help and protection, all Texas Rangers looked "mighty tall in the saddle."

McSWIGAN, MARIE. Snow Treasure. (rd5) Dutton, c1942. 179p. $3.50
(Paper, Scholastic Book Services, 50c)
The inspiring and exciting story, based on fact, about a brave group of children who helped the Underground smuggle out Norway's gold supply under the noses of the Nazis.

The symbol "rd" accompanied by the figure, in parentheses, following the title in each entry, indicates the estimated grade level of reading difficulty (see p. 18-19).

MEADER, STEPHEN WARREN. Phantom of the Blockade. (rd6) Harcourt, c1962. 190p. $3.25

The story of Anse O'Neal, who joined the crew of a Confederate blockade runner in the last year of the Civil War. Danger and excitement fill the book as Anse participates in catching a spy, is wounded in a battle, and engineers the delivery of ammunition to General Lee.

MICHENER, JAMES. The Bridges at Toko-Ri. (rd7) Random, c1953. 146p. $2.95 (Paper, Bantam, 40c)

The story of a brave jet pilot in Korea who wonders why he is one of the few who must put his life in danger. A short exciting story that is realistic and gripping.

O'DELL, SCOTT. Island of the Blue Dolphins. (rd5) Houghton, c1960. 184p. $2.75

A well-written account of the twenty years an Indian girl spent alone on the Island of San Nicolás off the coast of California. A romantic and historical tale of adventure.

O'SULLIVAN, MAURICE. Twenty Years A-Growing. (rd8) Viking, c1963 (rev. ed.). 298p. $4

This is a reissue of an unusual first-person account that has become a modern classic, telling of neolithic life in the Blasket Islands of Ireland.

PICARD, BARBARA LEONIE. Lost John: A Young Outlaw in the Forest of Arden. (rd8) Criterion, c1963. 224p. $3.50

This adventure story takes place in England during the reign of Richard Coeur de Lion. His legacy usurped by his stepfather, fifteen-year-old John Fitzwilliams runs away from home, is waylaid in the Forest of Arden, and joins a band of outlaws led by the colorful Rolf the Red.

RICHTER, CONRAD. The Light in the Forest. (rd7) Knopf, c1953. 179p. $3.50 (Paper, Bantam, 35c)

A white boy, reared by an Indian chief, is forced to return to his original home. His love for and loyalty to his Indian parents and his rejection of the white man's civilization arouse inevitable conflicts.

RIDLE, JULIA BROWN. Mohawk Gamble. (rd6) Harper, c1963. 209p. $3.50

The fictionalized story of the adventures of a young explorer and fur trader who was kept a prisoner by the Iroquois Indians. This fascinating true adventure tells of his captivity, attempted escape, and recapture.

RIGGS, SIDNEY N. Arrows and Snakeskin. (rd6) Lippincott, c1962. 160p. $3.25

The exciting adventures of an English boy who is captured by the Pequot Indians in Connecticut in 1637 and grows up with them.

SANDOZ, MARI. The Story Catcher. (rd5) Westminster, c1963. 175p. $3.25

Young Lance of the Oglala Sioux undergoes many winters of hardship, adventure, and sorrow before the village of Sun Shield recognizes him as Story Catcher and band historian. Depicts the life of the Plains Indians as they cling to the old ways on the tragic eve of their end.

SEYMOUR, ALTA. When the Dikes Broke. (rd5) Follett, c1958. 144p. $2.95 (Paper, Scholastic Book Services, 35c)
When, in 1953, Holland suffered the worst floods in five hundred years, a Dutch family had struggles and adventures that make a story of suspense.

SPEARE, ELIZABETH GEORGE. The Bronze Bow. (rd7) Houghton, c1961. 255p. $3.25
The story, set in Palestine during the time of the Roman Empire, is an account of Daniel Bar Jamin's journey from a blind hatred to his acceptance and understanding of love.

UNDERHILL, RUTH M. Antelope Singer. (rd5) Coward, c1961. 280p. $3.50
The story of a Connecticut family's adventures and relations with the Indians as they travel by covered wagon through Nevada to California at the time of the California Gold Rush.

WEBB, ROBERT N. We Were There on the Nautilus. (rd5) Grosset, c1961. 178p. $1.95
Realistic story, told in journalistic fashion, as an eyewitness account of the first atomic-powered submarine. An exciting and dramatic adventure. Similar stories may be found in other titles under We-Were-There Books in the Books in Series section.

WERSTEIN, IRVING. Jack Wade, Fighter for Liberty. (rd4) Doubleday, c1963. 143p. $2.50
Young Jack Wade joins a band of guerrilla rebels and proves his usefulness as a spy in this action-packed Revolutionary War story. (Signal Book Series)

ADVENTURE: Personal

CLARKE, TOM E. The Big Road. (rd6) Lothrop, c1963. 192p. $3
At odds with his stepfather, turned down by the Navy, jobless, and his money gone, Vic jumps on a freight train and becomes a hobo for several months. Based on the author's own experience during the depression of the 1930's.

DOSS, HELEN. The Family Nobody Wanted. (rd7) Little, c1954. 267p. $4.50
The true and heart-warming story of the woman who adopted twelve children of various nationalities, making a "one-family United Nations."

FLOHERTY, JOHN J., and MCGRADY, MIKE. Skin-Diving Adventures. (rd7) Lippincott, c1962. 192p. $3.50
Men and women who go under the sea tell of their adventures as they dive, some for the sport of it and some for the study of the ocean depths.

The symbol "rd" accompanied by the figure, in parentheses, following the title in each entry, indicates the estimated grade level of reading difficulty (see p. 18-19).

HEYERDAHL, THOR. Kon-Tiki. (rd7) Rand McNally, c1950. 304p. $5.95
(Paper, Permabook, 35c; Pocket, 50c)
Six young scientists travel 4000 miles across the Pacific on a raft in order to
prove a theory. In this book you can share their great experience on the high
seas.

KERN, JANET. Yesterday's Child. (rd7) Lippincott, c1962. 239p. $4.95
The amusing story of the daughter of a famous city doctor. She grows up
during the war years and manages to have a normal, well-adjusted childhood
in spite of the unsettling times.

MARSHALL, HOWARD. Men Against Everest. (rd7) Transatlantic,
c1954. 64p. $2.50
A gripping and exciting account of Mt. Everest, the world's highest and most
famous mountain, in the far-off Himalayas. For thirty years men tried to reach
its top, but none succeeded and many died before its ultimate, thrilling conquest by an Englishman in 1953.

PLATT, RUTHERFORD. Adventures in the Wilderness. (rd5) Harper,
c1963. 153p. $3.95
These vivid accounts were made by early white explorers of the North American continent when it was a wilderness. (American Heritage Junior Library
Series)

SCOGGIN, MARGARET C., ed. The Lure of Danger. (rd7) Knopf, c1947.
374p. $3
True adventure stories of men who challenged danger because it was part of
their jobs—and lived to tell of their experiences. Each chapter is taken from a
book to which it may serve as an introduction.

SELSAM, MILLICENT E., ed. Stars, Mosquitoes and Crocodiles: The
American Travels of Alexander von Humboldt. (rd7) Harper,
c1962. 170p. $3.50
A selection of excerpts from Alexander von Humboldt's American travel
journals, showing the maps he made, the plants he collected, the ocean cur-
rents he plotted, and the South American Indians he studied.

STEELE, WILLIAM OWEN. Westward Adventure: The True Stories of
Six Pioneers. (rd6) Harcourt, c1962. 188p. $3.25
The author tells of five very different men and one woman who moved westward from the Atlantic coast toward a broad new land. The adventurous and
hazardous aspects of the six stories are dramatically presented.

WESTBROOK, ROBERT. Journey Behind the Iron Curtain. (rd7) Putnam, c1963. 160p. $3.50
The author, a teen-age American boy, reports on his journey to Russia and her
satellites, Poland and Czechoslovakia, with a group of his classmates from
Putney School in Vermont.

ADVENTURE: Stories

AGLE, NAN HAYDEN, and WILSON, ELLEN. Three Boys and Space. (rd4) Scribner, c1962. 159p. $2.75

The triplets see the seven astronauts on television and decide to enter the school contest on space. They involve the whole town in their research on satellites and model rockets. Shepard's flight in the Freedom VII is also an exciting part of this amusing story.

AMERMAN, LOCKHART. Guns in the Heather. (rd7) Harcourt, c1963. 191p. $3.25

High adventure comes to a young American in this tale of espionage set in the Scottish Highlands. It is filled with humor and excitement, danger and courage, all of which make for a fast-moving story.

ANDREWS, ROY CHAPMAN. Quest in the Desert. (rd9) Viking, c1950. 192p. $3

Jack Benton goes to the Gobi Desert to hunt for dinosaur bones and traces of ancient man. His hair-raising experiences include incredible weather and danger from bandit attacks, poisonous snakes, and animal stampedes. His relation with his dog gives the book special appeal.

ANNIXTER, JANE and PAUL. Windigo. (rd5) Holiday, c1963. 196p. $2.95

Was it an evil spirit that robbed Andy's traps and scared his dog, as the Indians said? Was it an animal, a man, or a demon? Andy and his loyal dog conquer their fear in this outdoor mystery adventure.

ARNOLD, OREN. White Danger. (rd5) Holiday, c1962. 192p. $2.95

Modern science goes into the mountain wilderness and snow surveyors meet adventure in the high Rockies.

BALL, ZACHARY. North to Abilene. (rd5) Holiday, c1960. 190p. $2.95

A boy grows to manhood on a cattle ranch in the early days of Texas. Adventure comes on the long trail drive to a Kansas railhead.

BAMMAN, HENRY A. and WHITEHEAD, ROBERT. Lost Uranium Mine. (rd2) Benefic, c1964. 72p. $2

Two young men help an old prospector hunt for a lost uranium mine in the Rocky Mountains and have many exciting adventures. (World of Adventure Series)

BONHAM, FRANK. Deepwater Challenge. (rd7) Crowell, c1963. 192p. $3.50

A story of adventure in which Cam Walker, determined to earn money for his family, invests in a fishing boat and dives for abalone off the coast of Southern California. Some of Cam's adventures are dangerous and some are financially discouraging.

The symbol "rd" accompanied by the figure, in parentheses, following the title in each entry, indicates the estimated grade level of reading difficulty (see p. 18-19).

CASSIDAY, BRUCE. Blast Off! (rd4) Doubleday, c1964. 142p. $2.95

An interesting account of the rocketry adventures of three high-school boys. The book emphasizes the need for cooperation and consideration of the team. (Signal Books)

CHENEY, CORA, and PARTRIDGE, BEN. Rendezvous in Singapore. (rd5) Knopf, c1961. 111p. $2.79

A fast-moving adventure story. Link is traveling alone to meet his father in Singapore for a tiger hunt when he is unknowingly made part of a jewel theft. He has to think fast to get away from danger.

CRARY, MARGARET. Pocketful of Raisins. (rd7) McKay, c1964. 156p. $3.50

When Holly's friend Curt has his driver's license suspended, their high-school's natural history field trip to Yellowstone seems a good way for both to spend their time. With blistered and aching feet, Holly almost gives up, but the campfire companionship and the country's beauty give her new slants on life and love.

EISNER, LEONARD. Buried Gold. (rd2) Penns Valley, c1961. 58p. $2 (also published by Follett, $1.56)

Thrilling adventures of two teen-agers who find a lost fortune on a lonely island off the coast of New England. (Interesting Reading Series)

EVARTS, HAL G. The Secret of the Himalayas. (rd6) Scribner, c1962. 185p. $2.95

A team of American scientists is sent to Nepal to bring back the "abominable snowman." An unknown enemy tries to sabotage the expedition, adding suspense and tension to the search for the yeti.

FRANKEL, HASKEL. Adventure in Alaska. (rd4) Doubleday, c1963. 142p. $2.50

An exciting story with a setting of lonely mountains and valleys, great new roads, and forgotten mines in the wilds of Alaska. (Signal Books)

GUILLOT, RENÉ. Fofana. (rd7) Criterion, c1962. 145p. $3

A French schoolboy, Jean Luc, goes to live with his father in the African bush country. A young leader of the tribe and master of the elephants, a native boy, Fofana, becomes his close friend. Fofana is a boy of courage and dignity and teaches Jean about the forests, animals, and people of the Lobi tribe.

HALL, AYLMER. The Search for Lancelot's Sword. (rd6) Criterion, c1962. 160p. $3.50

Three youngsters, Hugh, Gwynn, and Mark, set out in search of the legendary sword of Sir Lancelot, reputedly buried somewhere on the grounds of the Welsh castle where they live.

JOHNSON, ANNABEL and EDGAR. Pickpocket Run. (rd8) Harper, c1961. 185p. $3.50

Seventeen-year-old Dix, unhappy at home and on the verge of delinquent behavior, finds over a holiday weekend that he has principles and that he has shown courage in upholding them. Good characterization and suspenseful action.

JOHNSON, JAMES RALPH. Wild Venture. (rd6) Follett, c1961. 176p. $3.15

Two Alabama teen-age boys spend a week in the woods with only a knife and a flint. They learn much from their experiences and from the "Possum Man."

McNAMES, JAMES. My Uncle Joe. (rd6) Viking, c1963. 63p. $2.95

A very short, interestingly written adventure story of the Northwest. The fun and trouble that the two main characters have are more important to the story than the true historical background.

MacPHERSON, MARGARET L. The Shinty Boys. (rd6) Harcourt, c1963. 224p. $3.25

A group of boys on the Isle of Skye try to earn money for equipment to play the game of shinty (a game like hockey). The events of one summer are described by Neil in an easy use of first-person narration.

MOLLOY, ANNE STEARNS. Secret of the Old Salem Desk. (rd4) Farrar, c1955. 243p. $2.95

A Maine boy, who wants to be an artist, has some mysterious and exciting times when he gets mixed up with antique thieves.

MOWAT, FARLEY. Lost in the Barrens. (rd7) Little, c1956. 244p. $3

Jamie Macnair and his Cree friend become separated from their hunting party in the wilds of northern Canada. They face a hard winter alone, and in their fight for survival learn to go along with nature. This is an engrossing adventure tale.

OBERREICH, ROBERT. The Blood Red Belt. (rd4) Doubleday, c1961. 143p. $2.95

Peter Casson, son of the manager of a fur trapping company, and an Iroquois Indian boy outwit two dangerous spies. (Signal Books)

PEASE, HOWARD. The Dark Adventure. (rd8) Doubleday, c1950. 229p. $2.95

A sobering account of what happened to Johnny Stevens, an amnesia victim, and Tony Berelly, a runaway, when they became involved in "hot rod" driving, dope peddling, and other demoralizing experiences from which they finally escaped.

PERSON, TOM. The Rebellion of Ran Chatham. (rd7) McKay, c1957. 185p. $2.75

The adventures of a sixteen-year-old who decides to run away and live in the woods of the Big Swamp rather than go to high school, which he thinks is a silly waste of time. Then he finds the life he has chosen is not very realistic though the snakes and animals, mosquitoes and unpleasant characters, and the terrible swamp heat are very real. He leaves the swamp with changed plans before school opens.

The symbol "rd" accompanied by the figure, in parentheses, following the title in each entry, indicates the estimated grade level of reading difficulty (see p. 18-19).

PEYTON, K. M. and MICHAEL. Sea Fever. (rd6) World, c1963. 240p. $3.50

A fifteen-year-old English boy has many exciting adventures when he tries to earn money to buy a fishing boat.

RADAU, HANNS. Illampu. (rd6) Abelard, c1962. 160p. $3

An Indian boy undertakes a long dangerous journey into the Bolivian Andes Mountains in search of his white llama, Illampu. A good adventure story in which Juan learns about the customs of the old Inca Indians who still cling to their ancient culture.

REESE, JOHN HENRY. Three Wild Ones. (rd7) Westminster, c1963. 188p. $3.25

Art Byfield, a troubled teen-ager who runs away from home after a family argument, becomes involved with an ex-convict turned horse trainer and other rough characters. "Sense rather than sentiment" in the matter of delinquency is stressed in Art's struggle for manhood.

SEE, INGRAM. The Jungle Secret. (rd4) Doubleday, c1961. 141p. $2.95

A young man faces danger in the jungles of Brazil when he tries to discover the secret that is ruining his father's rubber business there. (Signal Books)

SOUTHALL, IVAN. Hills End. (rd5) St. Martin's, c1963. 174p. $3.75

A fast-paced story of the adventures that befall a group of school children who are isolated by a flood in Australia.

SYKES, JO. Trouble Creek. (rd6) Holt, c1963. 217p. $3.50

When sixteen-year-old Ten Holland and his resented stepfather are hired to search for Alvin Brighton, mysterious events occur in this Western adventure story.

VINTON, IRIS. Look Out for Pirates! (rd2) Random, c1961. 63p. $1.95

The exciting, fast-moving story of how pirates were defeated by some good men. (Beginner Books)

WALDEN, AMELIA ELIZABETH. To Catch a Spy. (rd8) Westminster, c1964. 224p. $3.50

An obscure clerk in the CIA, Sally Templeton, bears a strong resemblance to Erika Buxton, suspected of anti-American espionage and now dead in a plane crash. Sally is chosen to impersonate her in order to help the United States counterintelligence, which results in a swift-moving story with romance, danger, and suspense.

WHITE, ROBB. The Lion's Paw. (rd5) Doubleday, c1946. 243p. $3.50 (Paper, Scholastic Book Services, 25c)

An adventure story about two orphans who make a sea escape and wind up finding their father. The suspense mounts as the search quickens for the mysterious Lion's Paw in Florida's forbidding Everglades.

WIER, ESTER. The Loner. (rd7) McKay, c1963. 153p. $3.75

An orphaned and nameless young migrant worker finds both a job and friends on a sheep ranch in Montana, where he strives to live up to the image of two ideals in his search for identity.

WILSON, HOLLY. Snowbound in Hidden Valley. (rd5) Messner,
c1957. 192p. $2.95 (Paper, Scholastic Book Services, 35c)
Two girls in a small Michigan town are friends, though one is a Chippewa Indian. When a mysterious fire breaks out, racial feelings run high until understanding of their Indian neighbors is achieved by the townspeople.

ANIMAL LIFE AND ADVENTURE: Birds and Fish

BOULTON, RUDYARD. Traveling With the Birds. (rd4) Donohue, c1933.
64p. $3.50
One of the best books explaining the whys and wherefores of bird migration,
written by a scientist connected with the Field Museum of Natural History.

McCLUNG, ROBERT M. Leaper: The Story of an Atlantic Salmon.
(rd4) Morrow, c1957. 61p. $2.75
One of nature's most dramatic stories, the life cycle of a salmon, in words and
pictures. Born in fresh water, the salmon, after two years, goes downstream to
the ocean and, after three years, returns to his birthplace. See also *Ruby
Throat: The Story of a Hummingbird* (rd5) Morrow, c1950. 46p. $2

MORGAN, ALFRED. Aquarium Book for Boys and Girls. (rd5) Scribner,
c1959 (rev. ed.). 209p. $3.50
All about water pets and their care. It includes good biological background
for better understanding of these creatures that live in water.

OGBURN, CHARLTON, JR. The White Falcon. (rd6) Houghton, c1955.
53p. $3 (Paper, Fawcett, 50c)
A boy defends an injured bird that causes trouble in the town. A charming
story of a boy's growing up.

PERRY, L. DAY, and SLEPICKA, FRANK. Bird Houses. (rd6) Bennett,
c1955. 96p. $2.75 (Paper, $1.75)
Detailed instructions on how to build bird houses for many different kinds of
birds. Interesting, informative material on bird habits and reasons for building houses in certain ways, and instructions for building winter shelters for
birds.

ZIM, HERBERT S. Homing Pigeons. (rd6) Morrow, c1949. 63p. $2.75
_____Owls. (rd4) Morrow, c1950. 60p. $2.75
_____Parakeets. (rd5) Morrow, c1953. 64p. $2.75
Simple text and pictures tell how to raise and train pigeons and parakeets. The
second book describes the keen sight, remarkable hearing, silent flight, and
usefulness of the owl.
_____and GABRIELSON, IRA N. Birds—A Guide to the Most Familiar
American Birds. (rd5) Golden, c1949. 160p. $3.95 (Paper, $1)
Fascinating information is given about the habits and habitats of birds along
with colored illustrations and maps.

The symbol "rd" accompanied by the figure, in parentheses, following the
title in each entry, indicates the estimated grade level of reading difficulty
(see p. 18-19).

ANIMAL LIFE AND ADVENTURE: Cats

BELTING, NATALIE M. Cat Tales. (rd5) Holt, c1959. 95p. $3
Folk tales about cats from Africa, Egypt, the Netherlands, Rumania, Russia, Ceylon, and other countries.

DeJONG, MEINDERT. The Last Little Cat. (rd3) Harper, c1961. 66p. $3.25
A little kitten, last of a litter of seven, is befriended by a blind old dog in this appealing story.

DOLCH, EDWARD and MARGUERITE P. I Like Cats. (rd1) Garrard, c1959. 63p. $2.25
A gay and amusing book about cats in fact and folk tale. (First Reading Books)

EMBRY, MARGARET. Mr. Blue. (rd3) Holiday, c1963. 71p. $2.75
Mr. Blue is an unusual and funny cat who visits a school class. He frightens the music teacher and causes some trouble but later becomes a hero and class mascot.

McGOVERN, ANN. Cats. (rd7) Maco, c1959. 80p. Paper, 35c
All the information a cat-owner needs to provide a happy, healthy life for his pet. Includes chapters on cat history, varieties of breeds, care and feeding, and criteria for selecting cats as pets. Outstanding cat photographs add to the book's attraction.

NEVILLE, EMILY. It's Like This, Cat. (rd5) Harper, c1963. 180p. $3.50
The humorous story of a teen-age boy growing up in New York City and of his love for a stray cat. His first girl, his companionship with an older boy in trouble, and a growing understanding of his father as a person are also part of this colorful, exciting tale.

RUSHMORE, HELEN. Ghost Cat. (rd4) Harcourt, c1954. 150p. $2.95
An Ozark Mountain community is the setting for this exciting story of Glory and the stray white cat that was supposed to bring bad luck.

SCHLEIN, MIRIAM. The Way Mothers Are. (rd2) Whitman, c1963. 32p. $2.75
A kitten is bothered as to how his mother can love him when he is naughty. The mother helps him to overcome his fears.

SEUSS, DR. (Geisel, Theodore Seuss). The Cat in the Hat. (rd2) Random, c1957. 61p. $2 (Houghton ed., $1.72)
What a wonderful cat this is that can balance so many things at once. An original and very funny book about what happens one dull, wet afternoon. Further adventures appear in The Cat in the Hat Comes Back. (Beginner Books)

ANIMAL LIFE AND ADVENTURE: Dogs

BALCH, GLENN. White Ruff. (rd6) Grosset, c1959. 235p. $1.95 (Paper, Scholastic Book Services, 50c)
A story of suspense that tells how a stolen collie escapes his captors and has many adventures, including some with a circus, as he travels hundreds of miles to find the boy who owns him.

BALL, ZACHARY. Bristle Face. (rd5) Holiday, c1962. 206p. $3.25
This notable and lively story about a boy and a dog in the South in 1900 is both moving and funny. Orphaned fourteen-year-old Jase adopts big, ugly Bristle Face, who fulfills the boy's fondest wish by developing into a fox dog.

BORLAND, HAL. The Dog Who Came to Stay. (rd6) Lippincott, c1962. 224p. $4.95
The relationship between a man, his dog, and nature is demonstrated in this moving story of the author's rabbit hound Pat.

BURNFORD, SHEILA. The Incredible Journey. (rd7) Little, c1961. 145p. $3.75
An exciting and heartwarming story of the travels and devotion of three unlikely companions—a bull terrier, a Siamese cat, and a Labrador retriever. The three pets, staying with a friend while their owners are abroad, disappear into the Canadian wilderness as they start their long trek homeward. This was made into a fine Walt Disney movie.

COATSWORTH, ELIZABETH. Jock's Island. (rd7) Viking, c1963. 80p. $2.75
A border collie and his flock are left on a lonely island when the threat of a volcanic eruption forces the villagers to evacuate their homes.

DAWSON, ALEC JOHN. Finn the Wolfhound. (rd6) Harcourt, c1963. 248p. $3.50
A champion dog, raised and trained in England, is separated from his beloved master and sent to Australia. There he has a hard life in a circus until he escapes to become leader of a pack of wild dogs and find his master in a dramatic climax that is filled with tension.

DUPRÉ, RAMONA DORREL. Too Many Dogs. (rd1) Follett, c1960. 32p. $1.60
One day Mr. and Mrs. White's two dogs bring home another dog and her nine puppies. They fill the house, eat up all the food, and dig up the garden until the Whites find a way to solve their problem happily. Amusing illustrations. (Beginning-to-Read Books)

GIPSON, FREDERICK BENJAMIN. Old Yeller. (rd5) Harper, c1956. 158p. $2.95 (Paper, Pocket Book, 35c)
The story of an ugly, mongrel dog who would tackle anything from an angry bear to a mad wolf in order to save his Texas frontier family.

_____Savage Sam. (rd6) Harper, c1962. 214p. $3
Sam, the son of Old Yeller, has a good trail nose and proves his worth in the rescue of two children captured by the Indians.

JOHNSON, MARGARET S. Gavin: A Scottish Deerhound. (rd6) Morrow, c1960. 95p. $2.75
A puppy travels from Scotland to an American ranch and leads a lonely life with a wolf cub as companion until they both run away. Gavin's adventures finally bring him the friendly pat and the human love he seeks with a kind ranch master and a vacationing college boy.

The symbol "rd" accompanied by the figure, in parentheses, following the title in each entry, indicates the estimated grade level of reading difficulty (see p. 18-19).

KJELGAARD, JIM. Big Red. (rd5) Holiday, c1956. 255p. $3.25 (Paper, Scholastic Book Services, 25c)
The adventures of a champion Irish setter and a trapper's son facing wilderness danger together. A favorite boy-dog story. Other exciting adventures about dogs by the same author are *Desert Dog, Double Challenge, Lion Hound,* and *Outlaw Red.*

———Boomerang Hunter. (rd6) Holiday, c1960. 172p. $2.95
An exciting story of a primitive Australian and his tame dingo who save a tribe from starvation after facing dangers of the desert.

———Irish Red; Son of Big Red. (rd5) Holiday, c1951. 224p. $3.25 (Paper, Scholastic Book Services, 25c)
The heart-warming story of a boy's love for a dog. A freezing ordeal atop a storm-swept mountain helps a playful Irish setter pup to become a magnificent champion.

KNIGHT, ERIC. Lassie Come-Home. (rd7) Holt, c1940. 248p. $3.50 (Paper, Grosset, 50c)
When the mines in Yorkshire close down, Joe's father has to sell Lassie, their prize collie. Lassie's four-hundred-mile journey back to Joe's family shows a dog's undying loyalty and amazing bravery.

MONTGOMERY, RUTHERFORD. Broken Fang. (rd6) Scholastic Book Services. (Caxton, c1935). 160p. Paper, 25c
The story of a dog that is branded a killer by everybody except his Sioux master, and of how the dog lived up to Sioux Charlie's trust.

STREET, JAMES. Good-bye, My Lady. (rd8) Lippincott, c1954. 222p. $4.50
A swamp boy catches a rare dog in the wilderness, trains and loves her, and through the loss of her gains a new maturity.

TERHUNE, ALBERT PAYSON. Lad: A Dog. (rd7) Dutton, c1949. 349p. $3.75 (First published in 1919)
Sunnybrook Lad was a real collie who lived on the author's estate. Terhune's stories of this and other collies are among the most popular of all dog books. A sequel to *Lad: A Dog* is *Further Adventures of Lad.*

ZION, GENE. Harry and the Lady Next Door. (rd2) Harper, c1960. 62p. $1.95
When the lady next door disturbs Harry with her singing, this unusual dog finds a way to handle the problem. (I-Can-Read Books)

ANIMAL LIFE AND ADVENTURE: Horses

ANDERSON, C. W. Blaze and the Indian Cave. (rd3) Macmillan, c1964. Unp. $2.50
Billy and Blaze appear in a new adventure. When the pony is stolen, it is up to Billy to find him and capture the thief.

BALCH, GLENN. Wild Horse Tamer. (rd6) Crowell, c1955. 179p. $3
(Paper, Scholastic Book Services, 25c)
A story of ranch life in Idaho. A brother and sister investigate the disappearance of their prized wild stallion. Plenty of action, rodeo thrills, good family relationships, and an authentic picture of western ranching all appear in this book.

CLARK, ANN NOLAN. Blue Canyon Horse. (rd4) Viking, c1954. 54p.
$2.75
A story of great beauty about a horse that at last comes home.

CROWELL, PERS. First to Ride. (rd6) Scholastic Book Services. (Originally published by McGraw as The First Horseman, c1948).
116p. Paper, 35c
A young caveman, fascinated by the strength and speed of the stallion Fleet Black, becomes the first horse tamer in history and is made the leader of his people. He has hair-raising adventures in a wilderness haunted by sabertoothed tigers.

FARLEY, WALTER. The Black Stallion. (rd7) Random, c1947. 330p.
$2.50
This is the first of a long series of books about the training and racing of a wild black Arabian stallion who is brought to the West. There is genuine love for and knowledge of horses, as well as plenty of action, including a shipwreck, a forest fire, and horse races.

HENRY, MARGUERITE. Stormy, Misty's Foal. (rd5) Rand McNally,
c1963. 224p. $3.95
Misty's foal is born just before a savage storm hits the island and Pony Ranch, bringing tragedy to herds of wild ponies. In this dramatic story Stormy and Misty help the island people recover from their losses.

HOLT, STEPHEN (Thompson, Harlan). Prairie Colt. (rd5) McKay,
c1947. 178p. $2.95 (Paper, Scholastic Book Services, 25c)
A fast-paced story of modern ranch life in Canada. Leif rides Red, a killer bronc, in the Stockmen's Race to win the ranch.

LAROM, HENRY V. Mountain Pony. (rd6) McGraw, c1946. Grosset
ed., c1951. 240p. $1.95 (Paper, Scholastic Book Services, 35c)
The story of a fifteen-year-old boy's devotion to a wild sorrel pony and his adventures with a gang of airborne poachers. High adventure plus excellent uncle-nephew relationship.

————Mountain Pony and the Rodeo Mystery. (rd6) McGraw,
c1949. Grosset ed., c1952. 228p. $1.95 (Paper, Scholastic Book Services, 25c)
A city boy's adventuresome attempts to recover a stolen rodeo bronc. Andy tracks his stolen horse from Castle Creek to Madison Square Garden—then has to prove that a "dude kid" can rope and tie a vicious outlaw!

The symbol "rd" accompanied by the figure, in parentheses, following the title in each entry, indicates the estimated grade level of reading difficulty (see p. 18-19).

Lyons, Dorothy. Golden Sovereign. (rd6) Harcourt, c1946. 259p. $3.25 (Paper, Scholastic Book Services, 35c)
A double-plotted story of a mean horse and a horse with a missing pedigree. Connie and Peter solve both problems. The story reveals a great deal about the business of training and handling horses.

Montgomery, Rutherford. Crazy Kill Range. (rd6) World, c1963. 224p. $2.95
The story of a black colt in the Nevada mountain country, and how he survives the dangers of the wild to challenge the veteran stallion, Big Baldy, for a herd of his own. The book contains the author's usual lessons about the need for conservation of wild life and wild lands.

Moody, Ralph. Come On, Seabiscuit. (rd5) Houghton, c1963. 172p $3.25
The true and fast-paced story of a gallant horse who was an outcast until an old-time cowboy saw in him the heart of a champion. Seabiscuit recovered from serious leg injuries time after time to become the greatest money-winner of the world. There is much here that shows the training, care, and handling of thoroughbreds.

Self, Margaret Cabell. The Complete Book of Horses and Ponies. (rd5) McGraw, c1963. 316p. $5.95
Many photographs and drawings make this a helpful reference book that is also delightful reading. Information is given on all a rider might need to know.

Simon, Tony, ed. Hit Parade of Horse Stories. (rd6) Scholastic Book Services, c1963. 156p. Paper, 25c
Fourteen stories about horses to be enjoyed by both boys and girls. Included among the fourteen authors are Will James, Jim Kjelgaard, MacKinlay Kantor, William Saroyan, and Quentin Reynolds.

Slaughter, Jean. Pony Care. (rd5) Knopf, c1961. 115p. $3.50
A handbook on the selection, care, and feeding of ponies. Information is given on training and handling, on equipment and housing, on food and exercise, on safety and first aid. Illustrated by many photographs.

Stuart, Jesse. Red Mule. (rd4) McGraw, c1955. 124p. $2.75
A man proves that despite the importance of machines in our times, tractors cannot replace mule power completely.

Townsend, Doris. Dinny and Dreamdust. (rd4) Doubleday, c1962. 142p. $2.50
Love of horses, hard work on a ranch, and a terrible stable fire all help lonely, motherless Dinny find friends and romance. (Signal Books)

ANIMAL LIFE AND ADVENTURE: Other Animals

Adamson, Joy. Forever Free. (rd7) Harcourt, c1963. 179p. $5.95
The third in a trio of books about an orphan lion cub, this is one of the most moving animal stories of all time. A woman and her game-warden husband in Kenya adopt an orphan cub, raise her as a pet, and finally set her free, as told in *Born Free*. The second book continues the story of Elsa and her cubs, when she still holds some affection for her human friends (*Living Free*). The third is the most touching as it tells of Elsa's death and of the Adamsons' efforts to protect her cubs until they are able to fend for themselves.

BRIDGES, WILLIAM. Zoo Pets. (rd3) Morrow, c1955. 94p. $2.95
This is an amusing presentation of the young animals in the Bronx Zoo, giving their habits in an appealing manner.

BULLA, CLYDE ROBERT. Three-Dollar Mule. (rd4) Crowell, c1960. 86p. $2.50
When a boy is given a mean mule for his birthday, he thinks he will have to give it up because the animal gets into so many scrapes. Then it saves Don's life, and the picture changes.

CARMER, CARL. Pets at the White House. (rd6) Dutton, c1962 (rev. ed.). 101p. $3
The favorite pets of eleven Presidents and their families are told about in this fascinating and often amusing book. They include Martha Washington's pet horse, Tad Lincoln's goats, the many pets of Theodore Roosevelt's six children, Franklin Roosevelt's famous little Scotty, and the Kennedy pets, especially the pony named Macaroni. Attractive illustrations add to the pleasure of the stories.

CAVANAH, FRANCES (comp. and ed.). Friends to Man: The Wonderful World of Animals. (rd7) Macrae, c1961. 252p. $3.50
An anthology of stories about animals, wild and domestic, real and fictional. Includes selections from well-known books, such as the original story, "My Friend Flicka," "I Like Skunks" from We Took to the Woods, and "Lora the Seal" from Seal Island.

CHAPIN, HENRY. The Remarkable Dolphin and What Makes Him So. (rd6) Scott, c1962. 96p. $2.75
The book describes the behavior of the dolphin in captivity, reaction to capture, response to training, and evidences of intelligence, humor, and affection shown by these animals. Some legends about dolphins from ancient times are included.

CHRYSTIE, FRANCES N. Pets; a Complete Handbook on the Care, Understanding, and Appreciation of All Kinds of Animal Pets. (rd5) Little, c1964 (rev. ed.). 274p. $3.95
A guide to the selection and care of pets. Included are the more orthodox types such as cats, dogs, parakeets, hamsters, etc.; wild animals; and farm animals. There is a new section on tropical fish. The final section discusses first aid and common diseases.

DARLING, LOIS and LOUIS. Turtles. (rd4) Morrow, c1962. 64p. $2.75
A brief survey of the varieties and habits of turtles living today—the care of pet turtles and a defense of their existence.

DARLING, LOUIS. Penguins. (rd5) Morrow, c1956. 64p. $2.75
This curious bird is made even more appealing in a book about his odd life and amusing habits. Penguin pictures have a humor all their own. Quite a few unfamiliar words.

The symbol "rd" accompanied by the figure, in parentheses, following the title in each entry, indicates the estimated grade level of reading difficulty (see p. 18-19).

DODD, ED. Mark Trail's Book of Animals. (rd7) Scholastic Book Services, abridged ed. (Hawthorn, c1955). 122p. Paper, 35c
Interesting text-and-picture discussion of nineteen wild North American mammals, based on the nationally syndicated cartoon strip. Full of unusual animal facts.

FENTON, CARROLL LANE. Reptiles and Their World. (rd6) Day, c1961. 128p. $3.50
Informative text and carefully captioned illustrations. The chapter division is on the basis of function or activity of reptiles—locomotion, finding mates, food habits, protection from danger, winter and summer rests, etc.

FOSTER, VIRGIL E. Close-up of a Honeybee. (rd3) Scott, W. R. c1960. 64p. $3
Beautiful photographs and simple text give a fine picture of this useful insect.

FROMAN, ROBERT. The Nerve of Some Animals. (rd6) Lippincott, c1961. 256p. $4.95
Animals may sometimes be smarter than people, as these funny and true stories about wolves, camels, dolphins, and coyotes show.

GALLICO, PAUL. Scruffy. (rd5) Doubleday, c1962. 299p. $4.50
The very amusing and highly unusual story of how the British Empire was saved by Scruffy and the Apes of Gibraltar.

GOUDEY, ALICE E. Here Come the Dolphins. (rd3) Scribner, c1961. 94p. $2.75
The fascinating story of the intelligent and appealing mammals of the sea who can be trained to do tricks.

HARRIS, LOUISE DYER and NORMAN DYER. Slim Green. (rd4) Little, c1955. 52p. $2.50
Here is information about different types of snakes, their habits, and the dangers they face, along with the adventurous life of Slim, one particular snake.

IPCAR, DAHLOV. Wild and Tame Animals. (rd2) Doubleday, c1962. Unp. $2.75
Fine illustrations and simple text combine to present the stories of many domestic and wild animals.

JAUSS, ANNE MARIE. Under a Green Roof. (rd5) Lippincott, c1960. 64p. $2.95
Pictures and words make clear this easily understood story of the birds and animals that live in our woods.

KJELGAARD, JIM. Haunt Fox. (rd7) Holiday, c1954. 220p. $3.25
An exciting wild animal story about a cunning red fox, Star, and the boy Jack and his foxhound, Thunder, who hunted the fox.

————Hidden Trail. (rd6) Holiday, c1962. 188p. $3.25
The adventures of a boy who photographs an elk herd as it migrates. This is a sequel to *Wildlife Cameraman*.

LANG, DON, and SAGE, MICHAEL. A New Star in the Big Cage. (rd7)
Lippincott, c1963. 160p. $3.75
An excellent and unusual story of a boy's desire to tame and train a wild
puma, and of his final success.

LATHROP, DOROTHY P. Let Them Live. (rd4) Macmillan, c1951. 80p.
$3.50
The habits of many birds and mammals along with their value to man and the
ways we can take to preserve them, form the conservation theme of this beautifully illustrated book.

LAWSON, ROBERT. The Tough Winter. (rd4) Viking, c1954. 128p. $3
Father and Uncle Analdas, Little Georgie and Willie Fieldmouse, and the
other Rabbit Hill animals have to deal with dire emergencies when "the
folks" leave for the winter.

LIPPINCOTT, JOSEPH WHARTON. The Wahoo Bobcat. (rd6) Lippincott, c1951. 250p. $3.95
With Florida swampland as background, this account of a bobcat and the boy
who had a strange friendship with it is simpler than *The Yearling* but has
something of the same appeal.

NORTH, STERLING. Rascal: A Memoir of a Better Era. (rd7) Dutton,
c1963. 189p. $3.95
A warm story which gives recollections of the author's life in a small midwest
town in Wisconsin at the close of World War I and introduces Rascal, his
mischievous pet raccoon. Sterling spent an adventurous year with Rascal.

SELSAM, MILLICENT E. How Animals Live Together. (rd5) Morrow,
c1963. 95p. $2.75
A study of social behavior in the animal kingdom. Group behavior (feeding,
breeding, hibernating, migrating, etc.) is discussed in the first chapters. Patterns of behavior are discussed in separate chapters for birds, mammals, and
insects. A final chapter discusses relationships between the different species.

_____The Language of Animals. (rd7) Morrow, c1962. 96p. $2.75
A discussion of the scientific findings on how animals communicate with each
other. The text is divided into chapters on fish; on frogs, snakes, and alligators; on birds; on mammals; and on insects.

SMITH, ARTHUR C. Western Butterflies. (rd5) Lippincott, c1961. 59p.
$2.95
You can find out how to collect and classify Western butterflies and learn
about their life cycle and habits.

WONG, HERBERT H. Ducks, Geese and Swans. (rd5) Lippincott,
c1960. 64p. $3.50
Illustrations and words together fully describe the fifty species of ducks,
geese, and swans that inhabit North America.

_____

The symbol "rd" accompanied by the figure, in parentheses, following the
title in each entry, indicates the estimated grade level of reading difficulty
(see p. 18-19).

ZIM, HERBERT S. Alligators and Crocodiles. (rd5) Morrow, c1952.
62p. $2.75 (Paper, Scholastic Book Services, 35c)
———Elephants. (rd3) Morrow, c1946. 60p. $2.75
———Frogs and Toads. (rd4) Morrow, c1950. 60p. $2.75
———Great Whales. (rd2) Morrow, c1951. 64p. $2.75
———Monkeys. (rd3) Morrow, c1955. 64p. $2.75
———Rabbits. (rd5) Morrow, c1948. 61p. $2.75
Sprightly and factual information about habits and habitats. Simple text and
interesting illustrations make these books inviting.
———Snakes. (rd5) Morrow, c1949. Unp. $2.75 (Paper, Scholastic
Book Services, 25c)
A complete, fact-filled book about all kinds of North American snakes. Ma-
ture in style and of interest to young high school scientists.

AVIATION

CAIDIN, MARTIN. The Silken Angels. (rd7) Lippincott, c1963. 264p.
$4.95
The true and exciting story of parachuting and of the men who learned to de-
pend on parachutes as protection against disaster.

CLARKE, TOM E. Puddle Jumper. (rd5) Lothrop, c1960. 191p. $3
A boy learns to fly a plane with his father, who is a bush pilot in Alaska. He
is opposed by the FAA officials because he is too young to get a pilot's license.

COLBY, CARROLL B. Bomber Parade: Headliners in Bomber Plane
History. (rd6) Coward, c1960. 48p. $2.50
Presents the history of bombing planes from World War I models to the most
recent types.

———Fighter Parade: Headliners in Fighter Plane History. (rd6)
Coward, c1960. 48p. $2.50
Describes the development of the modern jet fighter plane from the first shaky
aircraft back at the turn of the century. Good photographs.

———SAC: Men and Machines of Our Strategic Air Command.
(rd6) Coward, c1961. 48p. $2.50
An account in brief passages of text and large photographs of the history, activities, men, and machines of our Strategic Air Command. There is a section
on aircraft and missiles, followed by material on personnel, maintenance, and
security measures.

COOKE, DAVID CONE. Flights That Made History. (rd6) Putnam,
c1961. 70p. $2.50
A survey of some of the dramatic flights of aviation history: Blériot's flight
across the English Channel, flight of the NC-4, Lindbergh's solo Atlantic
crossing, and Wiley Post's globe-circling feats, among others.

FLOHERTY, JOHN J., and McGRADY, MIKE. Whirling Wings. (rd7)
Lippincott, c1961. 160p. $3
The story of the invention and development of the helicopter, an increasingly
important mode of transportation.

GREENWOOD, JAMES R. The Parachute: From Balloons to Skydiving. (rd6) Dutton, c1964. 183p. $3.50

The author, who made his first jump in 1938 and has since performed 236 free-fall exhibition leaps, traces the development of the parachute from its early appearance on Leonardo da Vinci's drawing board to its use with the Apollo space craft. There are chapters on skydiving techniques and on safety regulations. A good introduction to skydiving, a sport that is becoming more popular every year.

HAMRE, LEIF. Perilous Wings. (rd7) Harcourt, c1961. 128p. $2.75

A good adventure story for boys, written by an officer in the Norwegian Air Force. Recurrence of fires in the wings of the crashed planes of the supersonic plane Squadron 317 results in two courageous men risking their lives to take the machine out on a test flight. The mystery is solved when the two men find the fires to be caused by ice formation.

HOYT, EDWIN P. Whirlybirds: The Story of Helicopters. (rd5) Doubleday, c1961. 57p. $2.95

A book about helicopters, illustrated with drawings of old and new models. The first section gives the history of flying craft preceding the helicopter, followed by improvements made in more recent models, and some of the commercial, military, and future uses of the whirlybird.

PHLEGER, MARJORIE. Pilot Down, Presumed Dead. (rd5) Harper, c1963. 206p. $3.50

An exciting survival story about a pilot forced to make a crash landing on a deserted Pacific island.

BIOGRAPHY

BAKELESS, KATHERINE and JOHN. Spies of the Revolution. (rd5) Lippincott, c1962. 192p. $3.95

Thrilling true stories of English and American secret agents during the struggle for freedom in the American Revolutionary War.

BAKER, NINA BROWN. Nellie Bly, Reporter. (rd5) Scholastic Book Services (Holt, c1956). 120p. Paper, 35c

A biography of America's first woman reporter. A true story about a pretty young girl who made headlines, spearheaded social reforms, and won the applause of millions. Included is her famous race around the world in eighty days. (Winston Adventure Books)

BOYLSTON, HELEN. Clara Barton. (rd6) Random, c1955. 192p. $1.95 (Paper, Scholastic Book Services, 35c)

An exciting and true Civil War story of the woman who began the American Red Cross. (Landmark Books)

The symbol "rd" accompanied by the figure, in parentheses, following the title in each entry, indicates the estimated grade level of reading difficulty (see p. 18-19).

BROOKS, POLLY SCHOYER, and WALWORTH, NANCY ZINSSER. The World Awakes: The Renaissance in Western Europe. (rd6) Lippincott, c1962. 224p. $5.95

The story of the Renaissance told through the lives of leading personalities of that period. The brief sketches are aided by illustrations.

BROWN, MARION M., and CRONE, RUTH. The Silent Storm. (rd6) Abingdon, c1963. 250p. $3.25

A biography of Annie Sullivan, Helen Keller's teacher, detailing her childhood and young womanhood, ending with John Macy's proposal of marriage.

BUCK, PEARL S. The Man Who Changed China. (rd5) Random, c1953. 192p. $1.95

Not only describes the life of a great leader, Sun Yat-sen, but also creates an appreciation for the greatness of Chinese culture and the people's struggle for self-government. (World Landmark Books)

BURLINGAME, ROGER. Out of Silence Into Sound: The Life of Alexander Graham Bell. (rd5) Macmillan, c1964. 146p. $2.95

Unlike most biographies, this one begins in the present with Telstar, then shows how it is the "great-grandchild" of Bell, who started it all many years ago with the invention of the telephone. The story is generously illustrated with photographs.

BURNETT, CONSTANCE BUEL. Captain John Ericsson: Father of the "Monitor." (rd6) Vanguard, c1960. 255p. $3

A good biography of the famous Swedish-American engineer and designer of the "Monitor." Much information is given about his use of compressed air for power and his interest in solar engines, screw propeller, and railway locomotive.

CAMPION, NARDI R. Patrick Henry: Firebrand of the Revolution. (rd7) Little, c1961. 261p. $3.75

A lively biography, including Henry's youthful escapades and his eventual success. Portrays the development of his distinguished career and national prominence.

CARSE, ROBERT. The Young Colonials. (rd6) Norton, c1963. 223p. $3.50

Biographical sketches of little known and youthful heroes, stressing the courage and ability of youth to meet and cope with danger adequately. Almost all the accounts recall the adventures of young people in the early period of our country's history.

CAVANAH, FRANCES. Adventure in Courage: The Story of Theodore Roosevelt. (rd4) Rand McNally, c1961. 111p. $2.95

The story of Theodore Roosevelt's courage in overcoming poor health in his youth. It relates his family life and his adventures from the age of eight up to the time of his succession to the Presidency when McKinley died.

CLAPESATTLE, HELEN BERNICE. The Mayo Brothers. (rd7) Houghton, c1962. 180p. $1.95

A well-written biography of William and Charles Mayo, two doctors from Minnesota who became the most famous surgeons of their time. A good picture of the growth and improvement of medical services generally.

DALGLIESH, ALICE. The Columbus Story. (rd2) Scribner, c1955. Unp. $3.25

Here are the main adventures of Columbus' life from his boyhood to his second voyage.

DAVIDSON, BILL. President Kennedy Selects Six Brave Presidents. (rd6) Harper, c1962. 96p. $2.95

The book is based on the author's interviews with President Kennedy about the six American Presidents whose courage meant the most to him—Washington, John Quincy Adams, Lincoln, Johnson, Theodore Roosevelt, and Arthur. The courage evidenced is a less familiar kind, such as Chester Arthur's bravery in sacrificing his own political career by helping establish a Civil Service.

DEGERING, ETTA B. Seeing Fingers: The Story of Louis Braille. (rd6) McKay, c1962. 115p. $2.95

The magnificent story of Louis Braille, who spent his life developing a way to enable the blind to read. The system named for him is included in the book.

DEGRUMMOND, LENA Y., and DELAUNE, LYNN DEGRUMMOND. Jeb Stuart. (rd6) Lippincott, c1962. 128p. $3.25

A lively life story of a famous and colorful figure in the Confederate Army during the War Between the States.

DE LEEUW, ADÈLE. Richard E. Byrd, Adventurer to the Poles. (rd3) Garrard, c1963. 80p. $2.50

Our struggles to learn more about this little-known territory are told in this story of Byrd's adventures at the South Pole. (Discovery Books)

DOLSON, HILDEGARDE. William Penn: Quaker Hero. (rd5) Random, c1961. 186p. $1.95

The fictionalized story of the young Quaker who struggled for religious freedom and founded the city of Philadelphia in Penn's Woods, now known as the state of Pennsylvania. The book abounds in humor and adventure. (Landmark Books)

DOUTY, ESTHER M. America's First Woman Chemist, Ellen Richards. (rd7) Messner, c1961. 191p. $2.95

A biography of the woman who, shortly after the Civil War, was the first female to attend M.I.T., later taught there, was the first president of the American Home Economics Association, and was a leader in the field of public health and proper nutrition.

EDWARDS, CECILE P. Horace Mann: Sower of Learning. (rd5) Houghton, c1960. 192p. $1.95 (Paper, $1.32)

The biography of one of the most influential men in teaching and in the development of American schools. (Piper Books)

FANNING, LEONARD M. Fathers of Industries. (rd6) Lippincott, c1962. 256p. $4.75

The fascinating life stories, briefly told, of twenty-four inventors out of whose work developed the large industries of today.

The symbol "rd" accompanied by the figure, in parentheses, following the title in each entry, indicates the estimated grade level of reading difficulty (see p. 18-19).

FRIEDMAN, ESTELLE. Ben Franklin. (rd3) Putnam, c1961. 48p. $2
An easy-to-read biography of one of America's first great patriots who was also an international figure, inventor, author, and statesman.

GILBERT, MIRIAM. Henry Ford: Maker of the Model T. (rd5) Houghton, c1962. 191p. $1.95 (Paper, $1.32)
The story of the man who developed the automobile and assembly line production that made it possible for the working man to own one. (Piper Books)

GRAVES, CHARLES PARLIN. A World Explorer: Marco Polo. (rd4) Garrard, c1963. 96p. $2.75
The story of one of the most exciting and influential explorations ever made, and of one of the most colorful figures in world history. (World Explorer Books)

HICKOK, LORENA. The Story of Helen Keller. (rd4) Grosset, c1958. 181p. $1.95 (Paper, Scholastic Book Services, 50c)
The story of this remarkable woman who overcame a triple handicap with the help of her "miracle worker" teacher, Annie Sullivan. A braille manual and alphabet are included. (Signature Books)

JOHNSON, DOROTHY M. Famous Lawmen of the Old West. (rd7) Dodd, c1963. 151p. $3
Eleven biographies of lawmen, including Wild Bill Hickok, Big Foot Wallace, Bat Masterson, and Wyatt Earp.

JOHNSTON, JOHANNA. Thomas Jefferson, His Many Talents. (rd7) Dodd, c1961. 159p. $3.50
A portrayal of a great President and statesman, author of our Declaration of Independence. His many interests and abilities are discussed—his contributions as a naturalist, scientist, architect, inventor, and musician.

KAY, HELEN. Abe Lincoln's Hobby. (rd3) Reilly, c1961. 32p. $2.75
This book shows Lincoln's love of children and animals as his "hobby."

KEESING, NANCY. By Gravel and Gum: The Story of a Pioneer Family. (rd6) St. Martin's, c1964. 168p. $3.50
The dramatic account of an actual Australian family that pioneered in aboriginal territory in New South Wales. Interesting details of pioneer life, of a gold rush, of bush ranger raids, and of relations with the aborigines.

KELLY, REGINA Z. Henry Clay: Statesman and Patriot. (rd5) Houghton, c1960. 191p. $1.95 (Paper, $1.32)
The seldom-told story of a man who influenced the course of American history, one who would "rather be right than be President." (Piper Books)

————Paul Revere: Colonial Craftsman. (rd5) Houghton, c1963. 188p. $1.95 (Paper, $1.32)
An authentic tale of the famous American who was a fine silversmith as well as an outstanding patriot during the days of the American Revolution. (Piper Books)

LATHAM, JEAN LEE. Carry On, Mr. Bowditch. (rd7) Houghton, c1955. 251p. $3.25
The fascinating and lively biography of the man whose mathematical genius solved the complex problems of navigation in the days of sailing ships. Useful for supplementary reading in mathematics classes.

LAWSON, DON. Young People in the White House. (rd4) Abelard, c1961. 160p. $3

Little-known facts, exciting scenes, and amusing incidents appear in these brief pictures of the lively young people who have lived in the White House, from John Adams' time to John Kennedy's.

LOMASK, MILTON. Andy Johnson: The Tailor Who Became President. (rd7) Farrar, c1962. 160p. $2.95

A good biography of Andrew Johnson, from his boyhood in North Carolina through his role in the Civil War, the Presidency, and the impeachment trial.

McCALL, EDITH S. Explorers in a New World. (rd3) Childrens, c1960. 123p. $2.50

A fast-moving, easy-to-read book about the adventurous and brave men who dared to explore the New World that became America. It manages to be both exciting and factual. (Frontiers of America Books)

McKOWN, ROBIN. Thomas Paine. (rd6) Putnam, c1962. 192p. $2.95

The life of the writer and political philosopher whose pamphlet "Common Sense" had such a great influence on our American Revolution.

McNEER, MAY YONGE. America's Mark Twain. (rd5) Houghton, c1962. 159p. $3.75

A good biography that tells the story and catches the spirit of our country's greatest humorist. Inserted at intervals through the text are "Previews" of Twain's books, with a one-paragraph plot summary and an illustration appearing on each page.

_____and WARD, LYND. Armed With Courage. (rd6) Abingdon, c1957. 112p. $2.50

A series of seven sketches of well-known persons who dedicated their lives to the service of mankind. Included are Florence Nightingale, Father Damien, George Washington Carver, Jane Addams, Wilfred Grenfell, Mahatma Gandhi, and Albert Schweitzer.

_____Give Me Freedom. (rd6) Abingdon, c1964. 128p. $3

Stories of courage and faith appear in these brief biographies of seven men and women who have achieved greatness in the cause of freedom. The seven selected are William Penn, Thomas Paine, Elijah P. Lovejoy, Elizabeth C. Stanton, Edwin Markham, Marian Anderson, and Albert Einstein.

MEIGS, CORNELIA. Invincible Louisa: The Story of the Author of Little Women. (rd5) Little, c1933. 260p. $3.75 (Paper, Scholastic Book Services, 35c)

This story of the author of Little Women takes you behind the scenes to meet all the Alcotts. It brings to light Louisa's fierce fight to support the family when her father failed financially.

The symbol "rd" accompanied by the figure, in parentheses, following the title in each entry, indicates the estimated grade level of reading difficulty (see p. 18-19).

MERCER, CHARLES, with VERMEULE, CORNELIUS C., III. Alexander the
Great. (rd6) Harper, c1963. 156p. $3.95
The childhood, education, and thirteen years of conquest of Alexander the
Great, who became King of Macedon and had a vision of world unity as long
ago as 336 B.C. The many photographs of interpretations of his travels
that have been created through the centuries make a unique combination of
history and art. (Horizon Caravel Books)

MODEROW, GERTRUDE. People to Remember. (rd5) Scott, c1960. 296p.
$2.60
Stories of sixteen remarkable people who went on even when the odds were
against them: from Henry Ford to Anne Frank, from Helen Keller to Billy
Mitchell, from George Washington Carver to Marie Curie, from Gandhi to
Von Braun, from Churchill to Amundsen.

PATTERSON, LILLIE G. Booker T. Washington: Leader of His People.
(rd3) Garrard, c1962. 80p. $2.50
Fast-moving story of a boy who made his dream come true. In doing so he became a world-famous leader of his people as well as one of America's great
scientists. (Discovery Books)

PEARE, CATHERINE OWENS. The FDR Story. (rd7) Crowell, c1962.
245p. $3.75
An excellent biography of Franklin Delano Roosevelt, his forceful personality,
his shortcomings, his vigor, and his relationships with other people in his life.
The author discusses the quiet ease of inherited wealth of the Roosevelt clan,
the turmoil of Tammany fights, the bitterness of the Depression, and the tension of the war years during both World Wars.

PRINDIVILLE, KATHLEEN. First Ladies. (rd6) Macmillan, c1963 (rev.
ed.). 308p. $3.95
This revised and well-illustrated book provides interesting profiles of our First
Ladies, from Martha Washington to Jacqueline Kennedy. The author includes each one's family background, schooling, courtship and marriage, many
lively anecdotes, and the role she played in helping her husband.

RANDALL, RUTH P. I Jessie. (rd7) Little, c1963. 223p. $3.95
The biography of the beautiful and dynamic Jessie Benton, who defied paren-
tal authority to marry a famous Army explorer of the West, John Charles Frémont. The Frémonts lived at times in luxurious surroundings and sometimes
in rude frontier homes—at times honored by the leaders of their day and
sometimes in disgrace or in seclusion.

RICHARDSON, BEN. Great American Negroes. (rd7) Crowell, c1956.
339p. $3.95 (Revised by William M. Fahey)
New names have been added and some dropped in this revision. Many fields
are represented here: actors, musicians, writers, dancers, educators, doctors,
scientists, statesmen, and sportsmen.

SAMUELS, GERTRUDE. B-G, Fighter of Goliaths: The Story of David
Ben-Gurion. (rd7) Crowell, c1961. 275p. $3.50
An excellent biography of David Ben-Gurion of Israel by a distinguished staff
writer of the New York *Times*. Ben-Gurion's childhood is given briefly, but
his personal life as an adult is covered adequately. A good picture of the
formation of Israel and of problems encountered by the new nation.

SCHOOR, GENE. Young John Kennedy. (rd7) Harcourt, c1963. 253p. $3.95

A portrait of the young President from childhood to his election, often told through selections from his own letters and journals.

SEIBERT, JERRY. Dan Beard: Boy Scout Pioneer. (rd4) Houghton, c1963. 191p. $1.95 (Paper, $1.32)

The biography of the founder of the Boy Scout movement in the United States. It appeals to boys who are especially interested in scouting. (Piper Books)

SHULTZ, GLADYS DENNY. Jenny Lind: The Swedish Nightingale. (rd6) Lippincott, c1962. 352p. $6.50

A complete biography of the famous singer, the first one to include the entire story of her American tour under the management of P. T. Barnum.

SIMON, CHARLIE MAY. The Sun and the Birch. (rd7) Dutton, c1960. 192p. $3.50

The early lives of Crown Prince Akihito and Crown Princess Michiko are very different. In them and in their marriage we see the changing Japan and present-day life and customs.

SMITH, E. BROOKS, and MEREDITH, ROBERT, eds. Pilgrim Courage. (rd4) Little, c1962. 108p. $3.25

Episodes from William Bradford's firsthand account of the Plymouth Plantation along with selections from his journals and those of Edward Winslow. They have been adapted and edited for easy reading.

SOOTIN, HARRY. Twelve Pioneers of Science. (rd7) Vanguard, c1960. 254p. $3.50

Each of the twelve brief biographies is devoted to a man who was a pioneer in his field. Each biography has two parts—a reconstruction of the actual scene of discovery and a life history.

STERNE, EMMA GOLDERS. Vasco Núñez de Balboa (rd5) Knopf, c1961. 147p. $2.75

A retelling of the daring exploits of the man who discovered the Pacific Ocean.

SYME, RONALD. African Traveler. (rd5) Morrow, c1962. 191p. $2.95

An easy, interesting, humorous, and exciting biography of Mary Kingsley, a Victorian woman who was the first white person to explore much of West Africa in the 1890's.

THOMAS, HENRY. Franklin Delano Roosevelt. (rd6) Putnam, c1962. 191p. $2.95

The story of one of our most dynamic Presidents who rose to fame and great political power in spite of his physical handicaps. The text is devoted primarily to Roosevelt's years in the White House, but there are also anecdotes about personal matters and family life.

The symbol "rd" accompanied by the figure, in parentheses, following the title in each entry, indicates the estimated grade level of reading difficulty (see p. 18-19).

WHITE, DALE. Bat Masterson. (rd6) Messner, c1960. 192p. $3.25
The life of Bat Masterson, a buffalo hunter, Indian fighter, student, and friend of Wyatt Earp, and also one of the law enforcers in Dodge City and Tombstone.

WILKIE, KATHARINE E. Robert Louis Stevenson: Storyteller and Adventurer. (rd5) Houghton, c1961. 189p. $1.95 (Paper, $1.32)
The story of the beloved author of *Treasure Island, Kidnapped,* and *A Child's Garden of Verses,* who was himself a great adventurer though he was a semi-invalid all his life. (Piper Books)

WILLIAMS, BERYL, and EPSTEIN, SAMUEL. Plant Explorer: David Fairchild. (rd6) Messner, c1961. 192p. $3.25
An interesting biography of the famous botanist and plant explorer David Fairchild, who brought more than 200,000 species of plants from tropical countries into the United States and established what is now the vital New Crops Research Branch of the Department of Agriculture. His work took him to exotic places that are vividly described.

YATES, ELIZABETH. Amos Fortune: Free Man. (rd4) Dutton, c1950. 181p. $2.95
This is the true story of a man who, born free in Africa in 1710, was sold as a slave in America in 1725. In time he purchased his own freedom, then worked to free three other slaves.

CAREERS: Facts

ARNOLD, PAULINE, and WHITE, PERCIVAL. Clothes: America's Apparel Business. (rd5) Holiday, c1961. 360p. $4.50
All about the clothing industry from spinning wheel to wash-and-wear. The story of the design, fashion, and manufacture of clothes.

————Homes: America's Building Business. (rd5) Holiday, c1960. 379p. $4.50
Charts and illustrations aid in telling the story of housing through the years and of modern building, household appliances, and living habits.

————Money: Make It, Spend It, Save It. (rd5) Holiday, c1962. 229p. $3.95
This guide to personal finance is good preparation for understanding and using banks, budgets, insurance, investments, and other aspects of money.

BENEDICT, BART. Aluminum: The Story of an Industry. (rd5) Lippincott, c1961. 65p. $2.95
How aluminum was discovered and developed is told in this book about one of the country's big industries.

CHAMBERLIN, JO HUBBARD. Careers in the Protective Services. (rd9) Walck, c1963. 128p. $3.50
A comprehensive presentation of this growing career field, the range of work, the different qualifications and training requirements for policemen and detectives, fire fighters, guards, watchmen, doorkeepers, security officers with private agencies and with the Federal, state, and local governments, county sheriffs, marshals, constables, and bailiffs. Many and varied career possibilities for young people with education ranging from postgraduate degrees to high-school diplomas.

CLEMONS, ELIZABETH. Rodeo Days. (rd4) Lippincott, c1960. 64p. $2.95
The thrills of the rodeo and its many exciting events are told in easy-to-read manner with beautiful action pictures in color.

COMPERE, TOM, and VOGEL, WILLIAM P., JR., eds. The Air Force Blue Book. (rd7) Military Publishing Institute edition, by arrangement with Scholastic Book Services, c1959. 384p. Paper, 35c
The book answers questions about enlistment and training opportunities, with information on such subjects as missile men, air industry, women in the Air Force, etc.

CURTIS, FRIEDA STEINMANN. Careers in the World of Fashion. (rd7) Whiteside, c1953. 268p. $3.50
There are many fascinating aspects of a career in fashions, including dress designing as well as selling and style promotion. This book will help you find your place if this is a field that interests you.

DEMING, DOROTHY. Careers for Nurses. (rd7) McGraw, c1952 (2d ed.). 351p. $6
There are many possibilities open in the field of nursing, and this will guide you in finding one that appeals to you, whether it lies in a city hospital, in an industrial plant, or in a public health service.

DODGE, BERTHA. Engineering Is Like This. (rd7) Little, c1963. 199p. $3.95
Here is an explanation of engineering from the early-day, deep-well pump to the modern pump turbines that operate Niagara.

EVERS, ALF. Selective Service: A Guide to the Draft. (rd7) Lippincott, c1961 (rev. ed.). 191p. $3.25
A handbook that tells of the opportunities and systems of all branches of the service. It gives timely, detailed information acquainting teen-agers with facts they need to know—registration, classification, volunteers, reserves, mental and physical examinations.

FLOETHE, LOUISE LEE and RICHARD. The Cowboy on the Ranch. (rd4) Scribner, c1959. Unp. $3.25
A beautifully illustrated and informative book about the seasonal work of the cowboy on a large ranch.

FLOHERTY, JOHN J. Aviation From the Ground Up. (rd7) Lippincott, c1960 (rev. ed.). 160p. $3.95
Present-day aviation as a career is explained and illustrated with photographs. The latest models in jet propulsion and helicopters are included. One of a series on assorted vocations giving qualifications needed and opportunities available in each field. Titles include: *Deep Down Under, Flowing Gold, Forest Ranger, Get That Story, Men Against Crime, Search and Rescue at Sea, Television Story,* etc.

_____and McGRADY, MIKE. Youth and the F.B.I. (rd7) Lippincott, c1960. 159p. $3.50
This tells the story of how the F.B.I. deals with the problems of youth. There is an introduction by J. Edgar Hoover.

The symbol "rd" accompanied by the figure, in parentheses, following the title in each entry, indicates the estimated grade level of reading difficulty (see p. 18-19).

HUETHER, ANNE. Glass and Man. (rd6) Lippincott, c1963. 224p. $4.50
The story of glass as used in art, in science, and in industry. Many drawings and photographs add to its value.

HYDE, WAYNE. What Does a Cowboy Do? (rd5) Dodd, c1963. 64p. $2.50
For older readers who will enjoy the authentic humor and colorful life of the modern cowboy. There are excellent photographs, too. Other volumes tell about the work of divers, of parachutists, of secret service agents, and of others.

———What Does a Forest Ranger Do? (rd4) Dodd, c1964. 64p. $2.50
The book shows that forest rangers do many things besides fighting fires. They destroy tree-killing insects, supervise the cutting of timber, stop avalanches, guard national forests and parks, rescue animals and people, etc. Included is the true story of Smoky Bear.

IRVING, ROBERT. Electronics. (rd6) Knopf, c1961. 173p. $3.25
Direct application of electronics, in simple form, to industrial devices and equipment. Good in considering a job in the field.

KUHN, FERDINAND. Story of the Secret Service. (rd6) Random, c1957. 192p. $1.95 (Paper, Scholastic Book Services, 50c)
The exciting and amazing story of the men who guard the President of the United States and hunt down counterfeiters. (Landmark Books)

LINGENFELTER, MARY R., and KITSON, HARRY D. Vocations for Girls. (rd7) Harcourt, c1951 (rev. ed.). 364p. $3.75
The many occupations open to girls are given, along with qualifications, preparation, and opportunities.

McGRADY, MIKE. Crime Scientists. (rd7) Lippincott, c1961. 160p. $3.25
True stories about tracking down criminals by using scientific equipment in the laboratory. Shows the application of scientific principles to many different kinds of work involved in detecting crimes.

MOORE, MARY FURLONG. The Baby Sitter's Guide. (rd8) Crowell, c1953. 120p. $2.95
On the basis of her own experience, the author gives advice and suggestions for would-be baby sitters on making sitting arrangements, entertaining the children, serving them meals, etc. Includes tips for teen-agers on what the sitters should expect from parents and what parents have a right to ask of sitters. Average behavior patterns of children also described.

PEAKE, MIRIAM MORRISON. A Job for You! (rd6) Scholastic Book Services, c1964. 156p. Paper, 25c
What young people need to know about getting and keeping a job, from application form and social security card to on-the-job etiquette. Suggestions about free-lance jobs students can do on Saturdays and after school.

PINNEY, ROY. Careers With a Camera. (rd7) Lippincott, c1964. 128p. $3.75
Read about the various opportunities to use photography as a career. Also included are the careers of outstanding photographers, along with attractive photographic illustrations.

PUTNAM, PETER. The Triumph of the Seeing Eye. (rd6) Harper, c1963. 178p. $2.95

An interesting book about the work done at the Seeing Eye school to give independence to the blind, with an account of the two-way training of dog and master. The author himself has trained at The Seeing Eye. (Breakthrough Books)

ROSS, CARMEN F. Personal and Vocational Relationships in Practical Nursing. (rd7) Lippincott, c1961. 208p. $3.25 (Paper, $1.95)

Here are basic rules for behavior and interpersonal relationships in the vocation of nursing.

TAYLOR, ARTHUR S.; SUTTON, JACK; and BENEDICT, BART. Logging: The Story of an Industry. (rd5) Lippincott, c1962. 64p. $2.95 (Paper, $1.95)

The complete story of what happens to trees from the time they are cut down until they are made into products. Reveals the many career opportunities in this area.

YATES, ELIZABETH. Someday You'll Write. (rd7) Dutton, c1962. 94p. $2.75

A guide to creative writing for young people. It discusses such things as selection of subjects, development of stories, steps in literary construction, and the discipline required of a writer.

CAREERS: Fiction—Boys

BECHDOLT, JACK. On the Air: A Story of Television. (rd6) Dutton, c1950. 192p. $2.75

Three young people of varied talents join forces to create a successful skit for television.

BERG, JEAN HORTON. Pierre, the Young Watchmaker. (rd5) Bobbs, c1961. 191p. $3.25

Thirteen-year-old Pierre wanted to be a watchmaker, as all the sons in his Swiss family had always been. In spite of tremendous handicaps and with Grandpère's help, Pierre proved to himself and to his family that he would someday be the finest craftsman of them all.

FIORE, EVELYN. Nat Dunlap: Junior "Medic." (rd4) Doubleday, c1964. 144p. $2.95

Nat volunteers for hospital work and learns to accept the necessary disciplines against which he had rebelled. He earns a place for himself in the hospital even if he could not earn an M.D. (Signal Books)

The symbol "rd" accompanied by the figure, in parentheses, following the title in each entry, indicates the estimated grade level of reading difficulty (see p. 18-19).

FRITZ, JEAN. I, Adam. (rd7) Coward, c1963. 244p. $3.75
In Connecticut in 1850, Adam Crane struggles on a farm with the evil and shiftless Sharkey, the former owner. After a struggle with himself, Adam decides against both whaling and farming as careers and goes to college.

HAIG-BROWN, RODERICK L. Mounted Police Patrol. (rd8) Morrow, c1954. 248p. $2.95
A boy with a warped, antisocial background finds himself a permanent guest in the home of his uncle, a Canadian Mounted Policeman. An interesting account of the work of the Mounted Police and of a boy's growing up.

KJELGAARD, JIM. Wildlife Cameraman. (rd6) Holiday, c1957. 218p. $2.95
With his dog and his two cameras, a young photographer spends a summer in the wilderness. He not only meets plenty of adventure, but also learns much about the ways of wild creatures. He ends the summer with a job as photographer for a forest service publication.

KOOB, THEODORA. Surgeon's Apprentice. (rd7) Lippincott, c1963. 192p. $3.50
An exciting true-to-life story of a young man learning to be a country surgeon in the Virginia of the early 1800's.

MEADER, STEPHEN W. T-Model Tommy. (rd7) Harcourt, c1940. 305p. $3.25 (Textbook ed., $2)
Redheaded Tom Ballard builds up a thriving trucking business with his ancient Model T Ford truck.

SENSENEY, DAN. Austin of the Air Force. (rd4) Doubleday, c1962. 142p. $2.50
When two chums enter the Air Force together, they almost break up their friendship because one is slow to learn the need to follow rules. Exciting adventures appear in an authentic setting of basic training. (Signal Books)

————Scanlon of the Sub-Service. (rd4) Doubleday, c1963. 142p. $2.50
A story filled with adventure in which Pete Scanlon becomes not only a qualified submariner but a first-rate man as well. (Signal Books)

VINSON, KATHRYN. The Luck of the Golden Cross. (rd5) Lippincott, c1960. 144p. $3.25
This tells of the adventurous life of sponge divers in Florida, and shows a brave boy's heroism in his village.

WYCKOFF, JAMES. Kendall of the Coast Guard. (rd4) Doubleday, c1961. 141p. $2.50
A realistic, fast-moving story of a young man who joins the Coast Guard. (Signal Books)

CAREERS: Fiction—Girls

BATES, ZELDA M. Roses Are Blue. (rd6) Westminster, c1962. 203p. $3.25
A book suggesting a career in an unusual area—floral decorating.

BOLTON, CAROLE. The Stage Is Set. (rd5) Morrow, c1963. 224p. $3.25
A young girl in dramatic school learns to work hard at her career, but also finds time for romance and excitement in a colorful straw-hat theater.

BOYLSTON, HELEN D. Sue Barton, Rural Nurse. (rd7) Little, c1939. 254p. $3.50 (Paper, Scholastic Book Services, 35c)
Coming from big-city nursing, Sue plunges into the excitement of helping Dr. Bill Barry with his practice in rural Springdale. A good picture of the way a rural nurse serves a small town.

———Sue Barton, Senior Nurse. (rd7) Little, c1937. 220p. $3.50 (Paper, Scholastic Book Services, 35c)
The second in a famous series written by a former nurse. Vivacious, red-headed Sue meets romance and excitement in a big-city hospital. She faces an important decision: should she marry Dr. Bill or continue the nursing career she has always dreamed of having?

———Sue Barton, Student Nurse. (rd7) Little, c1936. 244p. $3.50 (Paper, Scholastic Book Services, 35c)
Gay, irrepressible Sue begins her career as an eager probationer. She loves every minute at the big-city hospital. In no time at all, she wins respect for her courage in risking her life to save two people.

COLMAN, HILA. Phoebe's First Campaign. (rd7) Morrow, c1963. 180p. $3.25
A fast-moving story of an eighteen-year-old girl's first job in a fund-raising office in New York City.

DOLIM, MARY. Miss Mac. (rd6) Van Nostrand, c1963. 168p. $3.50
"Miss Mac" is Jennifer Macmillan, a young student teacher, and this is the touching story of her first year in a high-school classroom—her feelings, hopes, and fears as she discovers the problems and rewards of teaching.

EDELL, CELESTE. Lynn Pamet: Caterer. (rd6) Messner, c1960. 192p. $2.95
Lynn comes from a talented family, but all she can do well is cook. She learns to start the hard way, from the bottom up, before she earns success in the cooking career that she makes glamorous and exciting.

FINLAYSON, ANN. A Summer to Remember. (rd4) Doubleday, c1964. 144p. $2.95
Peg Drummond spends a summer as a junior swimming counselor at a camp for children. Here she gets the opportunity she wants to train for the Olympic tryouts. (Signal Books)

FORBES-ROBERTSON, DIANA. Footlights for Jean. (rd4) Doubleday, c1963. 142p. $2.50
Jean Allen, who aspires to become an actress, learns many things about the theater—and about herself—at the Pine Tree Playhouse. (Signal Books)

The symbol "rd" accompanied by the figure, in parentheses, following the title in each entry, indicates the estimated grade level of reading difficulty (see p. 18-19).

FRIERMOOD, ELISABETH HAMILTON. Ballad of Calamity Creek. (rd8) Doubleday, c1962. 214p. $2.95

Ann Todd, resenting the fact that her father will send her to school for only one year, goes to a Kentucky mountain school to teach. Here she finds that she is doing as much learning as teaching, for she becomes fascinated by the customs and crafts of the mountain people. A romance with a young English teacher develops.

HARRIS, CHRISTIE. You Have to Draw the Line Somewhere. (rd6) Atheneum, c1964. 249p. $3.95

Linsey Ross-Allen decides early to be an artist, but it is many years before she reaches her goal of becoming a fashion illustrator in New York. The world of fashion and the trials that are part of growing up are interestingly presented here.

HILL, MARGARET. The Extra-Special Room. (rd7) Little, c1962. 312p. $3.50

A new story of Anne Hillsbro's experiences in the classroom. The students needing Anne's help are retarded children. A sequel to *Really, Miss Hillsbro*.

———Hostess in the Sky. (rd7) Little, c1955. 241p. $3

The exciting adventures of an airline hostess.

MEANS, FLORENCE CRANNELL. Knock at the Door, Emmy. (rd7) Houghton, c1956. 240p. $3.25

Pluck and determination help fifteen-year-old Emmy Lou Lane, the daughter of a family of migrant workers, to earn an education and a promising career in social service.

MILNE, RUTH. TV Girl Friday. (rd7) Little, c1957. 248p. $3

Susan wanted to be a TV actress, but she found an exciting career behind the scenes. A swiftly paced career story emphasizing the jobs behind the camera. Teaches the reward of diligence in overcoming disappointment.

NELSON, MARG. A Girl Called Chris. (rd7) Farrar, c1962. 192p. $2.95

Chris Ralston gets a job against the advice of her family. With her intelligence and hard work, she gets both a scholarship and the boy of her choice.

REYNOLDS, HELEN. Summer of Surprise. (rd7) Funk, c1960. 186p. $2.95

Insufficient funds for her senior year at art school force Penny Warburton to set up classes in leathercraft, weaving, ceramics, and tapestry weaving in her barn to earn money during the summer. Contains some romance and career ideas for girls interested in practical arts.

SHERBURNE, ZOA. Ballerina on Skates. (rd6) Morrow, c1961. 187p. $3.25

A fast-paced story of Karen, an orphan who becomes the star of an ice show. A realistic picture of the exciting career of a young girl who makes a life for herself as a professional skater and finds love in spite of the fact that she has the problem of being very tall.

TEMKIN, SARA A., and HOVELL, LUCY A. Jinny Williams: Library Assistant. (rd7) Messner, c1962. 192p. $2.95

Unable to attend college, Jinny is thrilled to be accepted as a junior assistant at the Public Library. Especially appealing to girls more interested in careers than in college.

THORVALL, KERSTIN. Girl in April. (rd8) Harcourt, c1963. 158p. $3

A small-town girl wins her parents' consent to embark on training for a designing career in Stockholm. She learns to understand herself, not in a mature way, but in a way an adolescent views her own development.

WEBER, LENORA MATTINGLY. Pick a New Dream. (rd7) Crowell, c1961. 256p. $3.75

Beany Malone learns about people from backgrounds different from her own when she finds a summer job in a community center.

WHITNEY, PHYLLIS. The Highest Dream. (rd7) McKay, c1956. 240p. $3.75

The story of Lisa Somers' training and experiences, and the people she meets while she is a guide at the UN, a job that lasts not more than two years. The author makes the UN a familiar place, busy with practical works as well as ideals of brotherhood.

CAREERS: Real People

BAKER, NINA BROWN. Big Catalogue. (rd4) Harcourt, c1956. 115p. $2.75

This is the story of Montgomery Ward and the mail order business. The farmers of the 1870's depended on catalogues to buy necessities and luxuries.

———Nickels and Dimes: The Story of F. W. Woolworth. (rd4) Harcourt, c1954. 134p. $2.50

The life and personality of the man who built the five-and-ten cent stores into a great business.

DHOTRE, DAMOO. Wild Animal Man. (rd6) Little, c1961. 154p. $3.50

The story of an animal trainer's career. Dhotre ran away from home at the age of nine, joined a circus in India, and later became the trainer for Ringling Brothers and Barnum and Bailey circus. Many incidents are filled with danger and suspense.

DOOLEY, THOMAS A. Dr. Tom Dooley, My Story. (rd6) Farrar, c1962 (rev. ed.). 176p. $2.95

This is the story of a young doctor's brief but courageous and exciting life dedicated to helping the people of Laos and Vietnam in their fight against poverty and disease. The story, also, of how Medico began. This is an abridgment for young people of Dr. Dooley's three books about his work.

The symbol "rd" accompanied by the figure, in parentheses, following the title in each entry, indicates the estimated grade level of reading difficulty (see p. 18-19).

FREEDMAN, RUSSELL. Teenagers Who Made History. (rd6) Holiday, c1961. 272p. $3.50

The accomplishments of eight famous people, all of whom achieved fame before they were twenty. They represent a variety of fields, including science, the arts, and sports. The eight are Braille, Colt, Galileo, Lafayette, Millay, Toscanini, Von Braun, and Zaharias.

GERSH, HARRY. Women Who Made America Great. (rd6) Lippincott, c1962. 224p. $4.50

The easy-to-read stories of ten brave women who were the first to break into fields once open only to men.

HUME, RUTH Fox. Great Men of Medicine. (rd5) Random, c1961 (rev. ed.). 192p. $1.95

The lives of ten outstanding medical men from earliest times up to the discovery and development of penicillin. (World Landmark Books)

McGRADY, MIKE. Jungle Doctors. (rd6) Lippincott, c1962. 192p. $3.95

The fascinating life stories, briefly told, of the heroic men and women who give medical help to people in far-off lands around the world. Photographs add to the attraction of this absorbing collection of biographies.

MANCHESTER, HARLAND. Trail Blazers of Technology: The Story of Nine Inventors. (rd5) Scribner, c1962. 215p. $3.50

The dramatic story of nine men whose new ideas had to be forced on a reluctant world. Machines and systems of the modern world resulted from the work of such men as Davenport, Diesel, Goodyear, Nobel, Lake, Maxim, Tesla, De Forest, and Sikorsky. They are not often written about, but without their work many present-day advances could not have been made.

PLACE, MARIAN T. The Copper Kings of Montana. (rd5) Random, c1961. 184p. $1.95

The story of the struggle of three men for control of the world's most important copper mining areas. (Landmark Books)

READ, KATHERINE L., and BALLOU, ROBERT O. Bamboo Hospital (The Story of a Missionary Family in Burma). (rd7) Lippincott, c1961. 224p. $4.25

The daughter of a medical missionary tells the moving and absorbing story of her parents, who went to Burma in 1892 and built a hospital.

RUTH, BABE, and CONSIDINE, BOB. The Babe Ruth Story. (rd3) Dutton, c1948. 250p. $4.95

There are photographs to illustrate this story of one of the greatest men in baseball.

STUART, JESSE. The Thread That Runs So True. (rd7) Scribner, c1958 (rev. ed.). 293p. $4.50 (Paper, $1.45)

The experiences of a Kentucky mountain school teacher.

TERKEL, STUDS. Giants of Jazz. (rd7) Crowell, c1957. 215p. $3.50
A fine introduction to jazz through the lives of the men who made it great.
Twelve of them are portrayed here, including Fats Waller, Benny Goodman,
and Bix Beiderbecke. You'll want to hear their records after reading their
lives.

THORNE, ALICE. Story of Madame Curie. (rd6) Grosset, c1959. 176p.
$1.95 (Paper, Scholastic Book Services, 50c)
An inspiring story of the Nobel prizewinning disoverer of radium and her life
as a scientist. (Signature Books)

YOUNG, ROSAMOND McPHERSON. Boss Ket: A Life of Charles F. Kettering. (rd7) McKay, c1961. 210p. $3.50
A good biography of the modest and persistent inventor, Charles Kettering,
who made a fortune from his inventions, the cash register and the automobile
self-starter, among other things, and for a time headed the companies that
produced them.

EXPLORING THE OUT-OF-DOORS

BUCK, MARGARET WARING. Along the Seashore. (rd4) Abingdon,
c1964. 72p. $3 (Paper, $1.75)
Clear text and accurate drawings introduce the young naturalist to the many
kinds of plant and animal life in or near the waters surrounding the conti-
nental United States. Material is arranged from the simplest form of marine
life to the most complex.

_____In Ponds and Streams. (rd4) Abingdon, c1955. 72p. $3 (Paper,
$1.75)

_____In Yards and Gardens. (rd4) Abingdon, c1952. 72p. $3 (Paper,
$1.75)
Good, simple description of the animal and plant life to be found in gardens,
and in, on, and around small bodies of water.

DOWDEN, ANNE OPHELIA TODD. Look at a Flower. (rd6) Crowell,
c1963. 128p. $4.50
The major part of the book is devoted to descriptions of flower parts and to
families of flowers. The book is profusely illustrated with drawings of plants
and plant parts.

HEADSTROM, RICHARD. Adventures With a Hand Lens. (rd6) Lippincott, c1962. 220p. $4.25
You can magnify the wonders of nature by means of the fifty easy experiments
described clearly with the help of many drawings.

_____Adventures With Insects. (rd6) Lippincott, c1963. 224p. $4.25
Easy-to-read descriptions of the way insects can be caught and studied. A
good beginning for a hobby or a vocation.

The symbol "rd" accompanied by the figure, in parentheses, following the
title in each entry, indicates the estimated grade level of reading difficulty
(see p. 18-19).

HUTCHINS, ROSS E. This Is a Flower. (rd6) Dodd, c1963. 152p. $3.50
The author describes reproductive methods, various means of pollination, re-
sponses to light, the way in which flowers attract insects, time of bloom,
sources of color, the perfume, size, shape, and names of flowers. Illustrated by
close-up photographs with good captions.

——This Is a Leaf. (rd6) Dodd, c1962. 121p. $3
Facts about leaves—how they change color, why they fall, strange leaf de-
fenses, cannibal leaves, and other wonders.

KANE, HENRY B. The Tale of a Pond. (rd5) Knopf, c1960. 110p. $3
A beautifully illustrated, artistic book about the life and use of a pond in
nature, as seen through the eyes of a boy through a year's cycle. He sees the
pond as a home for many water creatures, as a source of water for animals and
plants, and as a sanctuary for migrating birds.

POOLE, LYNN and GRAY. Weird and Wonderful Ants. (rd6) Obolensky, c1961. 117p. $3.50
A book about the ubiquitous insects, their intricate behavior patterns and their
highly specialized skills. The anatomy of the ant and the structure of the
colony are discussed first; descriptions of the specialized functions of bankers
(honey hoarders), herders, fighters, etc., follow.

WEAVER, HARRIETT E. There Stand the Giants: The Story of the Red-
wood Trees. (rd5) Lippincott, c1960. 64p. $2.95
The story of some of the oldest trees on earth, as told by a former ranger and
naturalist.

FAMILY AND COMMUNITY LIFE

ANNIXTER, JANE and PAUL. Horns of Plenty. (rd5) Holiday, c1960.
203p. $3.25
A family who lives in the wilderness of the Rockies has many adventures with
both human and animal neighbors.

AVERY, KAY. Goodbye, Blue Jeans. (rd5) McKay, c1963. 174p. $3.50
This is twelve-year-old Susan's story, how she earned money during the summer vacation in a small New England town, bought a typewriter, and with the
help of two boys started a weekly newspaper. A story of small town life with
all its disappointments, conflicts, and good fun.

BALL, ZACHARY. Kep. (rd5) Holiday, c1961. 207p. $3.25
A realistic novel of a motherless, sensitive youth who must learn to face life
after his father is killed in a hunting accident through the boy's own careless-
ness.

BOLTON, CAROLE. Reunion in December. (rd6) Morrow, c1962. 220p.
$3.25
The story of a fourteen-year-old girl who comes to grips with herself during a
Christmas vacation spent with her dead father's family. A story of compli-
cated relationships.

BRAGDON, ELSPETH. That Jud! (rd6) Viking, c1957. 126p. $2.50
Jud Lurvey, aged twelve, was an orphan and lived on the generosity of
Spruce Point, Maine. The author enlists the sympathy of the reader for the
lonely and unwanted Jud, who won the confidence and affection of the townspeople by an act of courage.

CARLSON, NATALIE SAVAGE. Jean-Claude's Island. (rd4) Harper,
c1963. 147p. $3.50
Jean-Claude's French Canadian family lives on an island in the St. Lawrence
River. The boy's father finds a way to persuade old Pepère that modern ways
of doing things are sometimes better than some old ways.

_____School Bell in the Valley. (rd4) Harcourt, c1963. 124p. $3.75
The story of a ten-year-old mountain girl of 1900 and her determination to
learn to read and to help her shiftless relatives in the valley.

CARR, HARRIET H. Rod's Girl. (rd7) Hastings, c1963. 190p. $3.50
A modern romance in which a group of high-school youngsters help to solve
a town problem. Marge and her town are both faced with growing pains in
this timely story of overcrowded schools, delinquency, local politics, and the
challenges young teen-agers are capable of meeting. How they manage is a
lesson for teachers as well as parents.

CAVANNA, BETTY. Accent on April. (rd6) Morrow, c1960. 256p. $3.25
A family story of the ups and downs of a teen-age girl's relationship with her
older brother. Good portrayal of adolescent perplexities.

_____Almost Like Sisters. (rd6) Morrow, c1963. 254p. $3.25
What can a sensitive young girl do when she must compete with her beautiful
young mother? She goes away to school in Boston in an attempt to escape being taken for her mother's sister. A well-written mother-daughter story.

CLARKE, JOHN. High School Drop Out. (rd4) Doubleday, c1964. 143p.
$2.95
Joe Bancroft, who is having trouble in high school where baseball interests
him more than studying, drops out, since he is big for his age and has a part-
time job. He soon realizes he is not ready to be a man in a man's world. (Signal Books)

CLEARY, BEVERLY. Sister of the Bride. (rd5) Morrow, c1963. 288p.
$3.25
When the teen-age daughter of the house plans a wedding, her romantic
younger sister becomes involved. Humor and warmth fill this family story
about the problem of early marriages.

CONE, MOLLY. Reeney. (rd8) Houghton, c1963. 131p. $2.75
Reeney takes over the household upon the death of her mother. At the end of
the book Reeney has changed very little—she has not become an excellent cook
and housekeeper, but she has learned that courage, humor, and understanding
help in difficult situations.

_____
The symbol "rd" accompanied by the figure, in parentheses, following the
title in each entry, indicates the estimated grade level of reading difficulty
(see p. 18-19).

DAHL, BORGHILD. This Precious Year. (rd7) Dutton, c1964. 159p. $3.25
The story of Helia Singstad's senior year at a small college in a North Dakota Norwegian settlement during the drought and the depression years of the 1930's. Depicts the struggles and sacrifices to get an education, the warm family and personal relationships, and the "not-so-long-ago" historical period.

DARINGER, HELEN. Adopted Jane. (rd4) Harcourt, c1947. 225p. $2.95
Jane, an orphan from the Home, has a hard decision to make when two families want to adopt her after she spends a summer with them.

DE ANGELI, MARGUERITE. Bright April. (rd4) Doubleday, c1946. 88p. $2.95
A Negro girl's life at home, with her Scout troop, and with her friends in a Philadelphia community.

DEJONG, DOLA. One Summer's Secret. (rd7) McKay, c1963. 184p. $3
A novel of youth today which describes the reactions of a group of Long Island teen-agers to the predicament presented by a frightened, runaway Negro girl of fifteen.

DICKSON, MARGUERITE. Only Child. (rd7) Longmans, c1952. 247p. $3.75
Trouble arrives when two orphaned cousins come to live with sixteen-year-old Gwen. Until that time she had been the center of attention.

DU JARDIN, ROSAMUND. Wait for Marcy. (rd7) Lippincott, c1932. 224p. $3.25 (Paper, Scholastic Book Services, 35c)
A story in which an understanding older brother helps a reluctant teen-ager to her first date. Excellent family relationship.

DUNCAN, LOIS. The Middle Sister. (rd6) Dodd, c1960. 180p. $3
Ruth has two attractive and talented sisters, while she feels plain and inferior. She loves them but also envies them, and must struggle to find her own place in life.

EYERLY, JEANNETTE. Drop-Out. (rd6) Lippincott, c1963. 192p. $3.50
The easy-to-read story of two confused teen-agers who reach wisdom only after some unhappy experiences following their decision to leave school.

———The World of Ellen March. (rd6) Lippincott, c1964. 192p. $3.75
A girl must learn to face the change made in her life by her parents' divorce. In doing so, she looks ahead to her own future.

FINLAYSON, ANN. Runaway Teen. (rd4) Doubleday, c1963. 143p. $2.50
Resentful of her new stepfather and unhappy over having to share her mother, Libby Canfield runs away to Chicago when she thinks they have forgotten her sixteenth birthday. (Signal Books)

FRIEDMAN, FRIEDA. Ellen and the Gang. (rd5) Morrow, c1963. 191p. $2.95
The adventures of a junior-high-school girl who lives in a housing project in New York City.

HALL, NATALIE. The World in a City Block. (rd5) Viking, c1960. 42p. $2.50

When a youth runs a bakery route in New York City, he learns about the colorful Old World background of the people he serves.

HARK, MILDRED, and McQUEEN, NOEL. A Home for Penny. (rd5) Watts, c1959. 202p. $2.95

An amusing and appealing story of Penny, who is often disappointed when other children in the orphanage find homes with families but she remains. She faces her problems and finally wins her own home.

KRUMGOLD, JOSEPH. Onion John. (rd7) Crowell, c1959. 248p. $3.95

The story is told from the point of view of twelve-year-old Andy, who is torn between loyalty to his father and attraction to the itinerant Onion John, whose strange, old-world ideas influence the boy.

LEE, HARPER. To Kill a Mockingbird. (rd8) Lippincott, c1960. 288p. $4.50

A young brother and sister in a small town in Alabama become involved in adults' conflicting views. The central problem is the town's attitude toward Negroes. When their father, a lawyer, defends a Negro on a rape charge, they are forced to hold their tongues and their fists when taunted by their townspeople and peers. During the trial they discover that their father is braver and much wiser than any other man they know.

LEE, MILDRED. The Rock and the Willow. (rd5) Lothrop, c1963. 223p. $3.50

The story of the struggle of a poor teen-age girl in rural Alabama to acquire an education. The writer makes a poor family seem rich to the reader of this story of the depression era.

L'ENGLE, MADELEINE. The Moon by Night. (rd6) Farrar, c1963. 224p. $3.25

A teen-age girl and her family take a camping trip to California and meet two kinds of friends. Problems of religion, prejudice, and conflicting loyalties help Vicky mature.

LIGGETT, THOMAS. The Hollow. (rd7) Holiday, c1958. 237p. $2.95

Juvenile delinquents learn how to help themselves in a work camp through the aid of a man who understands them.

LITTLE, JEAN. Mine for Keeps. (rd5) Little, c1962. 186p. $3.75

A warm family story about a child who returns to her home and friends after several years in a school for handicapped children. Describes the handling of the resentment and self-pity of a child who has cerebral palsy.

MEIGS, CORNELLA. Wild Geese Flying. (rd4) Macmillan, c1957. 194p. $2.95

A wandering family settle into the Vermont home left them by their grandfather and face the problem of being accepted by their community. This involves a mystery.

The symbol "rd" accompanied by the figure, in parentheses, following the title in each entry, indicates the estimated grade level of reading difficulty (see p. 18-19).

MUSGRAVE, FLORENCE. Two Dates for Mike. (rd7) Hastings, c1964.
150p. $3.25
Fifteen-year-old Mike has an assortment of problems—he thinks girls are pests
until he meets a girl who is a foreign exchange student, and he prefers school
dramatics to sports his father wants him to take part in. He finds out that he
needs a few adults giving guidance. Good treatment of teen-age problems and
emotional difficulties.

NIEHUIS, CHARLES C. Beegee. (rd7) Macrae, c1963. 187p. $3.25
Beegee is fleeing from his Cedar Rapids home where he felt the lack of identity with a warm family life and where he was involved in a violent gang
rumble. He starts a new and exciting adventure in self-discovery with a group
of men in the Arizona conservation service.

NIELSEN, JEAN. The Golden Dream. (rd7) Funk, c1959. 248p. $2.95
(Paper, Scholastic Book Services, 35c)
An interesting, warmhearted novel of family life in which teen-age Starli survives disappointments at school and home and, with the help of friends and
one admiring boy, looks to a golden future.

NORFLEET, MARY CROCKETT. Hand-Me-Down House. (rd5) Knox,
c1962. 96p. $2.50
A Negro doctor and his family move into a racially changing neighborhood
and make friends, even though they are uncertain at first of their acceptance.
A heartwarming story of a young boy who brings the gift of love to a lonely
old lady and happiness to his older brother and sister, winning for himself an
unexpected joy.

OGILVIE, ELISABETH. Becky's Island. (rd7) McGraw, c1961. 187p.
$3.25
A Maine story in which seventeen-year-old Vicky stumbles upon Becky's Island and its neglected people. Vicky is devoted to the neglected children on
the island and is successful in getting them a school and a teacher.

PHIPSON, JOAN. The Family Conspiracy. (rd5) Harcourt, c1964. 224p.
$3.50
The story of the adventures of four children on an Australian sheep ranch.
Their mother's operation and a severe drought lead them to conspire to earn
money for a hospital fund. Their plans prove to be often dangerous and
always difficult, and to require much resourcefulness.

RENDINA, LAURA COOPER. World of Their Own. (rd6) Little, c1963.
205p. $3.50
The reactions of a group of teen-agers from Florida to a summer of hard work
in a Connecticut tobacco camp. As the summer progresses, each learns something from the group experience: the rebel Pete, to be friendly; the popular
Kit, to understand why and how she has been trading on her charm; and shy
Paula, to relax enough to talk to a boy.

REYNOLDS, BARBARA LEONARD. Hamlet and Brownswiggle. (rd4)
Scribner, c1954. 203p. $3.50
Full of fun about forming a hamster club, this story also is concerned with
the troubles that face the person who is the "middle child" in the family.

SHERBURNE, ZOA. Stranger in the House. (rd5) Morrow, c1963. 192p. $3.25

After nine years in a mental hospital, Kathy's mother returns to her family, but finds she is treated as a stranger in her own house. Many problems result for the teen-age daughter and her brother until the family gradually comes together again.

SHOTWELL, LOUISA R. Roosevelt Grady. (rd4) World, c1963. 151p. $2.95

The story of a migrant farm boy who longs for a house and a school he can stay in. He makes friends with an orphan, and together they find a way to reach their goal.

SIMON, SHIRLEY. Cousins at Camm Corners. (rd4) Lothrop, c1963. 192p. $3

Marcy Sutton, pretty and pampered, comes from New York City to visit a noisy house full of cousins in a small town in Ohio. Her conflicts with a large family whose chief troubles are financial are very amusing.

SIMPSON, DOROTHY. New Horizons. (rd6) Lippincott, c1961. 192p. $3.50

A young girl discovers that she must meet new problems if she is to widen her horizons. She learns how to do this when she leaves her sheltered life on a Maine island and goes away to school on the mainland.

SMITH, IMOGENE. Egg on Her Face. (rd6) Lippincott, c1963. 192p. $3.50

Fun and seriousness combine in this story of the problems and pleasures of a girl's high-school years.

SORENSEN, VIRGINIA E. Miracles on Maple Hill. (rd4) Harcourt, c1956. 180p. $2.95

This award book tells the story of a man who has been a prisoner of war, and of how he and his family find understanding and happiness during some exciting years on their farm.

STEINBECK, JOHN. The Pearl. (rd8) Viking, c1947. 128p. $3 (Paper, Bantam, 40c)

The finding of a pearl of great value changes completely the lives of two simple people. Now people of wealth, they learn fear, treachery, and the agony of great human loss. There is no freedom until finally the pearl is cast back into the sea from which it came.

STERLING, DOROTHY. Mary Jane. (rd6) Doubleday, c1959. 214p. $2.95

A Negro teen-ager enters a newly integrated junior high school in the deep South and slowly begins to form friendships and good relationships with her classmates.

The symbol "rd" accompanied by the figure, in parentheses, following the title in each entry, indicates the estimated grade level of reading difficulty (see p. 18-19).

STOLZ, MARY. The Bully of Barkham Street. (rd5) Harper, c1963. 194p. $3.50

Martin learns to outgrow being a bully as we are given a look at the reasons he has become one. He begins to handle his weight problem, too, and to use his active imagination in the right way.

————Who Wants Music on Monday? (rd5) Harper, c1963. 267p. $3.50

This is a delightful story of a family with a beautiful, self-centered older sister, a college sophomore brother, and fourteen-year-old Cassie, who is plain but interesting and lively. The sisters share a room but irritate each other. Their college brother has two roommates, one English and one Negro, to whom people in the story react in different ways. Each has his problem as he struggles to find his place in a confusing world. This includes the parents as well as the young people in the story.

STREATFEILD, NOEL. Traveling Shoes. (rd5) Random, c1962. 245p. $2.95

The story of an artistic and talented family. The four Forum children toured with their father, an accompanist, and their mother, an artist. The prodigy of the family, Sebastian, gave violin concerts in London and their former, dearly loved Devonshire house became home again.

————A Vicarage Family; an Autobiographical Story. (rd7) Watts, c1963. 196p. $4.95

Although written in the third person, this is an autobiographical book and the story of a vicarage family at the turn of the century. Victoria, the author, is the rebel in a large English family. She is strong-minded, independent, and aware of the superior charms of her older sister and of the youngest, Louise, the family beauty.

STUCLEY, ELIZABETH. The Contrary Orphans. (rd6) Watts, c1962. 192p. $2.95

A book about a home for orphans in England. Most of the story concerns Carlotta—wily, tough, imaginative, and rebellious, and Frankie—awkward, rejected, stuttering, and shy. A realistic picture of one social group in a narrow environment.

SYKES, JO. Chip on His Shoulder. (rd7) Funk, c1961. 186p. $2.95

Hamilton Roark is an active member of the Red Whistler's gang. The new juvenile officer sends him to a Montana horse ranch for the summer in a last desperate effort to save the boy from delinquency. Here, new friends and a better environment help Roark learn the cost of gang life.

WARE, LEON. The Rebellious Orphan. (rd5) Westminster, c1964. 217p. $3.50

A touching story of loneliness and escape. Newly orphaned Bill Talbot has no choice but to live with his three aunts in a big house on an island at Newport Beach, California. Bill leads an increasingly oppressive life until he finds that he is legally the owner of the house.

WÄRNLÖF, ANNA LISA. The Boy Upstairs. (rd8) Harcourt, c1963. 128p. $2.75

The struggle of an impetuous girl, sixteen-year-old Frederika, to reestablish herself in a world made insecure by her parents' divorce. Martin, the boy upstairs, seems an enemy to Frederika.

WEBER, LENORA MATTINGLY. Tarry Awhile. (rd7) Crowell, c1962. 247p. $3.75

Through the experiences of her friends, a happily engaged Beany Malone learns that teen-age marriage has its problems. The book describes wholesome family life, good friendship values, and sensible attitudes toward all the problems of courtship and marriage.

WILLARD, BARBARA. Hetty. (rd5) Harcourt, c1963. 192p. $3.50

A story of family life in an English coastal town in the year of Queen Victoria's Diamond Jubilee. Thirteen-year-old Hetty Jebb, redheaded and impetuous, and her best friend, the daughter of a wealthy family, are major characters.

WRIGHT, ANNA MARIA ROSE. Land of Silence. (rd5) Friendship, c1962. 143p. $2.95 (Paper, $1.75)

Toby, a poor student in the seventh grade, rude and sloppy in dress, resentful and uncooperative, by chance sees the work being done in classes for the deaf. He becomes interested in education for the deaf and, as a result, feels more useful, becomes more cooperative and friendly, and improves in his own work.

WYNDHAM, LEE. Candy Stripers. (rd6) Messner, c1958. 192p. $2.95 (Paper, Scholastic Book Services, 50c)

The nurses' aides known as candy stripers perform a real service in today's world. Bonnie Schuyler becomes a junior aide in a medical center and has a variety of experiences.

FOLK TALES AND MYTHS

AULAIRE, INGRI and EDGAR PARIN D'. The d'Aulaires' Book of Greek Myths. (rd4) Doubleday, c1962. 192p. $4.95

The fascinating stories of the Greek gods and heroes are retold in simple words and in the interesting pictures of the d'Aulaires. Fun for any age.

BOTKIN, BEN, and WITHERS, CARL. The Illustrated Book of American Folklore. (rd5) Grosset, c1958. 99p. $3.95

Two hundred legends, hero stories, and superstitions in prose and verse from every part of the country. (Illustrated Books)

CARPENTER, FRANCES. African Wonder Tales. (rd5) Doubleday, c1963. 215p. $3.95

Here are folk tales from different African countries. They show how much alike human adventures and experiences are no matter what land they happen in.

DE LEEUW, ADÈLE. Indonesian Legends and Folk Tales. (rd4) Nelson, c1961. 160p. $2.95

A series of stories that helps us to understand the literary heritage of an important Eastern culture.

The symbol "rd" accompanied by the figure, in parentheses, following the title in each entry, indicates the estimated grade level of reading difficulty (see p. 18-19).

FRITH, HENRY. King Arthur and His Knights. (rd5) Doubleday, c1963. 416p. $1.49

The pageantry of King Arthur's court comes to life in this story of knights and their ladies, jousts and battles, magic spells and distressed ladies.

GUNTHER, JOHN. Jason and the Golden Fleece. (rd4) Random, c1959. 52p. $1.95 (Paper, Scholastic Book Services, 25c)

The exciting adventures of Jason and his Argonauts. Jason had a special reason for wanting to capture the Golden Fleece from the enemy—his kingdom was at stake.

HARRIS, CHRISTIE. Once Upon a Totem. (rd5) Atheneum, c1963. 148p. $3.50

Five vivid and dramatic legends of the North Pacific Indians shows the customs and beliefs of these early Americans. The courage of their young people is portrayed, along with their heroic traditions and highly developed culture.

HAZELTINE, ALICE ISABEL, comp. Hero Tales From Many Lands. (rd6) Abingdon, c1961. 475p. $5.95

An excellent collection of thirty tales from the best retellings of the world's great tales of epic heroes from Achilles and Odysseus to Ghengis Khan and Scarface—much material that is no longer in print.

ISH-KISHOR, JUDITH. Tales From the Wise Men of Israel. (rd5) Lippincott, c1962. 224p. $4

Ancient parables are told with simplicity and humor. The introduction by Harry Golden adds to the book's attraction.

LEODHAS, SORCHE NIC. Thistle and Thyme: Tales and Legends From Scotland. (rd5) Holt, c1962. 143p. $3.50

A delightful collection of ten Scottish tales which were handed down to the author by word of mouth and are told as entertainment at a feast. Excellent stories for reading aloud and a good source for storytelling material. Similar tales of the Scottish Highlands may be found in the same author's *Heather and Broom*.

McLEAN, MOLLIE, and WISEMAN, ANNE. Adventures of the Greek Heroes. (rd6) Houghton, c1961. 174p. $2.95 (Paper, $1.48)

This is a beautiful edition of the classical Greek hero tales, including those of Hercules, Perseus, Theseus, Orpheus, and the Argonauts.

MONIGOLD, GLENN W., comp. Folk Tales From Vietnam. (rd5) Pauper, c1964. 61p. $1

A delightful collection of folk tales from a country that is very much in the news. Some have familiar themes; some are totally different. There are beautiful and colorful illustrations in the Oriental manner, and a brief introduction tells about the country itself.

PICARD, BARBARA LEONIE. The Lady of the Linden Tree. (rd5) Criterion, c1962. 214p. $3.50
A collection of twelve new fairy tales filled with enchantment and magic and set in Europe and the Orient. The author has used many familiar basic themes: the ugly princess who becomes her beautiful self, the trading-at-a-loss story, the Cinderella theme, and the like.

——Tales of the British People. (rd5) Criterion, c1961. 159p. $3
A retelling of nine legendary stories of the British Isles, covering the period from the first Celtic invasion to the end of the fourteenth century. Each tale is prefaced by a brief historical introduction, linking the stories with the Normans, Saxons, Celts, Vikings, or Romans who first told them.

POTTER, ROBERT R. Myths and Folk Tales Around the World. (rd4) Globe, c1963. 371p. $3
Myths from Greece, Rome, and Northern Europe are told here, along with folk tales from all around the world.

RUSHMORE, HELEN. The Dancing Horses of Acoma and Other Acoma Indian Stories. (rd5) World, c1963. 192p. $4.50
Twelve old legends of the Acoma Indian tribes of New Mexico are written down for the first time. The illustrations are done in the style of the Acomas.

SCHREIBER, MORRIS. Stories of Gods and Heroes. (rd4) Grosset, c1960. 101p. $3.95
Almost half a hundred classical myths and legends of characters that include the American Hiawatha as well as the ancient Greeks and Romans.

GIRLS' STORIES

BAKER, LAURA NELSON. Somebody, Somewhere. (rd8) Knopf, c1962. 179p. $3
The story of Diana, her feelings about the junior year in a new school and the help she gave Chick, her boyfriend, when he was picked up by the police. A good picture of the relationship between the delinquent and the stable adolescent, and of the problems of loyalty to other girls, going steady, etc.

BOLTON, CAROLE. Christy. (rd5) Morrow, c1960. 217p. $3.25
Teen-age Christy's world is turned upside down by the arrival of a writer old enough to be her father, and dashing enough to capture her dreams. The humor and sadness of a first love are sympathetically pictured.

BRADBURY, BIANCA. The Amethyst Summer. (rd6) Washburn, c1963. 186p. $3.50
Sixteen-year-old Bayley's mother must leave to stay with a relative who is ill and Bayley has to keep house during the summer for her father and three brothers. She learns to organize her work, to pretend serenity for her father's sake, and to be more thoughtful of other people.

The symbol "rd" accompanied by the figure, in parentheses, following the title in each entry, indicates the estimated grade level of reading difficulty (see p. 18-19).

BRATTON, HELEN. It's Morning Again. (rd7) McKay, c1964. 215p. $3.95

Ruth Ashley, who had a sheltered life in her Missouri farm home, goes to live with her grandmother in the capital. Here she must meet the challenges of a larger high school, more sophisticated friends, and other socially demanding situations. Her story is typical of that of many young people today who have high ideals, intelligence, and a desire to learn and mature.

BROOKMAN, DENISE CASS. The Young in Love. (rd8) Macrae, c1962. 191p. $3.25

A story that treats of the problems of an adolescent girl. Jan loses David, the boy next door with whom she has been going steady, when she tries to attract an older boy. She is rebuffed and humiliated, but after a talk with David she gains perspective and maturity.

CAVANNA, BETTY. Fancy Free. (rd7) Morrow, c1961. 256p. $3.25 (Paper, Berkley, 45c)

An interesting and romantic story about a sixteen-year-old girl who goes to Peru with an archaeological expedition directed by her father.

————Paintbox Summer. (rd7) Westminster, c1949. 191p. $3.25 (Paper, Scholastic Book Services, 35c)

Kate Vale enjoys swimming, beach parties, a wharf apartment overlooking the bay, and a romance with a handsome Portuguese fisherman during an exciting summer at the famous Peter Hunt art colony at Cape Cod.

CLEARY, BEVERLY. Fifteen. (rd5) Morrow, c1956. 255p. $3.25

The story of fifteen-year-old Jane Purdy's romance with Stan Crandall, a de-livery boy, whom she meets while baby-sitting one afternoon. Boy-girl rela-tionships portrayed with humor and an understanding of teen-agers.

CRAIG, MARGARET MAZE. Trish. (rd7) Crowell, c1951. 242p. $2.50 (Paper, Berkley, 35c)

The story of Patricia Ingram, but it could be the story of any girl, anywhere, who falls in love for the first time and has decisions to make when faced with problems of a more serious nature. A tender and courageous story of first love.

DU JARDIN, ROSAMUND. One of the Crowd. (rd7) Lippincott, c1961. 192p. $2.95

One of the popular Tobey and Midge books, this one concerns the decision Midge, a high-school sophomore, must make between the smart set and the friends she has always known. Other titles in the series include *Practically Seventeen, Boy Trouble,* and *Wedding in the Family.*

————Someone to Count On. (rd7) Lippincott, c1962. 185p. $2.95

Fun, activities, and new friends help Twink gain maturity during the summer of her junior year in high school.

————Young and Fair. (rd7) Lippincott, c1963. 192p. $3.25

Love and success are won in this novel of a young girl living in the 1880's. She finds romance with the son of her boss in a Chicago department store.

EMERY, ANNE. First Love, True Love. (rd7) Westminster, c1956. 191p. $2.95

The story of Pat's junior year in high school and her struggle with the prob-lem of whether or not to go steady. Pat learns to curb her spendthrift ways and her habit of "arranging" things for other people. Other popular books by this author are *Going Steady; High Note, Low Note; Sweet Sixteen.*

EYERLY, JEANNETTE. More Than a Summer Love. (rd7) Lippincott, c1962. 192p. $3.50

When a girl unexpectedly spends a summer in Iowa as a companion to her grandmother, she runs into excitement and makes new friends.

FRANCHERE, RUTH. Hannah Herself. (rd7) Crowell, c1964. 176p. $3.50

Education is looked upon with suspicion in pre-Civil War Illinois. Sixteen-year-old Hannah from the East arrives in the rural Illinois of the 1830's to visit her sister and brother-in-law who are engaged in establishing a school for older boys. A good portrait of Hannah's growth from girl to woman.

GILBERT, NAN. The Unchosen. (rd7) Harper, c1963. 214p. $3.50

An interesting novel, told in first person by Ellen, a high-school senior. Debbie, Kay, and Ellen have never had a date; they are not attractive or happy girls. They embark on a program of self-improvement and thus make other friends—both boys and girls.

HARTWELL, NANCY. Something for Laurie. (rd7) Holt, c1962. 189p. $3

This is the story of a girl who is dissatisfied with herself. As she learns to do something about it, so may the reader who is not pleased with herself.

KISINGER, GRACE G. The New Lucinda. (rd7) Nelson, c1958. 192p. $2.95 (Paper, Scholastic Book Services, 35c)

A family move presents the opportunity for a shy, self-conscious teen-ager to change her personality. Shy, awkward Lucinda or "Beanpole" changes to smooth, sophisticated "Cindy."

LAMBERT, JANET. Star-Spangled Summer. (rd7) Scholastic Book Services (Dutton, c1941). 220p. Paper, 25c

Poor little rich girl Carroll hasn't been having a nickel's worth of fun until she is invited to spend a summer with Penny Parish. She enjoys her first horse show, first formal dance, and a moonlight picnic.

LEHR, DELORES. The Tender Age. (rd7) Lothrop, c1961. 205p. $3.50

The story of a shy girl who feels awkward talking to boys and wants, above all, to be liked.

MARSHALL, CATHERINE. Julie's Heritage. (rd6) McKay, c1957. 231p. $3.95

The story of Julie, a Negro girl, who finds that she can use her lovely singing voice to win friends in high school, to prove her worth, and to bring the races together.

MORSE, CAROL. Judy North, Drum Majorette. (rd4) Doubleday, c1963. 143p. $2.50

The way Judy faces up to her shyness and her desire to bid for the attention of the handsome captain of the football team make an interesting story. (Signal Books)

The symbol "rd" accompanied by the figure, in parentheses, following the title in each entry, indicates the estimated grade level of reading difficulty (see p. 18-19).

OGILVIE, ELISABETH. Blueberry Summer. (rd7) McGraw, c1956. 187p.
$3 (Paper, Scholastic Book Services, 50c)

One summer in the life of Cass, a plain, overweight, teen-age girl who discovers that sometimes when everything and everybody seem to be against
you, the fault is largely yours. Fate leads her to a charming artist named Jeff
Marshall, and Cass forgets her problems.

————Turn Around Twice. (rd6) McGraw, c1962. 160p. $3.25

When shy, sixteen-year-old Burnley Wilder wins a contest prize of either
$3,000 or a Maine island, her choice of the island involves her in mystery as
well as romance.

STOUTENBERG, ADRIEN. Window on the Sea. (rd7) Westminster, c1962.
159p. $2.95

The events that follow the meeting of Mollie Lucas and Kingsley Reynal show
Mollie that a whole new world of opportunity lies beyond her fishing pier.
Mollie meets an intelligent boy who helps her to realize that she needs to give
up mediocrity.

WEBER, LENORA MATTINGLY. Something Borrowed, Something Blue.
(rd7) Crowell, c1963. 288p. $3.75

Beany's elaborate wedding, planned by her step-grandmother, is not enthusi-
astically greeted by her fiancé, friends, or family. However, her wedding
evolves into a "day to remember."

WRIGHTSON, PATRICIA. The Feather Star. (rd6) Harcourt, c1963. 160p.
$2.95

From a remote and beautiful coastal district of Australia comes the story of
the summer in which fifteen-year-old Lindy Martin took the long step from
childhood into adolescence and learned a new appreciation of her parents and
of life.

HEALTH AND SAFETY

BENDICK, JEANNE, and LEVIN, MARCIA O. Pushups and Pinups: Diet,
Exercise and Grooming for Young Teens. (rd5) McGraw,
c1963. 127p. $2.75

A book that should make both boys and girls more conscious of their weight
and health. There are chapters on fitness, care of skin and body, appropriate
exercises for both boys and girls, calorie counting, sleeping, and vitamin
needs. Humorous and appealing illustrations.

BURGDORF, OTTO P. Adventure Book of Human Biology. (rd5)
Capitol, c1962. 94p. $3.95

This is helpful in understanding the human body and how it works. (Capitol
Adventure Books)

BUTLER, BEVERLY. Light a Single Candle. (rd7) Dodd, c1962. 242p.
$3.25

A good story about an adolescent girl's adjustment to blindness at fourteen—
her reactions of despair succeeded by determination, her gradual feelings of
security about being accepted, and her decreasing self-consciousness about
being different. An account of home, school, friends, and problems relating to
Cathy's handicap.

DIETZ, DAVID. All About Great Medical Discoveries. (rd5) Random, c1960. 140p. $1.95

Great medical discoveries that have affected the health of people around the world have come about as the result of cooperative efforts, even though men like Pasteur, Lister, Salk, and Fleming worked as individuals. This is their story. (Allabout Books)

FELSEN, HENRY GREGOR. To My Son, the Teen-age Driver. (rd8) Dodd, c1964. 124p. $3

A practical, informative guide for the young driver to help him (or her) understand his car, prevent accidents, and realize today's traffic problems. Invaluable tips and suggestions on operating cars that are generally not covered in training programs. *Must* reading for all teen-agers.

FLOHERTY, JOHN J. Watch Your Step. (rd6) Lippincott, c1950. 160p. $4.50

The simple rules of safety are dramatized through interviews and tours with police inspectors, garage mechanics, radio-car patrolmen, traffic officers, fire chiefs, and lifeguards.

GOODHART, ROBERT S. The Teen-ager's Guide to Diet and Health. (rd8) Prentice, c1964. 176p. $3.95

Tips on how to figure your "ideal" weight—how to gain, lose, or maintain weight, and how to count calories. The book contains a training table for athletes, advice on the care of skin, hair, and nails, plus questionnaires and charts. Valuable information for teen-agers on how to manage their own nutrition in their own way.

GRANT, BRUCE. Know Your Car and How to Drive: Hints and Tips to Stay Alive. (rd9) Rand McNally, c1962. 72p. $2.95 Paper, $1.50)

A compact, handy guide that emphasizes safety precautions. Included as well is information as to the mechanics of a car, emergency repairs, construction, operation, and maintenance. Advice on purchasing a car and on finance is also given.

GRUENBERG, BENJAMIN and SIDONIE. The Wonderful Story of You. (rd5) Doubleday, c1960 (rev. ed.). 182p. $3.50

A clear and unembarrassing telling of facts that puzzle young people. Especially helpful is the chapter on "Becoming Yourself," for it deals with the emotions and intellect in relation to their effect upon physical development.

HEMPHILL, JOSEPHINE. Fruitcake and Arsenic. (rd7) Little, c1962. 144p. $3.95

An account of the activities of the Federal agency that protects us from bad foods and dangerous drugs. The author also describes the day-to-day operations of Federal agents in visiting, investigating, testing, and tracing people, industrial plants, and products.

The symbol "rd" accompanied by the figure, in parentheses, following the title in each entry, indicates the estimated grade level of reading difficulty (see p. 18-19).

LEAF, MUNRO. Safety Can Be Fun. (rd3) Lippincott, c1961. (rev. ed.). 63p. $2.95

This amusing picture storybook has stick figures that emphasize basic health rules and show what may happen to a careless person.

McHENRY, E. W. Foods Without Fads. (rd7) Lippincott, c1960. 160p. $3.50

A useful guide to foods that are basic for good health. Also explained is the relationship of diet to health and disease.

MENNINGER, WILLIAM C., and others. How You Grow Up. (rd5) Sterling, c1957. 160p. $3.95

A famous psychiatrist discusses the facts about growing up. Getting along with others is one of the things emphasized.

MILLER, JAMES G. Adventure Book of the Human Mind. (rd5) Capitol, c1962. 93p. $3.95

The fascinating story of the human mind and the senses, of human behavior and psychology, told simply and understandably. (Capitol Adventure Books)

NEUMAYER, ENGELBERT J., ed. The Unvanquished: A Collection of Readings on Overcoming Handicaps. (rd8) Oxford, c1955. 145p. Paper, 85c

The unifying theme is the ability of brave men and women to win success in spite of crushing handicaps. The form is varied—short story, drama, poetry, biography.

SPINGARN, NATALIE DAVIS. To Save Your Life. (rd6) Little, c1963. 213p. $3.95

True stories of the U.S. Public Health Service show how the work of this group has saved lives many times.

SPORTS ILLUSTRATED, EDITORS OF. Sports Illustrated Book of Safe Driving. (rd5) Lippincott, c1962. 96p. $2.95

This is a valuable book in giving suggestions about driving conditions, dangers, and safety equipment, plus information on driving sports cars.

VALENS, EVANS G., and HURD, CLEMENT. Wildfire. (rd4) World, c1963. 32p. $3.75

The exciting and terrible picture of what happens when a great fire goes through the forest. It points up the need for safety precautions in forest areas and shows the behavior of animals in such a disaster.

WARD, RODGER, and YATES, BROCK. Rodger Ward's Guide to Good Driving. (rd7) Harper, c1963. 195p. $3.50

Young automobile enthusiasts learn about safe and skillful driving under any conditions, and also get advice on choosing a car. This book is designed to help teen-agers with their driving problems.

HISTORY AND GEOGRAPHY

ADAMS, BEN. The Last Frontier: A Short History of Alaska. (rd7) Hill, c1961. 181p. $3.50

A good history of Alaska and of the colorful people who have shaped her history. A quick survey of the climate, geography, and the peoples, illustrated by an Eskimo artist.

ADLER, IRVING. Tools in Your Life. (rd6) Day, c1956. 128p. $3

An account of man's development of tools from the earliest stone axe to atomic energy. The sociological effects that have resulted from the introduction of new inventions or from the clinging to old tools and old ways of doing things.

ANDRIST, RALPH K. Heroes of Polar Explorations. (rd6) Harper, c1962. 156p. $3.95

A survey of the adventures of pioneer polar explorers of the Arctic and the Antarctic, from Captain Cook through the International Geophysical Year. (Horizon Caravel Books)

COLVIN, GERARD. The Lands and Peoples of Central America; Guatemala—El Salvador—Costa Rica—Honduras—Nicaragua—Panama—British Honduras. (rd6) Macmillan, c1962. 96p. $2

The book covers the geography, history, political structure, economic resources, and recent developments in industrial and agricultural patterns, etc. Illustrations include twenty-nine photographs and a map. (Lands and Peoples Series)

DUPUY, TREVOR NEVITT. The Military History of World War II. (rd6) Watts

Several volumes, illustrated by photographs and maps, telling of the war on land, at sea, and in the air. Though easy to read, their chief appeal is to the older teen-ager or adult. Some titles are:
The Air War in the West: September 1939-May 1941. c1963. 76p. $2.50
The Air War in the West: June 1941-April 1945. c1963. 66p. $2.50
European Land Battles, 1939-1943. c1962. 91p. $1.95
European Land Battles, 1944-1945. c1962. 83p. $1.95
The Naval War in the West: The Raiders. c1963. 67p. $2.50
The Naval War in the West: The Wolf Packs. c1963. 60p. $2.50

FLOETHE, LOUISE LEE. The Indian and His Pueblo. (rd3) Scribner, c1960. Unp. $3.25

A colorful description in words and pictures of the life of the Rio Grande Indians from the past to modern times.

FRAZIER, CARL and ROSALIE. The Lincoln Country in Pictures. (rd4) Hastings, c1963. Unp. $3.50

Photographs of the environment in which Lincoln spent the most formative years of his life—places Lincoln lived and the things he might have used, with descriptive and anecdotal captions. Brief text with each picture.

GOETZ, DELIA. Tropical Rain Forests. (rd4) Morrow, c1957. 64p. $2.75

Covers the rain forest area of Asia, Africa, and South America—the teeming life and the important products. Soft green illustrations on every page.

The symbol "rd" accompanied by the figure, in parentheses, following the title in each entry, indicates the estimated grade level of reading difficulty (see p. 18-19).

HAMMOND, WINIFRED. Plants, Food and People. (rd6) Coward,
c1964. 160p. $3.95

The book points out man's dependence upon plants for his food, clothing, and
shelter. From man's early dietary habits, the author traces his progress to
modern mechanized farming, concluding with a brief chapter on plant research for space travel. Useful for reference and supplementary material in
applied sciences and social studies.

HIRSCH, S. CARL. The Globe for the Space Age. (rd6) Viking, c1963.
96p. $3.75

The history of the model globe and what it reveals about geography, the
seasons, weather, and the space program.

HOFSINDE, ROBERT. The Indian and the Buffalo. (rd4) Morrow, c1961.
96p. $2.75

The chapters deal with such topics as hunting methods, uses of buffalo for
food or tools, for robes or rawhide, and an interesting comparison of buffalo
dances in several different tribes.

HOGG, GARRY. Deep Down: Great Achievements in Cave Exploration.
(rd7) Criterion, c1962. 160p. $3.50

Descriptions of eight thrilling accounts of explorations "deep down" into some
of the world's most perilous caves, including the discovery of the Carlsbad
Caverns. Some of the explorations were successful; some ended in tragedy.

JOHNSON, GERALD WHITE. The Congress. (rd6) Morrow, c1963. 128p.
$2.95

The story of the legislative branch of American government. Given are the
tasks of the two Houses of Congress—the House of Representatives and the
Senate—and their relationship with other branches of the government.

———The Presidency. (rd6) Morrow, c1962. 128p. $2.95

An analysis of the executive branch of our government. A description of the
tasks that the President now has, the changes in the presidential role and
powers, and relationships between the presidency and other branches of the
government.

———The Supreme Court. (rd6) Morrow, c1962. 127p. $2.95

The author describes the role of the Supreme Court, its importance and power, its place in our system of government, and its effect on the lives of ordinary citizens. Policies of the Supreme Court in the years since the Civil War,
including the problem of segregation, are discussed.

JOY, CHARLES R. Young People of South America: Their Stories in
Their Own Words. (rd5) Duell, c1963. 236p. $4.50

This book contains twenty-six chapters by boys and girls from all the countries of South America.

KELLY, REGINA ZIMMERMAN. Chicago: Big-Shouldered City. (rd8)
Reilly, c1962. 176p. $3.50

The story of four generations of a Chicago family as it grew and prospered
with the city from 1811 to 1893. Two brief chapters at the end of the book
describe some of the changes since 1893 and cite places of interest to be seen
today.

LEAF, MUNRO. Geography Can Be Fun. (rd3) Lippincott, c1962 (rev. ed.). 64p. $2.95
Brief text and amusing drawings make geography an easy task in this book.

MEYER, EDITH PATTERSON. The Friendly Frontier. (rd6) Little, c1962. 296p. $4.75
Timely story of the not always friendly American-Canadian border we tend to accept so easily.

MILHOUS, KATHERINE. Through These Arches: The Story of Independence Hall. (rd5) Lippincott, c1964. 96p. $4.50
American history and "spirit" are revealed through many pictures and unusual text, from Indian days to the day Independence Hall became a national shrine. This tribute is a fitting and beautiful one. Both young people and adults will find facts of interest here.

NEWMAN, ROBERT. The Japanese People of the Three Treasures. (rd7) Atheneum, c1964. 187p. $4.25
The author introduces Japan and its people through a brief survey of their history and of their character.

PARKER, GORDON. Great Moments in American History. (rd3) Penns Valley, c1961. 48p. $2
Colorful and memorable incidents of American history are retold, such as Washington crossing the Delaware and Custer's last stand. (Interesting Reading Series)

PENDLE, GEORGE. The Land and People of Chile. (rd6) Macmillan, c1960. 96p. $2
Historical information and description of the country, its people, and its industries. Contains photographs and an appendix of useful information concerning population, exports, and the like. (Lands and Peoples Series)

PRATT, HELEN GAY. The Hawaiians: An Island People. (rd6) Tuttle, c1963. 193p. $3.50
In addition to depicting the geographical setting and island life in general, the author describes the arrival of the early Polynesian settlers, their occupations, crafts, food products homes, customs, sports and games, poetry and legends.

PROTTER, ERIC. Explorers and Explorations. (rd5) Grosset, c1962. 156p. $3.95
True and thrilling tales of exploration and discovery around the world. The early Phoenicians, the great period of discovery in the fifteenth and sixteenth centuries, and the most recent outer-space travel are all included.

ROESCH, ROBERTA. World's Fairs; Yesterday, Today, Tomorrow. (rd5) Day, c1962. 96p. $2.95
A thorough account of ancient, medieval, and modern international fairs, including the 1962-1963 Seattle fair and the 1964-1965 New York fair.

The symbol "rd" accompanied by the figure, in parentheses, following the title in each entry, indicates the estimated grade level of reading difficulty (see p. 18-19).

ROSENBAUM, MAURICE. London. (rd5) Rand McNally, c1963. 128p.
$2.75
> A description of the teeming life and history of London—the third book in the
> Cities of the World series. Good illustrations of buildings and several excellent
> street maps.

RUSSELL, FRANCIS. Lexington, Concord, and Bunker Hill. (rd5)
Harper, c1963. 156p. $3.95
> The account begins with the rides of Revere and Dawes, flashes back to
> the events that led to the American Revolution, and concludes with the bat-
> tles of Lexington, Concord, and Bunker Hill. (American Heritage Junior Li-
> brary Series)

SALE, J. KIRK. The Land and People of Ghana. (rd5) Lippincott,
c1963. 160p. $3.25
> A picture of the land and people of Ghana, the first of the African new coun-
> tries to gain independence. The country's heritage and rich traditions, the role
> of Ghana as a leader in the Pan-African movement, and the people and poli-
> tics are outlined. (Portraits of the Nations Series)

SALISBURY, HARRISON E. The Key to Moscow. (rd5) Lippincott,
c1963. 128p. $2.95
> A description of the capital of Russia, its historical and modern significance.
> (Keys to the Cities Series)

SASEK, MIROSLAV. This Is Edinburgh. (rd3) Macmillan, c1961. 59p. $3
> One of several books about famous and exciting cities around the world.
> (This Is——Series)

SMITH, FRANCES C. The World of the Arctic. (rd7) Lippincott, c1960.
128p. $3.25
> All about the Arctic region—its geography, exploration, geology, and native
> plant and animal life.

SPENCER, CORNELIA. The Yangtze: China's River Highway. (rd5)
Garrard, c1963. 96p. $2.75
> China's great river is its main highway, where one tenth of the human race
> lives. A colorful story of the drama of China's Main Street. (Rivers of the
> World)

TOOZE, RUTH. Cambodia: Land of Contrasts. (rd6) Viking, c1962.
192p. $4.50
> A description of contemporary life in Cambodia—its industries, natural re-
> sources, life in the capital city, national holidays, social customs—told against
> the background of this strategically important little country's history and tradi-
> tions. Profusely illustrated by photographs and prefaced by two clear maps.

TURNBULL, COLIN M. The Peoples of Africa. (rd7) World, c1962.
128p. $3.50
> A general discussion of the land itself and of the first men in Africa, followed
> by a description of groups of African peoples who live in the same way:
> hunters, nomadic pastoralists, and settled cultivators, from earliest times to
> the rapidly changing present. (A Major Cultures of the World book)

VAETH, J. GORDON. To the Ends of the Earth: The Explorations of
Roald Amundsen. (rd6) Harper, c1962. 219p. $3.50
An extensive account of Amundsen's explorations illustrated with photographs
and maps. Most of the source material is taken from Amundsen's own books.

WESTON, CHRISTINE G. Afghanistan. (rd7) Scribner, c1962. 162p.
$3.95
This kingdom situated at the crossroads of Asia is one of the lesser known
places in the world. Emphasis is placed on social customs and on recreation
rather than on historical and political details.

WILLIAMS, JAY. Knights of the Crusades. (rd7) Harper, c1962. 156p.
$3.95
A well-written account of the Crusades, the era of chivalry when the English
and French knights did battle against the infidel Saracen in the Holy Land.
The illustrations are reproductions of tapestries, drawings, manuscripts, etc.,
of the period. (Horizon Caravel Books)

HOBBIES—MAKING AND DOING THINGS

BANK-JENSEN, THEA. Play With Paper. (rd5) Macmillan, c1962. 48p.
$1.95
Making pictures, designs, toys, and decorations by folding and cutting paper
has been popular with young and old for hundreds of years and all over the
world. Easy directions are given in words and pictures.

BENDICK, JEANNE, and BERK, BARBARA. The First Book of How to Fix
It. (rd5) Watts, c1960. 69p. $2.65
A helpful book for every young person, with practical guides to fixing everyday items, and a cautious reminder about those not to be tampered with by
the inexperienced. (First Books)

BLOUGH, GLENN O. Bird Watchers and Bird Feeders. (rd3) McGraw,
c1963. 48p. $2.95
Many fine pictures, along with a simple text, will be useful to those interested
in helping birds. Bird menus are given for various types, and information
about bird banding and bird watching through all seasons is also offered.

BUSH-BROWN, LOUISE. Young America's Garden Book. (rd6) Scribner,
c1962. 280p. $4.50
Here is a practical but imaginative book on gardening for young people. The
thirty projects described are concerned with flowers, fruits, vegetables, ex-
perimental and general subjects, gardens for every season and for any section
of the country. Useful information is given at the end in tabulated lists.

CAMPBELL, ELIZABETH A. Nails to Nickels: The Story of American
Coins Old and New. (rd4) Little, c1960. 58p. $3
Fascinating story of American coins and the part money has played in our
history. Individual coins are also described. Helpful to the coin collector.

The symbol "rd" accompanied by the figure, in parentheses, following the
title in each entry, indicates the estimated grade level of reading difficulty
(see p. 18-19).

COLBY, CARROLL BURLEIGH. Musket to M 14: Pistols, Rifles, and Machine Guns Through the Years. (rd6) Coward, c1960. 48p. $2.25

Traces the development of hand guns, rifles, and light machine guns from the American Revolution to the latest models now in use.

COLLINS, HENRY HILL. The Bird Watcher's Guide. (rd6) Golden, c1961. 123p. $3.95

The text gives information for the bird watcher, such as equipment of all kinds, the classification of birds, bird photography, the building of baths and houses, devices to attract birds, favorite foods, keeping lists and taking a census, etc. Photographs, diagrams, and lists of bird clubs and state bird books are included.

DAVIS, CHARLOTTE L., and ROBINSON, JESSIE. Toys to Sew. (rd5) Lippincott, c1961. 96p. $3

A practical book with easy-to-follow directions and diagrams for making all kinds of toys and gifts for fun or for profit.

ENDICOTT, ROBERT F. Scrap Wood Fun for Kids. (rd6) Association, c1961. 223p. $4.95

The book contains 100 ready-to-use patterns for easy-to-make things constructed from wood for home, shop, and camp.

FROMAN, ROBERT. Wanted: Amateur Scientists. (rd7) McKay, c1963. 102p. $3.25

This book tells how amateur scientists can make important contributions to science, and how their hobbies can bring personal satisfaction and possibly be of value to science.

GILMORE, H. H. Model Rockets for Beginners. (rd5) Harper, c1961. 117p. $2.95

Complete easy-to-follow instructions are given for making scale models of sixteen rockets, with pictures and diagrams. The first part of the text gives basic principles of rocket flight and some historical material. Four pages are devoted to each of the sixteen models.

HAUTZIG, ESTHER. Let's Make Presents: 100 Gifts for Less than $1.00. (rd5) Crowell, c1962. 191p. $3.95

Careful directions and numerous diagrams for making gifts that are simple and inexpensive. The text is divided into sections on gifts for women, men, children, and a family. All instructions have been pretested by children. Recommended for arts and crafts classes and Scout groups.

HUGHES, TONI. Fun With Shapes in Space. (rd4) Dutton, c1960. (rev. ed.). 217p. $5.95

Easy-to-follow directions are given for making three-dimensional shapes out of paper, and opportunities are then offered for creating originals and for improvising.

JAEGER, ELLSWORTH. Nature Crafts. (rd6) Macmillan, c1950. 128p. $3.95

With only a few fundamental tools, such as a pocket knife, an axe, a saw, a bit and brace, a gauge or two, and scissors, one can create many useful and interesting things in the fields, woods, and vacant lots.

LEEMING, JOSEPH. Fun With Greeting Cards. (rd5) Lippincott, c1960. 96p. $4

One of many craft books covering a great variety of hobbies and interests. Directions are easy to follow and diagrams are helpful. Fun for all the family. Other volumes cover artificial flowers, clay, magic, leather, puzzles, shells, and wood. (Fun With——Series)

LEWIS, SHARI, and OPPENHEIMER, LILLIAN. Folding Paper Puppets. (rd5) Stein, c1962 (Distributed by Lippincott). 77p. $3.95

The popular originator of television's tender and amusing Lamb Chop and other puppets gives clear and brief directions for making attractive puppets that work. Well illustrated with both drawings and photographs.

MACFARLAN, ALLEN A. and PAULETTE. Fun With Brand-New Games. (rd5) Association, c1961. 255p. $3.50

More than 200 original new games for all types of play situations, complete with guides for leadership, with diagrams, and with lists of materials needed. There are fourteen chapters covering picnic games, those requiring no equipment, tag games, etc.

MICHEL, JOHN D. Small Motors You Can Make. (rd6) Van Nostrand, c1963. 99p. $3

Explicit, step-by-step directions from an arts and crafts teacher are given for building and operating small working motors constructed from such everyday materials as tin cans, paper clips, coat hangers, and plastic wood.

NEW YORK HERALD TRIBUNE HOME INSTITUTE. Young America's Cook Book. (rd7) Scribner, c1959 (rev. ed.). 312p. $4.50

A fine book prepared by experts. It contains useful general information as well as good recipes, planned meals, new ideas, and helpful illustrations.

PETERSON, HAROLD L. A History of Firearms. (rd5) Scribner, c1961. 56p. $3.50

The book traces the development of firearms from the early fourteenth century to the M-14 rifle adopted by the United States in 1957. The book closes with a page of advice on safety.

ROBERTS, CATHERINE. Who's Got the Button? Old and New Angles to Button Collecting. (rd6) McKay, c1962. 97p. $3.25

Old and new angles to button collecting to satisfy the heart of any collector.

SEVERN, BILL. Magic in Your Pockets. (rd6) McKay, c1964. 147p. $3.50

The magic tricks in this book are the kind you can carry with you anywhere you go to amuse and mystify your friends—you can pretend to be a mind reader, make a pencil float in midair, deliver a letter that was "mailed yesterday," make a friend seem to lose inches from his waist, etc. The book contains advice to help the young hobbyist create new tricks of his own.

————and SEVERN, SUE. Let's Give a Show. (rd4) Knopf, c1956. 178p. $2.75

For vacation-time fun, theatricals are exciting. Good help with makeup, rehearsing, and costuming for magic, minstrel, circus, or variety shows.

The symbol "rd" accompanied by the figure, in parentheses, following the title in each entry, indicates the estimated grade level of reading difficulty (see p. 18-19).

TURNER, JIM. Stamps: A Guide to Your Collection. (rd6) Lippincott, c1963. 112p. $3.50

For the beginning collector, here is an introduction to stamp collecting, along with a brief history of stamps and a description of the necessary workshop and equipment.

VAN RENSSELAER, ALEXANDER. Fun With Ventriloquism. (rd4) Doubleday, c1955. 61p. $1.50

Simple instructions for the beginner who is interested in learning ventriloquism. Detailed directions for the breathing and vocal exercises that must be mastered before attempts at real ventriloquism can be made. Various types of dummies described and a sample dialogue included.

WALTNER, WILLARD and ELMA. The New Hobbycraft Book. (rd4) Lantern, c1963. 144p. $4.95

Clear, step-by-step directions for many new useful and decorative projects, such as a rocket bank, fishing lures, circus wagon, space rug, etc., using simple tools and easy-to-get low-cost materials.

ZIM, HERBERT S., and BURNETT, WILL. Photography; the Amateur's Guide to Better Pictures. (rd5) Golden, c1956. 160p. $1.95 (Paper, $1)

A basic book for the beginning photographer of any age, for it will help you to take better pictures with any camera from Brownie to complicated models.

HUMOR: Cartoons

JAFFEE, AL. Tall Tales. (rd4) Scholastic Book Services (Berkley, c1960) 96p. Paper, 25c

More than a hundred "tall, thin" cartoons by a popular newspaper cartoonist. Tall, skinny laughs and zany cartoons that are nationwide favorites with everyone who loves to laugh.

KETCHAM, HANK. Dennis the Menace: Household Hurricane. (rd4) Holt, c1957. 64p. $1 (Paper, Scholastic Book Services, 25c)

A book of cartoons that capture the funny side of the war between youngsters and grown-ups. Dennis, the nation's favorite problem child, upsets home and neighborhood alike.

NEHER, FRED. Will-Yum. (rd7) Berkley, c1958. 96p. Paper, 35c

Cartoons about a comical teen-ager, Will-Yum, who will remind you that life can be hilarious. Filled with the mishaps and the funny side of being "twixt twelve and twenty."

NORMENT, JOHN, ed. Monkeyshines. (rd5) Berkley, c1960. 96p. Paper, 35c

A collection of nearly one hundred riotous cartoons about the jungle, featuring just about every animal, plus some of the wackiest hunters who ever beat a bush.

SHAFER, BURR. Through History With J. Wesley Smith. (rd6) Scholastic Book Services (Vanguard, c1950). 124p. Paper, 50c

More than a hundred hilarious cartoons about a man who makes history look like mass confusion. It is funniest to those who already know their history.

HUMOR: Jokes, Rhymes, and Riddles

ADAMS, JOHN PAUL, ed. We Dare You to Solve This. (rd6) Berkley, c1955. 128p. Paper, 40c

More than two hundred puzzles, riddles, anagrams, crossword puzzles, word games, tricks, mathematics problems, conundrums, and other tests of wits.

BLAKE, ROBERT, comp. 101 Elephant Jokes. (rd5) Scholastic Book Services, c1964. 96p. Paper, 25c

A hundred and one elephant jokes you have to know when the crowd starts trading laughs. Youngsters tell elephant jokes in order to use up all the crazy answers they have left from other questions.

CERF, BENNETT. Bennett Cerf's Book of Laughs. (rd2) Random, c1959. 61p. $1.95

Popular funny stories and jokes amusingly illustrated. (Beginner Books)

_____Bennett Cerf's Book of Riddles. (rd2) Random, c1960. 62p. $1.95

Gay, colorful illustrations add to the fun to be had from these riddles that all ages can enjoy. (Beginner Books)

_____Book of Animal Riddles. (rd2) Random, c1964. 62p. $1.95

Popular riddles and humorous illustrations that appeal to all ages. (Beginner Books)

_____Houseful of Laughter. (rd5) Random, c1963. 182p. $3.95

A collection of stories, verse, and anecdotes. James Thurber, Ogden Nash, Mark Twain, and Robert Benchley are among the humorists represented.

_____More Riddles. (rd2) Random, c1961. 64p. $1.95

More clever, funny riddles for young people, along with amusing illustrations. (Beginner Books)

CIARDI, JOHN. The Man Who Sang the Sillies. (rd4) Lippincott, c1961. 64p. $2.95

These two dozen nonsense poems are likely to please everyone because of their humor and rhythm. If you like these, you will also enjoy the same poet's *The Reason for the Pelican,* a collection of gay poems about animals.

CRAMPTON, GERTRUDE, comp. Your Own Joke Book. (rd6) Scholastic Book Services, c1957. 124p. Paper, 35c

The greatest collection ever of jokes, tongue twisters, smart comebacks, riotous newspaper slips, and awful, awful puns. There are also dozens of poems ideal for writing in autograph books, as well as anecdotes attributed to leading historical figures.

The symbol "rd" accompanied by the figure, in parentheses, following the title in each entry, indicates the estimated grade level of reading difficulty (see p. 18-19).

KOHL, MARGUERITE, and YOUNG, FREDERICA. Jokes for Children. (rd4) Hill, c1963. 116p. $3

Over 650 riddles, rhymes, puns, and jokes about teachers and pupils, children, families, and animals. All were tested on children. Some are old jokes and others are on up-to-date topics, such as beatniks, rock 'n' roll, and rocket stations.

LAUBER, PATRICIA, ed. Jokes and More Jokes. (rd5) Scholastic Book Services, c1955. 122p. Paper, 25c

More than four hundred jokes and cartoons chosen from *Scholastic* magazines, including hilarious puns, tall stories, and wisecracks. "How to Tell a Joke" introduction gives clues on good taste and courtesy in joke telling.

LIEBERS, ARTHUR, ed. School Daze. (rd5) Scholastic Book Services, c1958. 92p. Paper, 25c

Jokes, quips, and cartoons about life inside and outside the classroom. One very funny section has "Daffynitions."

McGOVERN, ANN, ed. Summer Daze. (rd5) Scholastic Book Services, c1961. 89p. Paper, 25c

Riddles, cartoons, jokes, all adding up to a pleasant nostalgia for the summer just past—making connections for Camp Laff-a-Lot, Tour Tickles, Beasts and Bugs, Daffy Definitions, and Way out West!

MORRISON, LILLIAN, ed. Remember Me When This You See. (rd5) Crowell, c1961. 182p. $3

A new collection of autograph verses for all occasions—can serve as an introduction to American humor and originality for those interested in folklore. The autographs are grouped by topic: love, friendship, graduation, etc.

_____Yours Till Niagara Falls. (rd4) Crowell, c1950. 182p. $2.95 (Paper, Scholastic Book Services, 25c)

Readers will want to start their own autograph books after reading these amusing rhymes, puns, and puzzles selected from actual autograph albums.

NORMENT, JOHN, ed. Laugh Along. (rd5) Berkley, c1963. 96p. Paper, 35c

A collection of crazy poems, daffy definitions, zany riddles, wacky jokes, and funny limericks.

REES, ENNIS. Riddles, Riddles Everywhere. (rd4) Abelard, c1964. 128p. $3.25

The riddles included in this collection are newly rhymed versions of prose originals drawn chiefly from British and American folklore. Two-color illustrations by Quentin Blake.

SEUSS, DR. (Geisel, Theodore Seuss). Dr. Seuss's ABC. (rd1) Random, c1963. 63p. $1.95

This may help the reader to enjoy sounds as well as learn the alphabet as he goes over the funny rhymes. It can be of help to the person with a serious reading problem.

_____Green Eggs and Ham. (rd1) Random, c1960. 62p. $1.95

Nonsense rhymes and zany pictures create fun for all ages. (Beginner Books)

WEIGLE, OSCAR, ed. Jokes, Riddles, Funny Stories. (rd3) Grosset, c1959. 105p. $1.95

Ever-popular riddles and jokes, plus rhymes and limericks, make this a book to read for fun.

HUMOR: Stories

ALLEN, MERRITT P. The Mudhen. (rd7) Scholastic Book Services (McKay, c1946). 192p. Paper, 25c

Crane, the inventor of the sidesplitting laugh and called "the Mudhen," works overtime hatching an assortment of mad, mad plots that turn the school into a hilarious comedy beyond repair.

BUTTERWORTH, OLIVER. The Enormous Egg. (rd5) Little, c1956. 186p. $2.95

The remarkable hatching of a dinosaur from the enormous egg laid by Nate Twitchell's hen raises problems. An extremely funny story.

ESPY, HILDA COLE. Look Both Ways. (rd6) Lippincott, c1962. 224p. $3.95

More amusing adventures of the four Espy children are related in this sequel to the delightful *Quiet, Yelled Mrs. Rabbit.* An adult book that young people can also enjoy.

FELSEN, HENRY GREGOR. Bertie Comes Through. (rd5) Dutton, c1947. 212p. $2.95 (Paper, Scholastic Book Services, 35c)

Bertie Poodle, built more for sportsmanship than sports, overcomes the stigma of the second team to become the hero of Heeble High and to win the applause of his classmates. A humorous story.

_____Bertie Makes a Break. (rd6) Scholastic Book Services (Dutton, c1949). 192p. Paper, 25c

Bertie needs money badly and becomes the unwilling party to a swindle, but later helps to trick the swindler. This experience helps Bertie to grow up. A humorous story.

FREEMAN, DON. Ski Pup. (rd2) Viking, c1963. 64p. $3.50

Amusing, gay pictures add to the fun in reading about the training of a young St. Bernard dog to do rescue work, and about what happens when he himself needs to be rescued.

HAYES, WILLIAM D. Project: Genius. (rd5) Atheneum, c1962. 135p. $3.25 (Paper, Scholastic Book Services, 25c)

When his school offered a prize to the student with the best outside project, Pete's efforts to win were unusual, exciting, and very funny. This is a book of adventure and humor that also has wisdom.

HIGHTOWER, FLORENCE C. Dark Horse of Woodfield. (rd6) Houghton, c1962. 233p. $3.25

A humorous story of the depression years. Maggie and her brother live at Woodfield with their aunt and their grandmother. Good family relationships prevail. A good horse story combined with a love story and a bit of mystery.

The symbol "rd" accompanied by the figure, in parentheses, following the title in each entry, indicates the estimated grade level of reading difficulty (see p. 18-19).

MASIN, HERMAN, ed. Baseball Laughs. (rd6) Scholastic Book Services, c1964. 160p. Paper, 25c
Humorous anecdotes about famous players, coaches, and umpires of baseball.

―――For Laughing Out Loud. (rd6) Scholastic Book Services, c1954. 90p. Paper, 25c
One hundred and fifty selections in pigskin humor, including anecdotes, limericks, and occasional cartoons. The funniest stories in football history, starring Knute Rockne, Jim Thorpe, Red Blaik, and other gridiron wits.

SCOGGIN, MARGARET C., comp. Chucklebait: Funny Stories for Everyone. (rd7) Knopf, c1945. 383p. $3 (Paper, Dell, 45c)
These twenty-two stories deal lightly and humorously with "growing pains," dating, school, problem parents, etc. Primarily intended for teen-agers.

HUMOR: Tall Tales

ARTLEY, A. STERL and MONROE, MARION. The New Tall Tales. (rd3) Scott, c1964. Parts I and II, 96p. each. $1.72 each
Collection of humorous short stories simply told for high-school students.

BOWMAN, JAMES CLOYD. Mike Fink. (rd6) Little, c1957. 147p. $3.50
The exploits of Mike Fink, tall-tale hero, from the time he first joined a keelboat crew on the Ohio River, to the time that he left the Mississippi River when the steamboats began to replace the keelboats.

McCLOSKEY, ROBERT. Burt Dow: Deep Water Man. (rd4) Viking, c1963. 64p. $4
A tall tale of the sea in which a whale gives Burt Dow and his dory refuge in exchange for a favor. A doughty Maine fisherman is deep in a whale's belly.

RIPLEY'S BELIEVE IT OR NOT, Ninth Series. (rd5) Pocket, c1961. 192p. Paper, 35c
Crammed with wonders collected from every corner of the globe! Odd facts about animals, ancient lands, human peculiarities, and superlatives of nature.

TURNEY, IDA VIRGINIA. Paul Bunyan, the Work Giant. (rd4) Binfords, c1941. 86p. $3
Paul Bunyan, an imaginary hero of the lumber camps, was famous for his deeds of cleverness and skill. He was never "stumped" and no job was ever too big or too hard for him to handle.

MUSIC AND ART

BAKELESS, KATHERINE L. Story-Lives of American Composers. (rd5) Lippincott, c1962 (rev. ed.). 292p. $4.25
Biographies of nineteen American composers, from Stephen Foster to the moderns, are told with the aid of photographs. Record and reading lists.

―――Story-Lives of Great Composers. (rd5) Lippincott, c1962 (rev. ed.). 288p. $4.25
The life stories of nineteen famous composers from Scarlatti to Sibelius are vividly related and illustrated with photographs. Record and reading lists are brought up to date.

BUNCHE, JANE. Introduction to the Instruments of the Orchestra. (rd5) Golden, c1962. 72p. $1.99
Musical sounds are described and a history of orchestra instruments is given in interesting fashion with helpful illustrations.

COHN, ARTHUR. The Collector's Twentieth-Century Music in the Western Hemisphere. (rd7) Lippincott, c1961. 224p. Paper, $1.95
An authority on the subject offers an excellent guide to the selection of records along with the story of this period and style of music. For other titles see the publisher's catalog. (Keystone Books in Music)

COMMINS, DOROTHY BERLINER. All About the Symphony Orchestra. (rd5) Random, c1961. 137p. $1.95
Here is much information for the music lover, including facts about orchestral instruments, what the conductor's work is, and the major forms of symphonic music. Brief biographies of great symphony composers are also part of the book. (Allabout Books)

GLUBOK, SHIRLEY. The Art of Ancient Egypt. (rd5) Atheneum, c1962. 48p. $3.95
This can be enjoyed at home or used in connection with museum visits. The pictures are beautiful and the text simple and not too long.
_____The Art of Ancient Greece. (rd5) Atheneum, c1963. 48p. $3.95
A book on the beautiful vases, statues, and buildings created by the ancient Greek people. Photographs and text give information about Greek life and changes in art techniques in ancient Greece.

JANSON, HORST W. and DORA J. The Story of Painting for Young People: From Cave Painting to Modern Times. (rd6) Abrams, c1952. 164p. $5
For those interested in art this is instructive and beautiful.

KAUFMAN, HELEN L. The Story of Haydn. (rd4) Grosset, c1962. 179p. $1.95
The interesting history of one of the world's great composers whose music, including symphonies, is still popular. If you like this, you might also enjoy *The Story of Mozart* by the same author. (Signature Books)

KING, MARIAN. A Gallery of Children; Portraits From the National Gallery of Art. (rd3) Lippincott, c1955. 48p. $2.50
Appealing, full-page reproductions of paintings having children as the principal subject, with a brief comment for each plus its history and biographical facts about the painter.

KRAVETZ, NATHAN. A Horse of Another Color. (rd3) Little, c1962. 57p. $2.95
A jolt to conformity—do we paint what we see? This can be enjoyed by all ages.

The symbol "rd" accompanied by the figure, in parentheses, following the title in each entry, indicates the estimated grade level of reading difficulty (see p. 18-19).

RIPLEY, ELIZABETH. Winslow Homer. (rd6) Lippincott, c1963. 72p. $3.50

The author presents the life and work of this famous American artist through a brief text and reproductions of some of his paintings. Other distinguished subjects of biographies by Ripley include Botticelli, Dürer, Picasso, Raphael, Titian, Goya, da Vinci, Michelangelo, Rembrandt, and Van Gogh.

SHIPPEN, KATHERINE B., and SEIDLOVA, ANCA. The Heritage of Music. (rd6) Viking, c1963. 448p. $6

The broad story of how music in the Western world developed from earliest times to the present. Interesting biographical material is included.

WEISGARD, LEONARD. Treasures to see. (rd3) Harcourt, c1956. 32p. $3

A fine and beautifully illustrated introduction to the museums of art.

ZAIDENBERG, ARTHUR. How to Draw Portraits: A Book for Beginners. (rd7) Vanguard, c1962. 60p. $3

A step-by-step explanation with illustrations to help beginning artists learn to capture likenesses and characteristics in drawing people. It also gives a basic analysis of general proportion needed in drawing the human face.

MYSTERY STORIES

AINSWORTH, NORMA RUEDI. Hit Parade of Mystery Stories. (rd6) Scholastic Book Services, c1963. 188p. Paper, 35c

A collection of stories of mystery and suspense, including tales by Agatha Christie, A. Conan Doyle, and Margery Allingham. Stories of counterfeiting, robbery, insurrection, murder, extortion, and other crimes.

BARRIE, DONALD C. Phoebe and the MacFairlie Mystery. (rd4) Lothrop, c1963. 208p. $3

When Phoebe is left an orphan, she goes to live with her father's people in Scotland. There she becomes involved in a mystery that has an exciting solution.

BONZON, PAUL JACQUES. Pursuit in the French Alps. (rd5) Lothrop, c1963. 157p. $3

Exciting mystery and adventure story that calls for the teen-age hero to show courage, strength, and human understanding. Vincent attempts to help Alberto, an Italian boy, who has been accused of stealing a gold cross from his village.

BOWEN, IRENE. Mystery of Eel Island. (rd5) Lippincott, c1961. 160p. $2.95

Two young people try to find out what causes the flickering light on a deserted island.

BRODERICK, DOROTHY M. Leete's Island Adventure. (rd5) Prentice, c1962. 128p. $3

While vacationing with their parents, fifteen-year-old Linda Barker and her brother encounter some strange events and help to solve a mystery involving smuggled jewels. Realistic and sympathetic relationships in Linda's family and especially between Linda and her brother.

CHENEY, CORA. The Mystery of the Disappearing Cars. (rd6) Knopf, c1964. 146p. $3.25

Two teen-age boys work during a summer at a Vermont hotel, where they become involved in the mystery surrounding the disappearance of antique automobiles. When they are suspected, they decide to solve the mystery and discover the secret of Model-T Mountain.

CORBETT, SCOTT. Cutlass Island. (rd5) Little, c1962. 151p. $3.25

Skip and Harvey, heroes of *Tree House Island,* are now hired to solve the mystery of the strange actions of the caretaker on Cutlass Island. They find themselves involved in another life-or-death adventure.

DEJONG, DOLA. The House on Charlton Street. (rd5) Scribner, c1962. 157p. $2.95

A good family and mystery story combined. The fun-loving Bartlett family move into an old Greenwich Village house with a mysterious past. When strange things begin to happen, they hunt for a solution to the problem.

DOHERTY, JOHN STEPHEN. The Mystery of Hidden Harbor. (rd4) Doubleday, c1963. 142p. $2.50

An adventure tale of a young man who finds a mystery under water in the harbor off Long Island Sound. He is able to stop an attempt at gunrunning in this fast-paced tale. (Signal Books)

DOYLE, SIR ARTHUR CONAN. The Boys' Sherlock Holmes. (rd7) Harper, c1961 (rev. ed.). 524p. $4.50

First published in 1936. This revised and enlarged edition contains some of the original material (*A Study in Scarlet, The Sign of the Four*), some material about the author and the man who served as a model for the detective, and three full-length novels, including *The Hound of the Baskervilles.*

EISNER, LEONARD. Mystery of Broken Wheel Ranch. (rd2) Penns Valley, c1961. 58p. $2 (Also published by Follett, $1.56)

An exciting thriller about the West, involving a mysterious stranger and a disappearing herd of valuable cattle. (Interesting Reading Series)

FULLER, LOIS HAMILTON. The Jade Jaguar Mystery. (rd5) Abingdon, c1962. 128p. $3

A good mystery and adventure story in pre-Columbian Yucatan. Tok, an Indian boy of a Mayan tribe in the days before Columbus, is caught up in a mystery involving a cave, a valuable map, and a small jade jaguar.

HOLDING, JAMES. The Mystery of the False Fingertips. (rd7) Harper, c1964. 250p. $3.50

A mystery adventure with a background of ancient history. Two sixteen-year-old boys become involved in a search for thieves who have stolen Egyptian art objects from the local museum.

The symbol "rd" accompanied by the figure, in parentheses, following the title in each entry, indicates the estimated grade level of reading difficulty (see p. 18-19).

HONNESS, ELIZABETH. Mystery of the Secret Message. (rd5) Lippincott, c1961. 192p. $2.95

This exciting mystery concerns some prying neighbors and a Japanese scroll. Then a disappearance involves the F.B.I. Other popular titles by the same author include *The Great Gold Piece Mystery, Mystery of the Auction Trunk,* and *Mystery of the Diamond Necklace.*

HOUSEHOLD, GEOFFREY. Mystery of the Spanish Cave. (rd4) Scholastic Book Services (Little, c1936). 160p. Paper, 35c

Dick Garland puts his life on the line to solve the mystery of the strange Cave of the Angels and the fate of four Spanish ships. Action, thrills, and shudders may be found in this science-fantasy mystery.

JANE, MARY C. Mystery Back of the Mountain. (rd5) Lippincott, c1960. 127p. $2.75

A brother and sister decide to become detectives in order to track down the mystery they discover in their summer home. Other titles by the same author include *Mystery at Pemaquid Point* and *Mystery on Echo Ridge.* All have New England settings.

———Mystery Behind Dark Windows. (rd5) Lippincott, c1962. 128p. $2.75

A group of young friends together solve a mystery in a New England mill town. One of this author's mysteries set in Maine is *Mystery at Dead End Farm;* one set in Canada is titled *Mystery in Old Quebec.*

JEFFRIES, RODERIC. Against Time! (rd6) Harper, c1964. 151p. $2.95

Detective Inspector Dunn has but twenty-four hours to find his kidnaped son. The police set about their task with almost no clues. A fast-paced story of detection by a popular English mystery writer. The reader, like the police, has his eyes on the clock.

JEWETT, ELEANORE. Hidden Treasure of Glaston. (rd6) Viking, c1946. 312p. $3.50 (Paper, Scholastic Book Services, 35c)

A historical mystery in which the boys find a secret vault in Glastonbury Abbey while searching for "King Arthur's Treasure."

KAY, MARA. In Place of Katia. (rd5) Scribner, c1963. 224p. $3.25

This exciting mystery tells of life in Russia during the last quarter of the eighteenth century. Girls especially will enjoy the book and will find some similarities with the novel *Caddie Woodlawn.*

MACDONALD, ZILLAH K. The Mystery of the Piper's Ghost: The Moaning Ghost of Piper's Pool. (rd5) Holt, c1954. 178p. $2.95 (Paper, Scholastic Book Services, 35c)

A readable juvenile mystery set in Nova Scotia. Mike and Willy work with the Canadian Mounties to trap the ghost that haunts the pool, get trapped in a blazing mine fire, and live through a lifetime of suspense in nine short hours.

MANUS, WILLARD B. The Mystery of the Flooded Mine. (rd4) Doubleday, c1964. 144p. $2.95

An adventure story involving skin diving which features the use of scuba technique to draw gold out of the earth—the most recent use to be made of this skill. (Signal Books)

MORRISON, LUCILE CURT. The Mystery of Shadow Walk. (rd6) Dodd, c1964. 183p. $3.25

Fifteen-year-old Jinny helps her father, a secret service agent for the United States Government, capture a quarry of counterfeiters, right under her family's own roof, by using secret passages connecting to deep dark caves, once part of the Underground Railway.

QUEEN, ELLERY, JR. Golden Eagle Mystery. (rd5) Scholastic Book Services (Lippincott, c1942). 200p. Paper, 35c

An umbrella with a carved claw for a knob, a faded letter, and a hollow cane become clues in this whodunit as the hero Djuna and his pal solve a family secret.

RAMBEAU, JOHN and NANCY. The Mystery of Morgan Castle. (rd2) Harr Wagner, c1962. 96p. $2.20

A boy's life is endangered when he finds a lot of counterfeit money as he hunts a summer job. Search, chase, and capture make a lively story. For other volumes with the same characters, see Morgan Bay Mysteries, in Books in Series section.

SEAMAN, AUGUSTA. The Mystery of the Empty Room. (rd6) Doubleday, c1953. $2.95. (Paper, Scholastic Book Services, 172p. 35c)

Mysteries pile up when Jean and Lois visit an uncle they never knew existed in a broken-down old house that is full of secrets and surprises.

VOIGHT, VIRGINIA FRANCES. The Missing $10,000 Bill. (rd6) Funk, c1960. 216p. $2.95

A fifteen-year-old girl and her youngest brother visit a cousin and encounter such mysterious problems as a missing $10,000 bill and a prowler on the land.

WHITNEY, PHYLLIS A. Mystery of the Golden Horn. (rd7) Westminster, c1962. 240p. $3.25

In Istanbul, Turkey, Vicki Stewart and Adria March, both problem children, become involved with gypsy fortunetellers and the missing, valuable horn-shaped pin.

_____Mystery of the Green Cat. (rd5) Westminster, c1957. 208p. $3.25 (Paper, Scholastic Book Services, 35c)

Thinking that the green cat holds the key to a man's disappearance and possible murder, teen-age detectives set out in San Francisco to find the truth. The chief clues are a thirty-five-year-old diary and a weird portrait.

_____The Mystery of the Hidden Hand. (rd5) Westminster, c1963. 234p. $3.25

On a visit to Rhodes, Gale and Warren Tyler encounter a mystery involving mirror signaling, broken tiles, a hand that appears and vanishes, a strange family secret, and a fascinating picture of historical Greece and modern Greeks.

_____

The symbol "rd" accompanied by the figure, in parentheses, following the title in each entry, indicates the estimated grade level of reading difficulty (see p. 18-19).

YOUNG, SCOTT. The Clue of the Dead Duck. (rd6) Little, c1962. 159p. $1.95

An exciting mystery and adventure story, told by Morgan, who lives as a foster child with Black Ab and his two children. When Black Ab goes to Toronto by bus, Morgan and Young Ab secretly go off on a forbidden duck hunt. A mystery develops which Morgan solves and he is then adopted by Black Ab.

OLD FAVORITES

ALCOTT, LOUISA M. Little Women. (rd6) Little, c1913. 397p. $3 (Paper, Penguin, 85c; paper, abridged, Scholastic Star Edition, 35c) (First published in 1868)

The story of Meg, Jo, Beth, and Amy. Almost every girl will make an effort to finish *Little Women* because she has heard so much about it from other girls. It is the best known and most read single title for girls. No age limit.

ALDEN, RAYMOND MACDONALD. Why the Chimes Rang, and Other Stories. (rd4) Bobbs, c1954 (new ed.). 146p. $2.50

A Christmas story about a kind act that brings delightful results.

BENSON, SALLY. Junior Miss. (rd6) Doubleday, c1941. 214p. $1.95

Judy, under fourteen, is a little too fat, snubbed by her older sister, alternately a joy and a pain to her parents, and very funny to read about.

BURNETT, FRANCES HODGSON. The Secret Garden. (rd5) Lippincott, c1949 (regular ed.). 256p. $3.50. Deluxe edition illustrated by Tasha Tudor. c1962. $5 (First published in 1911)

The well-loved story of willful, plain Mary who is sent to live in her uncle's big house. She does not know that waiting inside the hidden garden is a mystery she will solve, or that she will find friends and happiness for the first time in her lonely life.

CHUTE, MARCHETTE. Stories From Shakespeare. (rd7) World, c1956. 351p. $3.95 (Paper, New American Library, 75c)

The introduction gives an appreciation of Shakespeare's remarkable story-telling ability as well as a vivid account of the theater of his time. The plays are all told in brief story form that is both enjoyable and understandable. This is a good reference to use before seeing the plays on television or the stage.

DALY, MAUREEN. Seventeenth Summer. (rd8) Dodd, c1942. 255p. $3

The sweetness and the pain of first love—come and gone in a summer. Girls read it for the perfect mirror of themselves.

DICKENS, CHARLES. A Christmas Carol. (rd7) Macmillan, c1963. 128p. $2.95 (Paper, Scholastic Star Edition, 35c)

The beloved story about an old miser's change of heart as he learns the true meaning of Christmas. Scrooge, a mean, tight-fisted old man despises Christmas until three strange visitors take him, in the course of one night, into the past and into the future, and give him a glimpse of the present.

FISHER, DOROTHY CANFIELD. Understood Betsy. (rd5) Holt, c1916. 213p. $3 (Paper, Scholastic Book Services, $1.95)

When Elizabeth moves from the city to the country, she becomes Betsy, and gradually a spoiled little girl is changed into a self-reliant youngster. Girls from the fifth grade through junior high school enjoy this book immensely.

GATES, DORIS. Blue Willow. (rd5) Viking, c1940. 180p. $3 (Paper, Scholastic Book Services, 50c)

The daughter of a migrant worker longs to be able to stay in one place. To have a real home of her own she is willing to sacrifice her most precious possession, a beautiful blue willow plate. This family story depicts the unhappy days of the depression era.

GRAHAME, KENNETH. The Wind in the Willows. (rd5) Scribner, c1933. 312p. $2.95 (Deluxe edition, $6; paper, $1.45)

An old favorite, the ever popular story of Mole and Rat and their friends. It appeals to grown people who like imaginative reading, as well as to younger people.

HILTON, JAMES. Goodbye, Mr. Chips. (rd7) Grosset, c1938. 125p. $2 (First published in 1934 by Little)

Mr. Chips, master at an English school, earns the friendship of three generations of boys. For mature girls and boys.

JAMES, WILL. Smoky. (rd7) Scribner, c1926. 308p. $2.95

A memorable story of a cow pony, told in a cowboy's vernacular. Other books by James include *Big Enough, Lone Cowboy,* and *Sun Up.*

KIPLING, RUDYARD. Jungle Book. (rd7) Doubleday, c1932. 303p. $3.50 (First published in 1894)

The story of how the wolf pack raised Mowgli from a baby to a young man. "The White Seal" and "Rikki-Tikki-Tavi" are also in this collection.

MEDEARIS, MARY. Big Doc's Girl. (rd7) Lippincott, c1950 (rev. ed.). 191p. $3.95

A heartwarming story of a doctor's family and especially of Big Doc's daughter, who has to choose between a career in music and life among her own mountain people.

O'HARA, MARY. My Friend Flicka. (rd7) Lippincott, c1941. 349p. $4.50 (Paper, $2.69)

With help from his mother, Ken realizes his strongest desire—to obtain a colt of his own. A complete picture of an American family on a Wyoming ranch. *Thunderhead* (Lippincott, c1943) and *Green Grass of Wyoming* (Lippincott, c1946) continue the story.

PYLE, HOWARD. Merry Adventures of Robin Hood. (rd6) Scribner, c1954. 212p. $5

The author's selection from his complete book of Robin Hood. Much briefer text and simpler reading than the original.

RAWLINGS, MARJORIE K. The Yearling. (rd7) Scribner, c1938. Reissue, 1952. 427p. $4.50 (Paper, $1.65)

Young Jody Baxter lives a lonely life in the scrub forests of Florida until his parents reluctantly consent to his adopting an orphan fawn. When the fawn destroys the meager crops, Jody realizes that the situation is a grave one. In the sacrifice of what he loves best, he leaves his own yearling days behind.

The symbol "rd" accompanied by the figure, in parentheses, following the title in each entry, indicates the estimated grade level of reading difficulty (see p. 18-19).

SEWELL, ANNA. Black Beauty. (rd5) Lippincott. 237p. $3.50 (Paper, Dell, 45c) (First published in 1877)
The life story of a fine horse in nineteenth-century England.

SPYRI, JOHANNA. Heidi. (rd5) Houghton, c1923. 356p. $2.75 (Paper, Doubleday, 95c) (First published in 1880)
Heidi prefers simple life in the Alps to coldly formal city life.

TWAIN, MARK (SAMUEL L. CLEMENS). Adventures of Huckleberry Finn. (rd6) Harper, c1931. 404p. $3.50 (First published in 1884)
————Adventures of Tom Sawyer. (rd7) Harper, c1932. 319p. $3.50 (First published in 1875)
Tom and Huck carry out many daring schemes and have much fun. Both books available in Rainbow Classics, World Publishing Co., $2.50 each.
————The Prince and the Pauper. (rd7) Harper, c1881. 278p. $3.50 (First published in 1882)
A prince and a pauper have exactly the same features, and when they exchange roles a highly exciting story begins for "young people of all ages."
————Tom Sawyer, Detective. (rd5) Scholastic Book Services, c1959. 113p. Paper, 25c; paper, Dell, 45c (with *Tom Sawyer Abroad*) (First published in 1896)
Huck and Tom help Aunt Sally and Uncle Silas out of several predicaments.

VERNE, JULES. Twenty Thousand Leagues Under the Sea. (rd8) Scribner, c1925. 489p. $5 (First published in 1869)
Written during the nineteenth century when undersea craft were unknown, this book still holds first place among submarine stories.

WALLACE, LEW. Ben-Hur (adapted by Willis Lindquist). (rd6) Scholastic Book Services (Simon & Schuster). 116p. Paper, 25c (First published in 1880)
Doomed as a galley slave, Ben-Hur escapes and hunts the man who betrayed him. He avenges himself and his family in a great chariot race.

WYSS, JOHANN. Swiss Family Robinson (abridged). (rd6) Scholastic Book Services, c1960. 256p. Paper, 35c (First published in 1813)
Four boys and their parents, shipwrecked on a remote island, survive many dangers which test their courage and their will to live.

OUTER SPACE

ASIMOV, ISAAC. Satellites in Outer Space. (rd3) Random, c1960. 79p. $1.95
The thrilling story of man-made satellites. (Easy-to-Read Books)

BRENNA, VIRGILIO. The Moon. (rd7) Golden, c1963. 101p. $3.95
A compilation of the scientific knowledge gained about the moon—its origin,
substance, motion, and surface, based on known fact and unsolved problems
—what is known and what lunar explorers may find.

CAIDIN, MARTIN. By Apollo to the Moon. (rd7) Dutton, c1963. 183p.
$3.50
The tale of the United States' effort to place a man *on* the moon.
_____X-15: Man's First Flight Into Space. (rd6) Ridge, c1961. 64p.
Paper, 25c
An exciting story of the X-15, the rocket-plane built to carry the first man into
the fringes of space. Complete, nontechnical details on engineering and flight
potential of the manned space vehicle, plus many photos taken during actual
flight tests, make this a book that is hard to put down.

CHESTER, MICHAEL, and McCLINTON, DAVID. The Moon: Target for
Apollo. (rd6) Putnam, c1963. 192p. $3.50
Beginning in the third century B.C., the authors trace the history of lunar
studies to the plans for Project Apollo. Contains drawings and photographs.

CLARK, SARA MAYNARD. First Men in Space. (rd3) Follett, c1961 (rev.
ed.). 59p. $2
The exciting stories of the first brave men who made daring flights in balloons.
(Interesting Reading Series)

COLBY, CARROLL BURLEIGH. Count Down: The Story of Our Missile
Bases. (rd5) Coward, c1960. 48p. $2.50
In addition to describing missile bases, the book tells something about how
the missiles are assembled and serviced for firing. Contains many photographs.

GOODWIN, HAROLD L. All About Rockets and Space Flights. (rd6)
Random, c1964. 143p. $1.95
The history of rockets, earth and sun satellite mechanics, and space exploration discussed in simple language. The chapters describe specific launch and
booster rockets now being used and perfected, the various electronic and mechanical devices carried by rockets to observe and record all kinds of space
phenomena, and a glimpse into future craft that will replace rockets. (Allabout Books)

HILL, ROBERT. What Colonel Glenn Did All Day. (rd4) Day, c1962.
64p. $2.50
This tells the story of John Glenn's day in outer space from the moment he
entered the capsule until he was picked up from the sea.

MYRUS, DON. Keeping Up With the Astronauts. (rd6) Grosset, c1963.
93p. $1.95
The story of how America's first astronauts were selected, tested, and trained.
Accounts of the actual flights of four of them are included.

_____

The symbol "rd" accompanied by the figure, in parentheses, following the
title in each entry, indicates the estimated grade level of reading difficulty
(see p. 18-19).

PIZER, VERNON. Rockets, Missiles, and Space. (rd7) Lippincott, c1962. 160p. $3.95

This tells how man has tried to conquer space, explaining how rockets, missiles, and space vehicles work.

SCHNEIDER, LEO. Space in Your Future. (rd7) Harcourt, c1961. 260p. $3.75

A well-written science book that gives a detailed picture of the universe in which our world exists as a background for an explanation of human adjustment to space and space flight. The book includes discussion of the solar system, our galaxy, atmosphere and gravity, the work of astronomers, and the tools they use.

SHELTON, WILLIAM ROY. Countdown: The Story of Cape Canaveral. (rd6) Little, c1960. 185p. $3.75

An excellent account of some of the activities of the major United States rocket site in terms of specific rockets or launches, such as the Atlas, Vanguard, and Explorer series, Army moon attempts, Juno, and Titan.

STAMBLER, IRWIN. Project Gemini. (rd6) Putnam, c1964. 64p. $2.95

A history of Project Gemini, a step in the race to the moon. The discussion begins with the historical background and concludes with a projection into the future. Many illustrations.

————Space Ship: The Story of the X-15. (rd6) Putnam, c1961. 48p. $2.50

The fascinating and exciting report of the flight of the X-15, the plane that flies through space at incredible speed.

STINE, G. HARRY. Man and the Space Frontier. (rd7) Knopf, c1962. 149p. $3.50

A scientific and complete description of the problems of physical and emotional adjustment to various phenomena of space flight: pressure, humidity, acceleration, weightlessness, high intensity sound and vibration, radiation, and isolation. Discusses the actual physical and psychological preparations man undergoes prior to journeying into outer space. Diagrams and an index are included.

THRONEBURG, JAMES. Man on the Moon: Our Future in Space. (rd5) Knopf, c1961. 65p. $2.75

A timely account of our development in understanding about the moon, beginning with early mythological beliefs and going up to recent scientific explorations.

VERRAL, CHARLES S. Go! The Story of Outer Space. (rd5) Prentice, c1962. 71p. $2.95

For those interested in outer space, this will give a clear explanation with accurate illustrations. (Junior Research Books)

YATES, RAYMOND F., and RUSSELL, M. E. Space Rockets and Missiles. (rd7) Harper, c1960. 337p. $3.95

A good summary of rockets and missiles up to 1960. The book is made more useful by its inclusion of a glossary of terms, photographs, and lists of satellite and probe launchings.

PERSONALITY AND HOW TO BE POPULAR

AHERN, NELL GILES. Teen-age Living. (rd7) Houghton, c1960. 326p. $4.95

An informal book about teen-age problems and interests. Includes dating, home and social relationships, personal appearance, and personality development.

BAILARD, VIRGINIA, and STRANG, RUTH. Ways to Improve Your Personality. (rd5) McGraw, c1951. 246p. $4.50

Numerous concrete accounts of how to meet common social situations give young teen-agers help in handling their school and home relations in a more mature and satisfying way.

BOCKNER, RUTH. Growing Your Own Way: An Informal Guide for Teen-agers. (rd7) Abelard, c1959. 208p. $3.50

Valuable counseling for teen-agers is offered in readable fashion by a psychologist.

BOLL, ELEANOR STOKER. The Man That You Marry. (rd7) Macrae, c1963. 191p. $3.25

A companion volume to *The Girl That You Marry*, this aims to give help on a topic of vital interest to young people, being a guide to the elements that make for a successful marriage.

BOONE, PAT. 'Twixt Twelve and Twenty. (rd7) Prentice, c1958. 176p. $3.95 (Paper, Dell, 35c)

Pat Boone, the popular film, television, and singing star, mixes common sense, a deep religious faith, and a review of his own youthful experiences and mistakes to help teen-agers of today. He gives his personal opinions on going steady, on being yourself, on building your secret dream—on everything from religion to dating in order to make the best of the years " 'twixt twelve and twenty."

BOSSARD, JAMES H. S., and BOLL, ELEANOR STOKER. The Girl That You Marry. (rd7) Macrae, c1960. 190p. $3.25

Excellent book for both boys and girls. It is designed to help them understand why girls differ from boys in their approach to many details of living, especially in relation to courtship, marriage, and starting a family.

BRYANT, BERNICE M. Miss Behavior! (rd6) Bobbs, c1960 (rev. ed.). 192p. $3.25

Helpful suggestions to the teen-age girl who wants to be popular and to develop poise and personality.

DALY, SHEILA JOHN. Questions Teen-agers Ask. (rd8) Dodd, c1963. 237p. $3.25

A widely read syndicated columnist answers questions teen-age readers asked most often during the past seventeen years about dating, personality, parent problems, money, smoking, drinking, etc.

The symbol "rd" accompanied by the figure, in parentheses, following the title in each entry, indicates the estimated grade level of reading difficulty (see p. 18-19).

DUVALL, EVELYN RUTH M. Facts of Life and Love for Teen-agers. (rd9) Association, c1963 (new rev. ed.). 426p. $4.95
In a straightforward manner, the author describes the many problems faced by young people as they mature physically and emotionally. The contents are divided into four major parts: Becoming Men and Women; Getting and Keeping Dates; Loving and Being Loved; and Heading Toward Marriage.

HEAD, GAY. Boy Dates Girl. (rd5) Scholastic Book Services, c1949. 122p. Paper, 25c
A question-and-answer guide for both boys and girls on dating and social problems. Advice on grooming, clothes, and family relationships is included.

———Hi There, High School. (rd7) Scholastic Book Services, c1960. 94p. Paper, 25c
Hundreds of valuable tips for freshmen orientation—how to adjust to high school life, how to count with the crowd and in school life. Clothes, dating, manners, study habits, party etiquette, and keeping friends are among the topics discussed.

———Party Perfect. (rd6) Scholastic Book Services, c1959. 64p. Paper, 25c
Practical, imaginative party ideas for teens, collected from columns in *Scholastic* magazines.

MILLER, CLAIRE GLASS. What Boys Want to Know About Girls. (rd6) Grosset, c1962. 149p. $2.50
Answers to questions most often asked by boys about girls their age. Phone calling, date planning, and what to talk about on a date are some of the topics covered.

OSBORNE, ERNEST G. Understanding Your Parents. (rd7) Association, c1962 (reprint). 122p. Paper, 50c
Want to know what makes parents tick? This will promote understanding between youngsters and their parents so they can all have more fun together.

ROOSEVELT, ELEANOR (with FERRIS, HELEN). Your Teens and Mine. (rd7) Doubleday, c1961. 189p. $2.95
Kindly and helpful advice for teen-age girls of today based on the author's own experiences in getting along with people, in gaining self-confidence, in assuming family responsibilities, and in many other areas.

UNGER, ARTHUR, and BERMAN, CARMEL. What Girls Want to Know About Boys. (rd6) Grosset, c1962. 138p. $2.50
Over a hundred questions that teen-age girls ask about boys are answered in this book.

Von HESSE, ELISABETH. So to Speak. (rd6) Lippincott, c1959 (rev. ed.). 256p. $4.95
The author shows how better speech and voice can help to develop an effective personality.

WHITE, BETTY. Teen-age Dancebook. (rd7) McKay, c1963 (rev. ed.). 263p. $5.95
A guide for teen-agers who want to know about dancing. Its importance as a social grace and as a way of developing personality are other factors considered.

POETRY AND DRAMA

ARMOUR, RICHARD. Our Presidents. (rd5) Norton, c1964. 80p. $3.50
Lighthearted verses on each of the Presidents, from Washington through Johnson, some reverent, some hilarious, accompanied by witty drawings.

BURACK, A. S., ed. Four-Star Plays for Boys. (rd6) Plays, Inc., c1957. 237p. $3.75
These fifteen one-act plays for all-boy casts offer a wide range of settings (Sherwood Forest, a modern newspaper office, a circus, etc.) and a variety of characters (cowboys, clowns, pirates, spacemen, and American teen-agers). Easy to produce.

CARLSON, BERNICE WELLS. Act It Out. (rd3) Abingdon, c1956. 160p. $2 (Paper, $1.60)
Dramatic games, pantomimes, stunts, tableaux, skits, pageants, and plays, along with marionettes and puppetry, make this a helpful book for those who like to "act it out." Useful for club and hobby groups.

CHUTE, MARCHETTE, and PERRIE, ERNESTINE. The Worlds of Shakespeare. (rd8) Dutton, c1963. 128p. $3.50 (Paper, $1.25)
Bits of Shakespeare's plays have been combined into a two-act play, with emphasis upon Shakespeare's love scenes and his music.

COLE, WILLIAM, ed. Poems for Seasons and Celebrations. (rd5) World, c1961. 224p. $3.95
A collection of over 140 poems, modern and traditional, honoring the four seasons and twenty-two important celebrations of the year. Some selections are from poets of the past, but the majority are the work of recent or contemporary writers. Attractive illustrations.

FENNER, PHYLLIS R. and HUGHES, AVAH, eds. Entrances and Exits: A Book of Plays for Young Actors. (rd6) Dodd, c1960. 276p. $3.75
Fifteen plays, including "Mr. Popper's Penguins," "Dick Whittington," and "Ali Baba and the Forty Thieves."

GROHSKOPF, BERNICE, comp. Seeds of Time: Selections from Shakespeare. (rd8) Atheneum, c1963. 59p. $3.25
These are lyric pieces and songs from Shakespeare's work, being short selections that appeal to young people and that may lead to an interest in the plays.

GROSS, EDWIN and NATHALIE. Teen Theatre. (rd7) McGraw, c1953. 245p. $3.25
Discussion of problems of directing, acting, costumes, scenery, props, makeup, lighting, special effects, and publicity. It includes six nonroyalty plays with production directions simple enough to be used without adult leadership.

The symbol "rd" accompanied by the figure, in parentheses, following the title in each entry, indicates the estimated grade level of reading difficulty (see p. 18-19).

HOLLANDER, JOHN, ed. The Wind and the Rain: An Anthology of Poems for Young People. (rd7) Doubleday, c1961. 264p. $3.50

An anthology of poems from the fourteenth century through the nineteenth with some material from the twentieth century, but not contemporary poetry. The book is divided into five sections: one of poems about wind and rain, the other four about the seasons.

HOWARD, VERNON. Humorous Monologues. (rd5) Sterling, c1955. 122p. $2.50

More than fifty original monologues that are good fun. They can be used for entertainment at parties or for classroom dramatics.

MANNING-SANDERS, RUTH, ed. A Bundle of Ballads. (rd6) Lippincott, c1961. 256p. $3

A fine collection of many kinds of ballads with prizewinning illustrations.

MILLER, HELEN LOUISE. Prize Plays for Teen-agers. (rd7) Plays, Inc., c1956. 504p. $5

A group of one-act plays—comedies, holiday, and everyday plays for young people. Sparkling dialogue and entertaining true-life situations.

NASH, OGDEN, ed. Everybody Ought to Know. (rd7) Lippincott, c1961. 192p. $3.75

A collection of poems, both serious and humorous, that a famous poet thinks everyone should know.

O'NEILL, MARY. Hailstones and Halibut Bones: Adventures in Color. (rd3) Doubleday, c1961. 59p. $2.95

Imaginative, colorful poems that are gay and appealing.

SCIENCE: Astronomy

HABER, HEINZ. Stars, Men and Atoms. (rd7) Golden, c1962. 188p. $3.99

An interesting book about the universe in which we live, especially our own planet. The author discusses carbon-14, space frontiers, life on other planets, the sun and the planetary system.

LA PAZ, LINCOLN and JEAN. Space Nomads: Meteorites in Sky, Field and Laboratory. (rd5) Holiday, c1961. 187p. $4.50

Wanderers of the sky are meteorites, whose nature, history, and space-age importance are described and illustrated here. The book also explains how to locate and identify them.

REY, HANS AUGUSTO. Find the Constellations. (rd5) Houghton, c1954. 72p. $3.50

Help in seeing the constellations is given through pictures of them as they are in the sky and with lines drawn to show their outlines. There are also timetables and a sky chart, along with some facts about the solar system and space travel.

SCHEALER, JOHN M. This Way to the Stars. (rd5) Dutton, c1957. 181p. $3.25

The exciting picture of how our knowledge of the universe developed, from the Greeks to the present. Information is also given on the characteristics of the sun, planetary motions, the instruments that help us learn about the sky, and the calculations that indicate there are millions of inhabited planets.

SIMON, TONY. The Search for Planet X. (rd6) Basic, c1962. 128p. $3.75

A description of the long years of patient hunting for Pluto, the outermost planet. This story of its discovery in 1930 describes the contributions of Newton, Leverrier, Lowell, and Tombaugh.

ZIM, HERBERT S. Comets. (rd4) Morrow, c1957. 64p. $2.25

The discovery of comets through the years, and the advance in knowledge concerning their orbits and frequency of appearance, simply described.

SCIENCE: Experiments

BEELER, NELSON FREDERICK. Experiments in Sound. (rd6) Crowell, c1961. 130p. $2.95

How sounds are made, how they travel, sound absorption, musical chords, and measure of the speed of sounds are some of the topics covered in this comprehensive book. Suggestions are given for home demonstrations and simple experiments.

DISRAELI, ROBERT. New Worlds Through the Microscope. (rd7) Viking, c1960 (rev. ed.). 160p. $4

The author's photographs reveal the marvels and beauty to be found in nature under the microscope. The book contains diagrams and simple household experiments.

FERAVOLO, ROCCO V. Junior Science Book of Weather Experiments. (rd3) Garrard, c1963. 64p. $2.50

Simple experiments that show how fascinating weather can be. Questions are answered about how clouds and rain are made, why the wind blows, and why frost makes patterns on windows. (Junior Science Books)

FREEMAN, MAE and IRA. Fun and Experiments With Light. (rd4) Random, c1963. 58p. $1.95

Forty well-illustrated experiments with light and directions for making a microscope and a periscope, all simple to do at home. The experiments clarify many of the scientific facts known about light. (Fun With—Books)

————Fun With Chemistry. (rd5) Random, c1944, rev. 1957. 64p. $1.95 (Paper, Scholastic Book Services, 25c)

Illustrated experiments giving elementary principles of chemistry, using things which can be found around the house. They show how to make invisible ink, how to watch plants breathe, and how to do dozens of other exciting, simple experiments. (Fun With—Books)

The symbol "rd" accompanied by the figure, in parentheses, following the title in each entry, indicates the estimated grade level of reading difficulty (see p. 18-19).

GOLDBERG, LAZER. Adventure Book of Chemistry. (rd5) Capitol, c1962. 94p. $3.95

This is a good description of the chemistry of atoms, elements, compounds, water, and color. Simple experiments aid in understanding. (Capitol Adventure Books)

HERBERT, DON. Mr. Wizard's Science Secrets. (rd5) Hawthorn, c1963. 264p. $3.95

The new, updated edition of a popular television personality's best-selling book discusses hundreds of home experiments and educational tricks, using simple materials and ingredients for hours of entertainment and education. The book shows that science can be fun.

KADESCH, ROBERT R. The Crazy Cantilever and Other Science Experiments. (rd6) Harper, c1961. 175p. $3.95

Forty practical experiments, all easy to perform, requiring only inexpensive or easily available material. Provides clear and simple instructions and practice in careful observation.

KEEN, MARTIN L. The How and Why Wonder Book of Science Experiments. (rd5) Grosset, c1962. 48p. $2.78 (Deluxe edition, $1; paper, 50c)

Questions are answered and illustrated for young teen-agers interested in science. (How and Why Wonder Books)

MORGAN, ALFRED. Adventures in Electrochemistry. (rd6) Scribner, c1959. 288p. $3.50

This represents a good introduction to electrochemistry and provides clear instructions for homemade apparatus to use in more than forty experiments.

———The Boys' Third Book of Radio and Electronics. (rd7) Scribner, c1962. 277p. $3.50

This is more advanced than elementary radio books and magazines but is still good for the novice. There are many projects, including how to build and operate practical radio receivers and portable record players.

———First Chemistry Book for Boys and Girls. (rd7) Scribner, c1950. 179p. $3.50 (Paper, $1.25)

Many easy-to-perform and fascinating experiments are described along with an introduction to the field of chemistry.

SWEZEY, KENNETH M. Science Shows You How: Exciting Experiments That Demonstrate Basic Principles. (rd7) McGraw, c1964. 96p. $3.50

Experiments illustrating general scientific principles are given with emphasis on their application to modern space science. Simple apparatus from readily available materials is required. Many good illustrations.

WYLER, ROSE, and AMES, GERALD. Prove It! (rd2) Harper, c1963. 64p. $1.95

Here are experiments the reader can do with water, air, sound, and magnets —all by using ordinary household items. (I-Can-Read Books)

SCIENCE: General

ADLER, IRVING. Monkey Business: Stories of Hoaxes in the Name of Science. (rd7) Day, c1957. 128p. $3

Accounts of the frauds in science describe how medicine grew from witchcraft and magic, astronomy from astrology, and chemistry from alchemy. The young scientist is alerted to the importance of testing and challenging all sources of information.

ARNOV, BORIS. Oceans of the World. (rd5) Bobbs, c1962. 192p. $3.50

A narrative study of the sea covering its history, its exploration, and its inhabitants. A final chapter describes some of the possible future benefits man may gain from the oceans—industrial products, food and minerals, energy for power, oil, and fresh water.

BELL, THELMA HARRINGTON and CORYDON. The Riddle of Time. (rd7) Viking, c1963. 160p. $3.50

There are many faces of time as related to astronomy, biology, geology, physiology, and psychology. The text is readable and the pictures are attractive and helpful.

BENDICK, JEANNE. Electronics for Young People. (rd6) McGraw, c1960 (rev. ed.). 190p. $3.50

This new edition of a popular book includes later developments in the field. New work in electronic weapons, television, etc., is described and illustrated.

———and BENDICK, ROBERT. Television Works Like This. (rd6) McGraw, c1959 (3rd rev. ed.). 64p. $2.75

This new edition includes later developments in television. The book gives a clear, easy-to-understand explanation of how television works. It is aided by illustrations and diagrams.

BURTON, VIRGINIA LEE. Life Story: A Play in Five Acts. (rd5) Houghton, c1962. 67p. $5

An unusual and striking way to present the evolution of the earth and seasons of the year. Beautiful pictures add to its value as the book shows the changing face of the earth from the first upheavals through the various ages.

CARSON, RACHEL. The Sea Around Us (adapted by Anne Terry White). (rd6) Golden, c1959. 165p. $4.95 (Paper, Mentor, c1960. 50c)

A rare and beautiful book about marine life. In this version adapted for young people, the emphasis is on outstanding photographs. The author captures both the magic and the science of the sea.

CHAMBERS, ROBERT W., and PAYNE, ALMA SMITH. From Cell to Test Tube. (rd7) Scribner, c1960. 216p. $3.50

An understandable telling of an important area of scientific research—biochemistry and its application to industry and medicine.

The symbol "rd" accompanied by the figure, in parentheses, following the title in each entry, indicates the estimated grade level of reading difficulty (see p. 18-19).

FARADAY, MICHAEL. The Chemical History of a Candle. (rd7)
    Crowell, c1957. 158p. $2.75
A famous series of lectures addressed to a group of young people by the
"prince of experimenters" has become a classic. Unbeatable for style, for clear
explanation, and for sustained interest. Using the candle in simple experiments, he gives an idea of a great array of scientific information and the manner in which the experimenter works.

FERMI, LAURA. The Story of Atomic Energy. (rd5) Random, c1961.
    184p. $1.95
The evolutionary exploration of the long-held theories of atomic energy that
finally ended in the splitting of the atom in recent times. (World Landmark
Books)

FREEMAN, IRA M. All About Sound and Ultra-Sonics. (rd5) Random,
    c1961. 139p. $1.95
Sound we can hear and sound beyond the ability of people to hear are considered in this easy-to-read volume. (Allabout Books)

FREEMAN, MAE and IRA. The Story of the Atom. (rd5) Random,
    c1960. 81p. $1.95
The development of knowledge about an important branch of science that
has changed our lives in every way. (Easy-to-Read Books)

_____The Story of Electricity. (rd5) Random, c1961. 79p. $1.95
An explanation in simple form of the miracle work that electricity performs
to make our own work and lives simpler. Includes a few easy experiments.
(Easy-to-Read Books)

GRAMET, CHARLES. Light and Sight. (rd6) Abelard, c1963. 160p. $3.75
An excellent book which explains in readable style how we see, the importance
of light to all forms of life (even to one-celled plants and animals), how the
human eye sees, and how scientists have invented instruments to extend the
range of man's sight to almost unbelievable horizons.

HITTE, KATHRYN. Hurricanes, Tornadoes and Blizzards. (rd4) Ran-
    dom, c1960. 82p. $1.95
Fascinating facts about some of nature's most dangerous storms. Illustrations
add to the understanding of the text. (Easy-to-Read Books)

HOGBEN, LANCELOT. The Wonderful World of Energy. (rd7) Double-
    day, c1957. 69p. $2.95
Outstandingly good introduction to the wonderful story of physics without
being too technical and with magnificent illustrations. It tells the story of
man's long struggle to find the energy to do his work, from the days of the
sledge to those of steam, electricity, and the atom.

HYDE, MARGARET OLDROYD. This Crowded Planet. (rd8) McGraw,
    c1961. 159p. $3
A study of some of the ways in which science can provide more food, minerals, and energy from the earth, sea, and sky in an overcrowded world.

IRVING, ROBERT. Electronics. (rd6) Knopf, c1961. 173p. $3.25
An easy-to-read explanation of electronics from the vacuum tube to the latest in television, weapons, and thinking machines.

———Hurricanes and Twisters. (rd5) Knopf, c1953. 143p. $3.29
(Paper, Scholastic Book Services, 35c)
The exciting story of the big storms—what they are, where they come from, how they are forecast, and what damage they do. Charts, maps, diagrams, and photographs help explain, making the description of these destructive elements more vivid.

KLEIN, H. ARTHUR. Masers and Lasers. (rd7) Lippincott, c1963. 184p. $3.50
A readable explanation of these wonderful beams of light—their construction and use as well as the underlying principles. They can be used in performing delicate surgery, in sending a message to a satellite, in shattering a diamond, or in destroying a missile. Clear pictures and diagrams help in understanding the text.

LOTH, DAVID. Crime Laboratory: Science Turns Detective. (rd7) Messner, c1964. 247p. $4.95
Excitement and suspense in the laboratory as mysteries are solved by methods ranging from the more familiar fingerprinting and chemical analysis to spectroscopy, voiceprinting and infrared light.

McKOWN, ROBIN. Fabulous Isotopes: What They Are and What They Do. (rd6) Holiday, c1962. 189p. $4.50
Drawings and photographs aid the explanation of the way isotopes are used in research, medicine, industry, and agriculture.

SCHNEIDER, HERMAN and NINA. Science Far and Near. (rd3) Heath, c1961 (2nd ed.). 288p. $3
This, along with two other volumes (Science for Here and Now and Science for Work and Play), presents challenging material and interesting activities in a great variety of topics in science.

VOGEL, HELEN WOLFF, and CARUSO, MARY LEONARD. Ocean Harvest: The Future of Oceanography. (rd7) Knopf, c1961. 144p. $3
A book about marine resources, giving information about world oceans and about the explorers of marine life. Some topics discussed are mineral resources, food resources from fish and seaweed, converting salt water to fresh, and producing algae cheaply enough to use them as a source of food.

WOHLRABE, RAYMOND A. Crystals. (rd6) Lippincott, c1962. 128p. $3.50
Photographs and diagrams add to the value of this clear explanation of the theory and experiments in the science that studies crystals.

WOODBURN, JOHN H. Radioisotopes. (rd7) Lippincott, c1962. 128p. $3.50
A clear and simple explanation of radioisotopes is given by an expert. Photos and diagrams are helpful.

The symbol "rd" accompanied by the figure, in parentheses, following the title in each entry, indicates the estimated grade level of reading difficulty (see p. 18-19).

SCIENCE: Machines and How They Work

ARNOLD, PAULINE, and WHITE, PERCIVAL. The Automation Age. (rd5) Holiday, c1963. 197p. $3.95
A nontechnical explanation of how automated devices have developed and are used in factories, homes, and offices; in air, sea, and space. Computers are explained and the future of automation is presented in relation to its effect on society.

BERGAUST, ERIK. Rocket Power. (rd6) Putnam, c1962. 48p. $2.50
A good, simply written book on rocket engines. Contains descriptions and technical data on all major rocket engines developed in the United States. A one-page glossary is appended.

BRADLEY, DUANE, and LORD, EUGENE. Here's How It Works. (rd6) Lippincott, c1962. 157p. $3.95
Experiments and easy-to-understand explanations show why machines we use in everyday life work.

COLBY, JEAN POINDEXTER. Tear Down to Build Up: The Story of Building Wrecking. (rd5) Hastings, c1960. 56p. $2.95
Good description of machinery and processes of building demolition with drawings and diagrams. Interesting to all ages, especially in large cities where demolition is a part of the current landscape.

HIRSCH, S. CARL. This Is Automation. (rd5) Viking, c1964. 128p. $3.75
A clear, interesting account of what automation is, tracing its development as a logical outgrowth of the Industrial Revolution and explaining what new skills are needed to prepare for the changes it is bringing in the way people live and work.

HOGNER, DOROTHY CHILDS. Water Over the Dam. (rd6) Lippincott, c1960. 256p. $3.95
From the smallest and earliest to the present-day giants, dams have affected people's lives. Here is their story.

MEYER, JEROME SYDNEY. Engines. (rd5) World, c1962. 80p. $2.75
An introduction to all kinds of engines: the steam, gasoline, diesel, turbine, electric, and jet, with a final chapter on engines of the future using atomic or solar energy. Illustrated by diagrams and with an index appended.

SCIENCE: Mathematics

GARDNER, MARTIN. Mathematical Puzzles. (rd7) Crowell, c1961. 128p. $2.75
Puzzles covering many areas of mathematics are presented with full explanations of their solutions. The book is divided into such areas as money puzzles, geometry puzzles, speed puzzles, etc. Suggestions for further reading are given.

HOGBEN, LANCELOT. The Wonderful World of Mathematics. (rd6) Doubleday, c1955. 69p. $2.95
How man discovered mathematics to help him sow crops, navigate, build cities, and even measure the distance of planets.

LAUBER, PATRICIA. The Story of Numbers. (rd4) Random, c1961. 80p. $1.95

An account of the development of man's most efficient counting system from earliest times. (Easy-to-Read Books)

RAVIELLI, ANTHONY. An Adventure in Geometry. (rd7) Viking, c1957. 117p. $3

Here is fun not usually associated with this branch of mathematics. Not concerned with "proofs" here, the reader is given many varieties of beauty and utility around him, all of them having geometrical forms. Here mathematics and art become a fascinating combination. Besides the usual two-dimensional forms, we see less well-known cycloids, involutes, and spirals.

SCHNEIDER, HERMAN and NINA. How Big Is Big? (rd4) Scott, W.R., c1954 (rev. ed.). 48p. $2.75

An attractive way to present comparison, size, and space relationships in everything from stars to atoms.

SCIENCE: The Prehistoric World

ANDREWS, ROY CHAPMAN. In the Days of the Dinosaurs. (rd4) Random, c1959. 80p. $1.95

Stories of animal life in prehistoric times, as told by a man who spent many years exploring in strange lands. (Easy-to-Read Books)

CLYMER, ELEANOR. Search for a Living Fossil; the Story of the Coelacanth. (rd6) Holt, c1963. 126p. $3.50

An account of the dramatic fourteen-year search for the "living fossil" fish, the coelacanth, thought to be extinct for thirty million years. The discovery of these fish off the coast of South Africa electrified the scientific world. The book combines a good "detective" story with actual scientific adventure.

EDEL, MAY. The Story of Our Ancestors. (rd7) Little, c1955. 199p. $3

_____The Story of People; Anthropology for Young People. (rd7) Little, c1953. 197p. $3

An introduction to anthropology for young people. The account of the experiences of scientists in putting together bits of evidence to give us the history and development of man is told clearly and interestingly.

EVANS, EVA KNOX. Adventure Book of Archaeology. (rd5) Capitol, c1962. 93p. $3.99

The thrilling and fascinating story of how archaeologists put together facts about the various ways of life that were so commonplace for people who lived ages ago. (Capitol Adventure Books)

The symbol "rd" accompanied by the figure, in parentheses, following the title in each entry, indicates the estimated grade level of reading difficulty (see p. 18-19).

GEIS, DARLENE. The How and Why Wonder Book of Dinosaurs and Other Prehistoric Animals. (rd5) Grosset, c1960. 48p. $2.78 (Deluxe edition, $1; Paper, 50c)

This tells of dinosaurs and other prehistoric animals on the earth in the past. It answers questions most often asked about them and is amply illustrated. It aims to stimulate young people to explore further in the field of science. (How and Why Wonder Books)

HOGBEN, LANCELOT. The First Great Inventions. (rd5) Lothrop, c1951. 36p. $1.75

———How the First Men Lived. (rd4) Lothrop, c1950. 36p. $2

How early man lived before the days of modern inventions such as steamboats, automobiles, etc.; how he learned to make fire, develop tools, build a shelter, catch his food; and how he discovered the principle of the wheel.

SWINTON, WILLIAM ELGIN. The Wonderful World of Prehistoric Animals. (rd7) Doubleday, c1961. 23p. $2.95

The text is divided into four parts: one each on the formation of the earth's crust, the deposit of fossil material, the development of paleontology as a science, and information about fossil hunting, the preserving and reconstructing of fossil remains.

WHITE, ANNE TERRY. The First Men in the World. (rd5) Random, c1953. 192p. $1.95 (Paper, Scholastic Book Services, 35c)

In the past century exciting clues to man's first existence were discovered—weapons made of stone, skeletons of strange beasts and humans. Archaeologists explored caves and earth deposits the world over and pieced together the development of man up to the first era of recorded history. (World Landmark Books)

WYLER, ROSE, and AMES, GERALD. The Story of the Ice Age. (rd4) Harper, c1956. 81p. $2.95

An exciting account of the various ice ages of the earth—their place or meaning in history. Discusses how the ice ages came about and their effect on plant, animal, and human life. Ends with a speculation as to the possibility of an ice age of the future.

SCIENCE FICTION

BERNA, PAUL. Continent in the Sky. (rd6) Abelard, c1963. 192p. $3.50

A young teen-ager stows away on a radio-navigation station and goes to a moon base, where he has some adventures that prove his courage.

BLISH, JAMES. A Life for the Stars. (rd7) Putnam, c1962. 224p. $3.50

A science fiction tale of the future in which entire cities leave the earth to find gainful employment in space. The story concerns Chris's experiences with competition among the cities in training for citizenship.

BONHAM, FRANK. The Loud, Resounding Sea. (rd7) Crowell, c1963. 224p. $3.50

A well-written junior novel, partly science fiction, but with some scientific basis, about a young boy who has a firsthand opportunity to observe a dolphin and its rapport with people. Interesting details about dolphins and Skip's relationships with his rolling-stone father.

BULETTE, SARA. An Adventure in Space. (rd3) Follett, c1961 (rev. ed.). 59p. $2

The thrilling adventures of some teen-agers who visit Gog's solar system and destroy a monstrous machine. (Interesting Reading Series)

CLARKE, ARTHUR C. Dolphin Island. (rd7) Holt, c1963. 186p. $3.50

Adventure story for the science-minded, this tells of dolphins in the Great Barrier Reef who can communicate with each other. An unusual science fiction story, different from most. (Winston Science Fiction Series)

HEINLEIN, ROBERT A. Citizen of the Galaxy. (rd7) Scribner, c1957. 302p. $3.50

An imaginative mystery story of the responsibilities of a young citizen of the future. Other titles by this popular author are *Tunnel in the Sky, Starman Jones, Space Cadet,* and *Rocket Ship Galileo.*

L'ENGLE, MADELEINE. A Wrinkle in Time. (rd5) Farrar, c1962. 211p. $3.25

Learn about the strange fifth dimension and the delightful stranger who brings to the Wallaces and their friend Calvin an adventure in space and time as they search for Meg's father, a famous scientist who has disappeared.

ORMONDROYD, EDWARD. Time at the Top. (rd6) Parnassus, c1963. 176p. $2.95

A good science fiction story in which Susan takes the elevator to the top floor of her apartment building and finds herself at the same spot in 1881. She persuades her widowed father to travel with her to the top. The author finds an old family group picture from the 1880's and there are Susan and her father.

SILVERBERG, ROBERT. Revolt on Alpha C. (rd5) Crowell, c1955. 148p. $2.50 (Paper, Scholastic Book Services, 35c)

Larry Stark, a young space patrolman, becomes involved in a revolt on Alpha C, a planet similar to Earth. The war is very like the American Revolution. A fast-paced action story.

————The Time of the Great Freeze. (rd6) Holt, c1964. 192p. $3.50

When the polar ice cap advances, the people move their city underground. After several hundred years, some of the under-the-ice inhabitants come out and travel by solar sled to England, which was not frozen. This is an exciting and different story. (Winston Science Fiction Series)

TODD, RUTHVEN. Space Cat and the Kittens. (rd4) Scribner, c1958. 94p. $2.75

This continues the amusing story of Flyball, who goes with the pilot on a rocket ship. This time his wife and two kittens go with him to a strange planet where there are tiny prehistoric animals.

The symbol "rd" accompanied by the figure, in parentheses, following the title in each entry, indicates the estimated grade level of reading difficulty (see p. 18-19).

SEAFARING

ARMSTRONG, RICHARD. Ship Afire. (rd6) Day, c1961. 192p. $3.50
An exciting story in which young apprentice "Bull" Barlow salvages the tanker "Cape Wrath" in convoy to England and saves the men in his care.

ARMSTRONG, WARREN. Sea Phantoms. (rd6) Day, c1961. 224p. $3.50
True stories of ghost ships, haunted ships, and haunted lighthouses.

BALL, ZACHARY. Salvage Diver. (rd5) Holiday, c1961. 220p. $3.25
Skin diving appears to be both an adventure and a science in this story of salvage work for sunken wrecks off the Florida Keys.

BUEHR, WALTER. Ships and Life Afloat. (rd6) Scribner, c1953. 116p. $3.50
A fully illustrated and informative account of ships "from galley to turbine." It is a fascinating tale of life at sea over the centuries.

COLEMAN, JAMES C., and others. Danger Below. (rd4) Harr Wagner, c1962. 97p. $2.12
Highly popular thriller in an adventure series that older boys enjoy. Salvage work, smuggled diamonds, and a sunken ship keep tension high. Earlier titles also make exciting reading. (Deep-Sea Adventure Series)

COSGRAVE, JOHN O'HARA. America Sails the Seas. (rd5) Houghton, c1962. 95p. $5
A book about American ships from the Indian canoe to a Polaris missile-launching nuclear submarine. Many of the individual ships famous in American naval history are described and illustrated. Over 200 illustrations in color together with diagrams and glossary.

HEMINGWAY, ERNEST. The Old Man and the Sea. (rd7) Scribner, c1952. 140p. $3.50 (Special text edition, $1.65)
The old fisherman struggles to keep his fish from the sharks and the elements and loses all but his courage.

HOYT, EDWIN P. From the Turtle to the Nautilus: The Story of Submarines. (rd6) Little, c1963. 134p. $3.50
An easy-to-read history of submarines, of the men who build them, and of those who man them.

KLEIN, DAVID. Beginning With Boats. (rd8) Crowell, c1962. 213p. $3.95
Instructions on how to buy, build, maintain, and operate canoes, rowboats, sailboats, and powerboats. Concluding chapters describe safety rules, marine manners, crewing, cruising, and the use of navigation charts.

MANUS, WILLARD. Sea Treasure. (rd4) Doubleday, c1961. 139p. $2.50
An exciting tale of a treasure hunt under the sea, of a desperate fight with a shark, and of a man who loved gold too much. (Signal Books)

MEADER, STEPHEN W. Whaler 'Round the Horn. (rd6) Harcourt, c1950. 245p. $3.25
The stirring tale of a whaling voyage by a favorite author.

MEHDEVI, ANNE SINCLAIR. The Leather Hand. (rd7) Knopf, c1961. 182p. $3

An absorbing and unusual story about a boy's adventures in skin diving for treasure lost in the Mediterranean.

POOLE, LYNN and GRAY. Danger! Icebergs Ahead. (rd4) Random, c1961. 81p. $1.95

The story of the International Ice-Patrol Service and man's attempt to learn about and master the dangers of the iceberg menace through cooperative effort. (Easy-to-Read Books)

RACHLIS, EUGENE. The Story of the United States Coast Guard. (rd5) Random, c1961. 176p. $1.95

Activities and history of what is a peacetime as well as a wartime government service. (Landmark Books)

RIFKIN, IDA. First Adventure at Sea. (rd3) Penns Valley, c1961. 48p. $2

A short novel set in the late 1700's when the young United States Navy battled against French pirates. (Interesting Reading Series)

TUCKER, ERNEST E. The Story of Fighting Ships. (rd6) Lothrop, c1963. 256p. $3.95

A good introduction to the ships and methods of naval warfare for each era up to the present, followed by a short story which uses this information in its plot. A companion volume to *The Story of Knights and Armor.*

WASSERMANN, SELMA and JACK. Sailor Jack. (rdPP) Benefic, c1960. 48p. $1.60

———Sailor Jack and the Jet Plane. (rdP) Benefic, c1962. 64p. $1.68

———Sailor Jack and the Target Ship. (rd2) Benefic, c1960. 96p. $1.68

Popular stories about a sailor assigned to an atomic submarine and his parrot. They are filled with action and humor, and have an authentic background. (Sailor Jack Series)

SHORT STORIES

ACEI [ASSOCIATION FOR CHILDHOOD EDUCATION INTERNATIONAL]. Told Under the Stars and Stripes. (rd5) Macmillan, c1962. (rev. ed.). 347p. $3.50 (Special edition, $1.95)

An old but good collection of stories about the different people from many lands and of different races who make up America.

AKIN, VIRGINIA. The Dream Years. (rd7) Chilton, c1964. 126p. $3.50

A collection of ten short stories taken from such magazines as *American Girl, Woman's Day, McCall's,* etc., about young girls and their problems. Among the characters are Terry, who loves one teacher and hates another; Dorothy, who baby-sits and learns responsibility; Susie, who takes part in the school play; Susannah, the girl in the glamorous "cartwheel hat."

The symbol "rd" accompanied by the figure, in parentheses, following the title in each entry, indicates the estimated grade level of reading difficulty (see p. 18-19).

ALDRICH, BESS STREETER. Journey Into Christmas and Other Stories. (rd8) Meredith, c1963 (rev. ed.). 239p. $4.95

Twelve of the author's favorite Christmas stories, written at various times in her long career, are heartwarming and brimming with the spirit of our great holiday season.

BERGER, ERIC, ed. Best Short Shorts. (rd6) Scholastic Book Services, c1958. 183p. Paper, 25c

Thirty-five fine short stories with surprise endings, many of which appeared in *Scholastic* magazines. Espionage as practiced by a wily Oriental; a boy's terror as he is trapped in a flooding submarine; the boy-catching dreams of the girl next door. Included are tales of adventure, romance, humor, mystery, science fiction, and sports.

———For Boys Only. (rd6) Scholastic Book Services, c1960. 192p. Paper, 35c

Twelve fast-moving short stories by such authors as Howard Pease and Jesse Stuart, selected especially for their appeal to boys, although the title may prove an irresistible magnet for girls. The tales involve adventure, humor, mystery, suspense, sports, and the supernatural, including a singlehanded fight with a shark in the Indian Ocean and a baseball pennant race decided by a baboon.

BRADBURY, RAY. R Is for Rocket. (rd7) Doubleday, c1962. 233p. $2.95

A collection of seventeen science fiction short stories, most of which have been previously published in books or magazines. The collection is varied in subject, locale, and style.

BRAND, CHRISTIANNA, ed. Naughty Children. (rd5) Dutton, c1963. 314p. $4.50

An anthology, chiefly of British authors, comprising the adventures of genuinely naughty children in stories and poems by such authors as Mark Twain, P. G. Wodehouse, O. Henry, Dickens, and Saki.

BUCK, PEARL S. Fourteen Stories. (rd7) Day, c1961. 256p. $4.95

These stories deal with love and marriage in East and West.

COLBY, CARROLL BURLEIGH. Strangely Enough. (rd6) Sterling, c1959. 125p. $3.50 (Paper, abridged, Scholastic Book Services, 25c)

More than eighty short, hair-raising tales about apparitions and spirits, flying saucers, mysterious disappearances, and incredible events.

DALE, EDGAR. Stories for Today. (rd3) U.S. Armed Forces Inst. c1954. 137p. 45c

———Stories Worth Knowing. (rd5) U.S. Armed Forces Inst. c1954. 190p. 45c

Short, simple stories for adults; carefully controlled vocabulary.

DEARMAND, FRANCES ULLMAN, ed. When Mother Was a Girl: Stories She Read Then. (rd7) Funk, c1964. 209p. $3.50

Fifteen stories chosen from several hundred magazines published for teenagers and their mothers in the 1940's. Space-age life seems very different from life twenty years ago, but such problems as dating, relationship with parents and teachers, and learning to make decisions are much the same.

FENNER, PHYLLIS R., ed. The Dark and Bloody Ground; Stories of the American Frontier. (rd7) Morrow, c1963. 223p. $3.50

Ten stories of pioneers on the American frontier. Many distinguished authors, such as Stephen Vincent Benét, Conrad Richter, A. B. Guthrie, Jr., etc., are represented here.

FERRIS, HELEN, ed. The Brave and the Fair: Stories of Courage and Romance. (rd7) Holt, c1960. 241p. $3.50

These dramatic stories show the strength and character of the young women who settled our wilderness.

————Time of Understanding. (rd7) Watts, c1963. 256p. $3.95

A collection of stories about teen-age girls and their relationships with their parents, friends, and beaux. Among the topics discussed are dating, girls with only one parent, problem daughters and problem parents, young love, and the growth of understanding.

FUTRELLE, JACQUES. The Thinking Machine. (rd5) Scholastic Book Services, c1959. 120p. Paper, 25c

Three suspense-packed stories about the world's greatest scientist-detective, Professor Augustus S. F. X. Van Dusen, alias The Thinking Machine. He claims he can escape from any locked cell in any prison in a week.

HUMPHREVILLE, FRANCES, and FITZGERALD, FRANCES. On Target. (rd4-5) Scott, c1963. 288p. $3.20

Good collection of easy-to-read stories for and about teen-agers.

————Top Flight. (rd4-5) Scott, c1961. 320p. $3

Short stories adapted for teen-agers to read easily and with pleasure.

SCHAEFER, JACK. The Plainsmen. (rd7) Houghton, c1963. 252p. $3.25

A collection of stories, some of which approach the tall tale, written about the moments of crisis in the lives of plainsmen.

SCHLEYEN, MILTON. Stories for Today's Youth. (rd4) Globe, c1958. 217p. $2.80

A dozen stories about Sandy Gordon, his family, and his friends. Fast-moving and entertaining tales about family problems, neighborhood problems, friendship problems at home and at school.

SCHUMAN, SYLVIE, ed. For Girls Only. (rd6) Scholastic Book Services, c1957. 153p. Paper, 35c

Eleven short stories of teen-age romance from leading magazines chosen for their insight into the uncertainties common to all teen-age girls.

STIRLING, NORA B. Exploring for Lost Treasure. (rd3) Doubleday, c1960. 56p. $2.50

Here are ten thrilling stories of adventurers, pirates, and seekers of lost treasure.

The symbol "rd" accompanied by the figure, in parentheses, following the title in each entry, indicates the estimated grade level of reading difficulty (see p. 18-19).

STOLZ, MARY SLATTERY. The Beautiful Friend, and Other Stories.
(rd6) Harper, c1960. 179p. $3.50
A collection of nine well-written short stories which reveal the author's understanding of teen-age problems and emotions. All the stories have appeared in
Seventeen, The Ladies' Home Journal, or *McCall's.*

STOWE, AURELIA, ed. It's a Date; Boy-Girl Stories for the Teens. (rd6)
Random, c1950. 215p. $2.95
Highlights problems of first date, prom worries, telephone waiting, etc. Very
light but universal in appeal and simply written.

————When Boy Dates Girl. (rd7) Random, c1956. 224p. $2.95
Ten new and different short stories about teen-age dating, written from the
masculine point of view.

————When Boy Likes Girl. (rd5) Random, c1962. 239p. $2.95
A collection of eleven stories, all of which unfold from the boy's angle. Many
are taken from *Seventeen* magazine. This anthology for teen-agers includes
stories by such authors as Laura Nelson Baker, Jesse Stuart, Keith Winter,
Janet Roberts, and Robert C. Ackworth.

STRANG, RUTH, and others. Teen-age Tales. Books 1, 2, 3, 4, 5, and 6
(rd5-6); Books A, B, and C (rd3-4). Heath, c1954-1962. 248p.
$2.96 each
These nine volumes contain stories about teen-agers and their interests—
stories of adventure, suspense, sports, science, animals, school life, boy-girl
relationships—carefully chosen for their appeal to the teen-ager of today.
Stories on a high-school level of interest, but on an elementary level of
difficulty. Colorful illustrations add to the appeal. A teacher's manual for each
book contains many helpful suggestions and exercises for reading skills
development.

VETTER, MARJORIE, ed. Stories to Live By: A Treasury of Fiction From
The American Girl. (rd5) Platt, c1960. 280p. $2.95
This collection of stories by well-known authors is concerned with the problems of young people—going steady, being ashamed of the family, having a
stepmother, being tall or being plain, being unable to afford college, dealing
with brothers and sisters, facing discouragement, having courage to be one-
self, being overweight, facing integration, feeling parents don't understand.
Some are based on true incidents.

SPORTS: Fact

ALLEN, MAURY. Ten Great Moments in Sports. (rd3) Follett, c1961
(rev. ed.). 58p. $2.08
Popular with older boys, these are exciting stories of some of the sports world
immortals, including Ben Hogan, Babe Ruth, Lou Gehrig, and others. (Interesting Reading Series)

ALLEN, MEL, and GRAHAM, FRANK, JR. It Takes Heart. (rd7) Harper,
c1959. 266p. $4.95
The reader follows the disappointments and struggles and shares in the
triumphs of top sports figures as they courageously overcome obstacles and
reveal their good sportsmanship.

ANDERSON, CLARY. The Young Sportsman's Guide to Baseball. (rd5) Nelson, c1963. 94p. $2.75

A nationally known high-school coach describes what baseball is and how it is played. (Young Sportsman's Library)

ARCHIBALD, JOE. The Richie Ashburn Story. (rd6) Messner, c1960. 192p. $3.25

A sports portrait of Richie, giving details of his education, family life, and participation in civic affairs.

BROWN, CONRAD. Skiing for Beginners: A Complete and Simple Method for Children and Their Parents. (rd6) Scribner, c1951. 63p. $3.50

Photographs are very helpful in this guide to learning how to ski.

COOKE, DAVID C. Better Bowling for Boys. (rd5) Dodd, c1961. 64p. $2.75

Easy text combined with sequence photographs and diagrams for the beginning bowler includes techniques and tips for the expert. The most complete book on the sport written for young bowlers.

DALEY, ARTHUR. Kings of the Home Run. (rd6) Putnam, c1962. 256p. $3.95

A well-written book by a sportswriter for the New York *Times*. Descriptions of the greatest home-run hitters in baseball history from Babe Ruth to Roger Maris. Record and photographs of each man are included.

DAVIS, MAC. Greatest in Baseball. (rd6) Scholastic Book Services, c1962. 96p. Paper, 35c

A collection of short biographies of thirty-two amazing personalities who caught "baseball fever" as boys, and never stopped until they made the Hall of Fame.

DURANT, JOHN. The Sports of Our Presidents. (rd7) Hastings, c1964. 149p. $3.95

An interesting account of the sports in which each President of the United States participated. The author begins with George Washington's fox hunting and continues on through President Kennedy's touch football to President Johnson's deer hunting. Includes charts of physical descriptions, date of Presidency, and varied interests of the Presidents.

EVANOFF, VLAD. A Complete Guide to Fishing. (rd6) Crowell, c1961. 206p. $3.75

A useful book about fishing in fresh or salt water. Here the complete novice or advanced amateur can learn something of the techniques of bait casting, fly casting, spinning, and fish identification.

GARAGIOLA, JOSEPH. Baseball Is a Funny Game. (rd6) Lippincott, c1960. 176p. $3.50

A former major league player tells amusing stories about the game and its teams.

The symbol "rd" accompanied by the figure, in parentheses, following the title in each entry, indicates the estimated grade level of reading difficulty (see p. 18-19).

GARDNER, FRANK.The Young Sportsman's Guide to Wrestling. (rd7)
Nelson, c1963. 96p. $2.75
A step-by-step guide to wrestling designed for each member of a wrestling
squad or for the individual wrestler. Emphasizes the balance, speed, and
timing so important to championship performances on the mat. (Young
Sportsman's Library)

GAULT, WILLIAM CAMPBELL. Two-Wheeled Thunder. (rd7) Dutton,
c1962. 184p. $2.95
The story of motorcycle racing with its thrills, drivers, and mechanics.

HARMON, TOM (with BENAUGH, JIM). Tom Harmon's Book of Sports
Information. (rd5) Scholastic Book Services, c1963. 152p.
Paper, 35c
A compendium of sports information. A thousand and one questions and
answers. Quizzes on thirteen different sports, arranged by the months in which
they are usually played.

HOUGH, RICHARD ALEXANDER. Great Auto Races. (rd9) Harper, c1961.
198p. $3.50
An anthology of international automobile racing by British and American
automotive writers. Includes Le Mans, Mille Miglia, Tourist Trophy, and the
Indianapolis 500. The statistics and technical details indicate that the best
audience is the racing fan.

HYDE, MARGARET OLDROYD and EDWIN. Where Speed Is King. (rd6)
McGraw, c1961 (rev. ed.) 144p. $3
A discussion of various interests involving speed: airplanes, bicycles, boats,
bobsleds, horses, hot rods, ice boats, pigeons, racing cars, skates, sailboats,
skis, sports cars, track, swimming, water skis, rockets, and spaceships. Health
and safety factors are discussed, and some of the personalities identified with
each sport are included.

JACKSON, CAARY PAUL. How to Play Better Baseball. (rd6) Crowell,
c1963. 160p. $3.50 (Paper, $1.75)
This baseball manual offers a clear explanation of the rules and positions of
the game, and gives playing tips that are helpful.

JACKSON, ROBERT B. Sports Cars. (rd4) Walck, c1963. 64p. $2.75
An explanation of the workings of a car and its parts, with emphasis on the
safety features of sports cars.

KAHN, ROGER. Inside Big League Baseball. (rd7) Macmillan, c1962.
98p. $1.95
The book traces the history of America's big league baseball teams. Some
chapters describe the training of a rookie, the travel patterns of a big-league
team, the race for the pennant, the World Series, and spring training.

KIERAN, JOHN, and DALEY, ARTHUR. The Story of the Olympic Games:
776 B.C. to 1960 A.D. (rd7) Lippincott, c1961 (new ed.).
416p. $6.95
Here is a new edition, well illustrated, of a fine book about the famous Olympic Games, including all of those in 1960.

LINDSAY, SALLY. Figure Skating. (rd6) Rand McNally, c1963. 96p. $2.95 (Paper, $1.50)

A study of the requirements in training and skill necessary for a champion figure skater. The book covers all aspects from starting-age groups and proper wearing apparel to entrance in competitions. Professionals such as Carol Heiss, Tenley Albright, and Hayes Jenkins in various skating positions are shown in the book.

MACPHERSON, TOM. Dragging and Driving. (rd7) Putnam, c1960. 160p. $2.95

A driver's handbook for the teen-ager. Important information to have on the day the license is received.

MASIN, HERMAN. How to Star in Baseball. (rd5) Scholastic Book Services, c1960. 64p. Paper, 25c

Keep up with the game, learn trick plays, read about the history of baseball, and view photos of leading professional players. A well-written guide for boys who want to improve their baseball skill.

————How to Star in Basketball. (rd5) Scholastic Book Services, c1958. 64p. Paper, 25c

Learn how to play a better game. Diagrams of trick plays and a history of the game are included.

————How to Star in Football. (rd5) Scholastic Book Services, c1959. 64p. Paper, 25c

Good tips on improving your game, along with an explanation of trick plays and a brief history of the sport and of some professional players.

MOKRAY, WILLIAM G. Basketball Stars of 1964. (rd6) Pyramid, c1964. 160p. Paper, 40c

Inside stories of the great pros and college stars and their crowd-thrilling plays, plus photos, records and statistics, and glimpses into their homes and lives.

MOORE, ARCHIE. Archie Moore Story. (rd6) McGraw, c1960. 240p. $4.95

A poor boy with a criminal record is able to overcome this handicap through a love of boxing, determination to win, and the courage to stick to his decision to become a champion light heavyweight boxer.

MUSIAL, STAN. "The Man's" Own Story, as Told to Bob Broeg. (rd6) Doubleday, c1964. 328p. $4.95

"Stan the Man," recently appointed director of the President's Physical Fitness Program and former Cardinal star, has been much admired both as a person and as a baseball player. This is the story of Musial's rise from Donora, Pennsylvania, sandlots to the crowd-cheering days in St. Louis and major league fame.

O'CONNOR, W. HAROLD. How to Star in Track and Field. (rd5) Scholastic Book Services, c1961. 64p. Paper, 35c

Keys to success and tips for improvement make this a valuable guide for the young sportsman interested in track events.

————

The symbol "rd" accompanied by the figure, in parentheses, following the title in each entry, indicates the estimated grade level of reading difficulty (see p. 18-19).

PRATT, J. LOWELL, ed. Sport, Sport, Sport. (rd6) Watts, c1960. 256p.
$2.95 (Paper, Pratt, 50c)
An unusual sports anthology, filled with stories of crises in the lives of American athletes, revealing them to be not only great champions, but also outstanding personalities. Interesting material about such athletes as Bob Feller, Roy Campanella, Babe Didriksen Zaharias, Jim Thorpe, and others. (Terrific Triple Title Series)

ROBINSON, RAY, ed. Baseball Stars of 1964. (rd6) Pyramid, c1964.
160p. Paper, 40c
The thrilling moments and inside stories of today's baseball greats—Mays, Mantle, Spahn, and others, plus official statistics, action photos, and lifetime records of outstanding major league players.

ROWAN, CARL T. Wait Till Next Year: The Life Story of Jackie Robinson. (rd6) Random, c1960. 339p. $4.95
A Negro boy from a sharecropper's cabin displays the courage and intelligence to fight prejudice through his ability as a baseball player. He plays so well that fans and team forget his color and think only of his ability.

SCHOOR, GENE. Lew Burdette of the Braves. (rd6) Putnam, c1960.
192p. $2.95
After success in the minor leagues, Lew wins his way into the major leagues and fame.

————Willie Mays: Modest Champion. (rd6) Putnam, c1960. 192p.
$2.95
The story of a happy young player who can inspire his teammates to do better as he distinguishes himself in the game. See also the same author's *Jackie Robinson: Baseball Hero.*

SHAPIRO, MILTON J. Gil Hodges Story. (rd6) Messner, c1960. 192p.
$3.25
A boy from the Indiana coal mines develops muscles because of his hard work there and then learns to bat as he plays different positions on the Dodgers team.

SILKS, DONALD K. Boxing for Boys. (rd5) Knopf, c1953. 44p. $1.75
Helps for the beginner on techniques, equipment, and practices.

WEBER, DICK, and WHITE, GORDON, JR. The Young Sportsman's Guide to Bowling. (rd6) Nelson, c1963. 96p. $2.75
A lively introduction to a sport that is popular the year around with all ages. Written by a member of the 1961-62 All-American Bowling Team and a New York *Times* sportswriter. (Young Sportsman's Library)

YATES, BROCK. The Indianapolis 500: The Story of the Motor Speedway. (rd7) Harper, c1961 (rev. ed.). 182p. $3.50
A revised "Golden Anniversary" edition of the exciting story of the Indianapolis motor speedway. Includes a complete list of records.

SPORTS: Fiction

ALLISON, BOB, and HILL, FRANK. The Kid Who Batted 1000. (rd6) Doubleday, c1951. 238p. $3.50 (Paper, Scholastic Book Services, 35c)

The funny, fast-moving story of Dave King, the seventeen-year-old St. Louis Chicks' batting wonder who never misses. The Chicks romp toward the pennant, and then comes the hilarious World Series payoff!

ARCHIBALD, JOE. Outfield Orphan. (rd6) Macrae, c1961. 208p. $3.25

Baseball story of suspense and action. Benjie's spirits sag when he begins to play badly. He feels there has been only trouble for the team since he joined the big league ball club as its first Negro player. Benjie wins through and learns to overcome his own prejudices as he attains a top place on the team. Other titles by the same author include *Backfield Twins* and *Big League Busher*.

ARMER, ALBERTA. Screwball. (rd5) World, c1963. 192p. $3

The heartfelt story of a crippled boy's struggle to compete with his athletic twin brother. Michael, the crippled twin, has a mechanical flair which brings victory in the eliminations of the Detroit Soap Box Derby.

BETHELL, JEAN. Barney Beagle Plays Baseball. (rd3) Grosset, c1963. 60p. $1.58 (Paper, 59c)

A story of interest to baseball fans, told simply and illustrated attractively. It has special appeal to boys with limited reading ability.

BISHOP, CURTIS. Lonesome End. (rd6) Lippincott, c1963. 192p. $3.50

Jim has many disappointments before he learns to understand himself and others. Only then is he able to help prepare his football team for two important games.

_____Rebound. (rd6) Lippincott, c1962. 160p. $3.25

When Rob does not make the varsity basketball team he is unhappy, but he rebounds to new victories. An accident, a girl, and a wise coach help him meet with success.

_____Sideline Quarterback. (rd6) Lippincott, c1960. 192p. $2.95

This popular sportswriter tells the story of a boy who finds he can help his team to win even though he is unable to be a member of it.

BOWEN, ROBERT S. Dirt Track Danger. (rd4) Doubleday, c1963. 141p. $2.50

A young racing enthusiast, Johnny Blake, has promised his father to quit racing if he doesn't make good, and now he has only two races left in which to prove himself. (Signal Books)

_____Perfect Game. (rd6) Lothrop, c1963. 190p. $3

After pitching a perfect no-hit game on graduation day, Johnny Brown is offered a major league contract, but tough luck prevents him from signing that contract for almost two years.

The symbol "rd" accompanied by the figure, in parentheses, following the title in each entry, indicates the estimated grade level of reading difficulty (see p. 18-19).

BRENNAN, JOE. Hot Rod Thunder. (rd4) Doubleday, c1962. 144p. $2.50

A swift action story which points out hot rodding as a useful hobby when rules are followed. (Signal Books)

CAMPBELL, R. W. Drag Doll. (rd6) Funk, c1962. 192p. $2.95

A story about hot rodders who value knowledge about automobile design and courtesy on the road more than speed.

CARSON, JOHN F. The Coach Nobody Liked. (rd6) Farrar, c1960. 224p. $2.95

A boy gives up scholastic recognition for athletic success to please his domineering father, a former basketball champion. The school coach helps Sid's father see the true value of sports beyond winning games.

CARTER, BRUCE. Fast Circuit. (rd7) Harper, c1962. 181p. $3.50

Nick Bailey runs into some mysterious setbacks as he races his automobile and strives to win the world championship at the Grand Prix.

COX, WILLIAM R. Tall on the Court. (rd7) Dodd, c1964. 209p. $3.25

Samuel Boone and Peter Harleoff, basketball teammates, are very much unlike in background, disposition, financial status, and the ability to get passing marks in school. Consequently, there are many clashes, both on and off the court.

DECKER, DUANE WALTER. Rebel in Right Field. (rd7) Morrow, c1961. 190p. $3.25

A good baseball story about the Blue Sox, in which Danny Redd, a rookie with all the makings of a major leaguer except one—the courage to take a risk —knocks himself out in a sixteen-inning game and saves the day.

FELSEN, HENRY GREGOR. Hot Rod. (rd7) Dutton, c1950. 188p. $2.95

An eloquent bid for careful driving among young people; any reader will thank the kind fortune that put him in his own, and not in Bud's shoes. Another popular book by the same author is *Street Rod*.

FENNER, PHYLLIS, ed. Kickoff: Stories of Football. (rd5) Knopf, c1960. 174p. $3.50

A collection of football stories stressing cooperation and teamwork and containing such items as a chance to sit on the bench with Knute Rockne, report of Red Grange's famous Philadelphia game, and an opportunity to meet a goat named Matilda, who once saved a football game for Columbia University.

FRICK, CONSTANCE H. Patch. (rd7) Harcourt, c1957. 188p. $3

The informal and the serious are combined in this track story of a hairbrained miler who becomes a reliable member of the high-school track team and a record breaker. Another sports story by the same author is *Tourney Team*.

FRIENDLICH, DICK. Line Smasher. (rd6) Westminster, c1952. 194p. $3.25 (Paper, Scholastic Book Services, 25c)

A close friendship between Cliff Gear and Bill Devlin, two college freshmen, is endangered by suspicions of headline-grabbing on and off the field. A fast-paced football story.

———Relief Pitcher. (rd7) Westminster, c1964. 176p. $3.25

Pete Conroy, utility fielder, injures his knee in a collision with a teammate. Although it looks as if his major league career has ended, he later proves his worth as a relief pitcher in an emergency. Another popular book by this author is *All-Pro Quarterback*.

GAULT, WILLIAM CAMPBELL. The Checkered Flag. (rd7) Dutton, c1964. 192p. $3.25

The story of three boys of different backgrounds in a midwestern city who team up with their own racing car to win a big race. They also succeed in a business undertaking. An exciting, action-packed story.

————Dirt Track Summer. (rd5) Dutton, c1961. 191p. $2.95

For auto racing fans, this story is an action-filled tale of sportsmanship and dirt track racing at its best. The two sons of a former racing mechanic, along with a friend, plan for a try at the big race and bring their car to an exciting victory.

————Drag Strip. (rd4) Dutton, c1959. 185p. $3.25

Sixteen-year-old Terry, who has been interested in racing cars since he was seven, forms a club with a Mexican boy from the slums and others who work on their cars together. They finally prove to the city their need for a drag strip.

————Road-Race Rookie. (rd7) Dutton, c1962. 186p. $3

A sports car racing story emphasizing the importance of sportsmanship, tolerance, and teamwork.

————Thunder Road. (rd7) Dutton, c1952. 188p. $2.95 (Paper, Scholastic Book Services, 25c)

Exciting action story of a young hot-rodder who goes from drag races on outlaw tracks to fighting for speed supremacy on the Indianapolis Speedway, known as Thunder Road. He determines to make automotive engineering his career.

GELMAN, STEVE. Baseball Bonus Kid. (rd4) Doubleday, c1961. 141p. $2.50

The story of Bobby, the $60,000 bonus kid of a big-league ball club, and how he grows up and proves his ability. (Signal Books)

————Football Fury. (rd4) Doubleday, c1962. 140p. $2.50

Tim finds that college, where he must study on his own, is very different from high school. He learns to make friends, to keep up with his studies, and to win a place on the football team as well. (Signal Books)

GIBSON, MICHAEL. Le Mans: Twice Around the Clock. (rd6) Putnam, c1964. 191p. $3.50

A realistic novel about a young English racing driver's initial success on the severe Le Mans course, a twenty-four-hour endurance test with fifty or more cars in competition. Authentic description of the course, thrilling dedication of drivers and mechanics, and convincing climax.

GILBERT, NAN. Champions Don't Cry. (rd6) Harper, c1960. 198p. $3.50

Teen-age Sally must learn to control herself if she hopes to become the tennis champion she longs to be.

GREEN, ANNE. The Valley Cup. (rd6) Nelson, c1962. 208p. $2.95

A story of steeplechase racing in which Ben Anders learns that it takes courage and sacrifice to realize his talents.

The symbol "rd" accompanied by the figure, in parentheses, following the title in each entry, indicates the estimated grade level of reading difficulty (see p. 18-19).

HARKINS, PHILIP. Argentine Road Race. (rd7) Morrow, c1962. 221p.
    $3.25
  Young Pedro Thompson learns about driving, but worries about the irrespon-
  sibility of his employer as tension mounts during the Grand Prix race.
————The Day of the Drag Race. (rd7) Morrow, c1960. 223p. $3.25
  The hero of this humorous story, packed with information about hot rods and
  auto races, is a skinny freckle-faced teen-ager.
————Where the Shark Waits. (rd7) Morrow, c1963. 191p. $3.25
  The humorous adventure story of a teen-age skin diver in California and
  Mexico. Most of the excitement occurs underwater and involves sharks.

HEUMAN, WILLIAM. Wonder Boy. (rd6) Scholastic Book Services
    (Morrow, c1951). 192p. Paper, 35c
  Seventeen-year-old Ad is big league material, the fastest pitcher the baseball
  scouts have ever seen. Action-packed baseball story about a has-been catcher
  who discovers a teen-ager with great potential. The boy's future depends on
  the man's overcoming his own fears.

JACKSON, CAARY PAUL. Stock Car Racer. (rd6) Follett, c1957. 224p.
    $2.95
  When Chet Carter and his friend Skip wreck the sports car they built, Chet's
  father sends them to a farm where stock car races are held. Chet learns about
  this kind of racing, and, more important, he learns that saving someone from
  a crash is better than winning a race. Some later books by the same author
  include *Pro Hockey Comeback* (c1961) and *Bud Baker, Racing Swimmer*
  (c1962).

JOHNSON, ALLAN L. Hot Rod Reporter. (rd8) Duell, c1961. 152p.
    $2.95
  A Colorado boy combines his hobbies of hot-rodding and photography and
  helps capture a group of criminals in an exciting adventure.

KNOTT, BILL. Junk Pitcher. (rd5) Follett, c1963. 224p. $2.95
  An exciting account of a young major league pitcher who, in spite of his fast
  ball, is sent to the minors where he must develop a whole new style of pitching to work his way back to the majors. Emphasizes that baseball is a business as well as a game, and success depends on drive and desire as well as
  on talent.

LEONARD, BURGESS. Stretch Bolton: Mister Shortstop. (rd6) Lippin-
    cott, c1963. 192p. $3.50
  An exciting, easy-to-read story about big-league baseball and Stretch's troubles with a new team. This shows how the character and sportsmanship of
  champions are developed. Other books about Stretch include *Stretch Bolton's
  Rookies* and *Stretch Bolton Comes Back*.

NEIGOFF, MIKE. Nine Make a Team. (rd4) Whitman, c1963. 128p.
    $2.50
  The story of a boy who learns the importance of cooperation with the other
  players and with the coach in order to have a successful team.

OLGIN, JOSEPH. Backcourt Atom. (rd5) Houghton, c1960. 120p. $2.75
  One of Shorty McLean's problems is his height, but it is not his chief problem.
  Becoming part of a basketball team, learning how to work with others, and
  making friends in a new school all help him become a champion.

OLSON, GENE. The Roaring Road. (rd7) Dodd, c1962. 183p. $3

A story of sports car racing—its thrills and the skill it demands. Dave Falconer trains for a race, comes into conflict with his mother over racing as a career, and is involved in a poor boy-rich girl romance. The theme is perseverance: "Work hard and you will win."

PHILLIPS, MAURICE. Lightning on Ice. (rd4) Doubleday, c1963. 143p. $2.50

A fast-paced story in which hockey player Kim Morgan learns the true meaning of friendship and sportsmanship. (Signal Books)

SANKEY, ALICE. Basketballs for Breakfast. (rd4) Whitman, c1963. 128p. $2.50

Larry loses his place on the junior high basketball team and thinks he will never play again. After joining a group at the Y, he learns much about the sport and is then qualified for his school team.

SCHOLZ, JACKSON. Dugout Tycoon. (rd7) Morrow, c1963. 254p. $3.25

A baseball story with play-by-play accounts, with fast-moving plot on and off the diamond, and with interesting dialogue and characters.

TUNIS, JOHN R. Buddy and the Old Pro. (rd3) Morrow, c1955. 189p. $3.25

A youthful baseball team learns that it is more important to show good sportsmanship than it is to win.

————Go, Team, Go. (rd7) Morrow, c1954. 215p. $3.25

Fast-paced basketball action is intensified when tensions develop between an overconfident team and a coach who refuses to compromise. The theme is one of self-discovery and personality growth.

VERRAL, CHARLES SPAIN. Champion of the Court. (rd7) Scholastic Book Services (Crowell, c1954). 154p. Paper, 25c

Rocky Rockland, a spoiled brat and the best basketball player Pineville ever had, sparks the team's fight for a championship until his hot temper and show-off stunts almost wreck their chances. Plenty of action for players and fans.

ZANGER, JACK. Baseball Spark Plug. (rd4) Doubleday, c1963. 143p. $2.50

A baseball story with plenty of action, and a diamond filled with interesting players. (Signal Books)

TRANSPORTATION AND COMMUNICATION

BERGERE, THEA and RICHARD. Automobiles of Yesteryear; a Pictorial Record of Motor Cars That Made History—Pioneer, Antique, Classic, and Sports Models. (rd6) Dodd, c1962. 160p. $3.50

A book that describes and gives detailed drawings of outstanding cars from 1893 through 1940, depicting their history from the earliest horseless carriages. The text is divided into three periods: "The Pioneer Years," "The Antiques," and "The Classic Era." On some pages there is a brief paragraph giving information about the times; for example, 1923, "This year's hit tune is 'Yes! We Have No Bananas!'"

The symbol "rd" accompanied by the figure, in parentheses, following the title in each entry, indicates the estimated grade level of reading difficulty (see p. 18-19).

BILLINGS, HENRY. Construction Ahead. (rd8) Viking, c1951. 158p. $3
The history of road making and the work of men who plan and build roads today told in clear, simple text with dramatic pictures.

FLEMING, ALICE. Wheels: From Ox Carts to Sports Cars. (rd6) Lippincott, c1960. 192p. $3.75
Absorbing story of man's most important invention, the wheel, as used for vehicles. Many pictures add to the clear text.

FLOHERTY, JOHN JOSEPH. Men Against Distance: The Story of Communications. (rd7) Lippincott, c1954. 148p. $3.75
Telephone, telegraph, radio, and television history and wonders are summarized along with research and general vocational information in these fields.

FRANKEL, LILLIAN and GODFREY. 101 Things to Do With a Bike. (rd7) Sterling, c1961. 128p. $2.95
A practical guide to cyclists on the handling of a bike.

LAIRD, HELENE and CHARLTON. The Tree of Language. (rd6) World, c1957. 233p. $3.50
The authors discuss the growth and development of language—the making of the alphabet, the beginnings of writing, the influences that keep language alive. Included are the histories of more than a hundred individual words.

MURRAY, DON. Man Against Earth: The Story of Tunnels and Tunnel Builders. (rd7) Lippincott, c1961. 192p. $3.95
From earliest days to the present, man has been digging his way through the earth. This is the story of one area in engineering.

ROBBIN, IRVING. Great Cars of All Time. (rd7) Grosset, c1960. 209p. $4.95
This is a Hall of Fame for automobiles over the past sixty-five years. With the history and design of each car is given a full-page picture in color.

ROGERS, FRANCES. Painted Rock to Printed Page. (rd7) Lippincott, c1960. 175p. $3.50
The history of communication by means of printing is given from earliest to modern times.

SOLOMON, LOUIS. Telstar: Communication Break-Through by Satellite. (rd6) McGraw, c1962. 63p. $2.95
A good report on the development of the communications satellite, the drama of the first transmission, and the ways in which the ground stations and the satellite function. Many illustrations with photographs and diagrams. A final chapter describes future projects now planned by the Space Agency.

ZIM, HERBERT S. Codes and Secret Writing. (rd5) Morrow, c1948. 154p. $2.75 (Paper, Scholastic Book Services, 35c)
Codes and ciphers as related to language development; number and letter codes and how to break them; secret writing and invisible inks—all appear in this useful and entertaining volume.

WAR STORIES

BONHAM, FRANK. War Beneath the Sea. (rd7) Crowell, c1962. 264p.
$3.75
The fictional story of a boy who experiences the conditions of submarine warfare in the Pacific Theater of Operations during World War II.

BRICKHILL, PAUL. Reach for the Sky. (rd6) Norton, c1954. 312p. $4.95
Here is the exciting story of Douglas Bader, who twice escaped from Nazi
prison camps and became a top air ace although he had lost both legs. The
amazing, and often funny, adventures of a born leader who would not let disaster tie him to a wheelchair. Photographs show Bader and his exploits.

BRUCKNER, KARL. The Day of the Bomb. (rd7) Van Nostrand, c1962.
189p. $3.50
A vivid account of the Hiroshima holocaust as seen through the eyes of two
Japanese children who survive the atomic bombing of their city. Ten years
later, Shigeo's lively teen-age sister succumbs to unsuspected radiation sick-
ness. Realistic fiction.

GALLICO, PAUL. The Snow Goose. (rd6) Knopf, c1941. 57p. $1.75
At the famous battle of Dunkirk during World War II, a snow goose aids
both the British Army and a man who is running away from himself. He finds
himself in part by aiding his country. A charming brief novel.

HERSEY, JOHN. A Bell for Adano. (rd6) Knopf, c1944. 269p. $3.95
(Modern Library, $1.25; paper, Avon, 50c)
The short novel and appealing story of an American Army major who defied
red tape in order to help a defeated village come back to life and usefulness.

LECKIE, ROBERT. The War in Korea: 1950-1953. (rd6) Random, c1963.
173p. $1.95
An account of the war in which troops of the UN acted as a police force to
fight an aggressor nation. Good treatment of the drama of small moments—
the numbing "knife-edged winds" that were the setting of this war. (World
Landmark Book Series)

LOOMIS, ROBERT D. Great American Fighter Pilots of World War
II. (rd5) Random, c1961. 208p. $1.95
It took brave and well trained men to gain air control during the Second
World War, as this exciting book reveals. (Landmark Books)

MONTAGU, EWEN. The Man Who Never Was. (rd7) Lippincott, c1954.
160p. $4.75
Here is the true cloak-and-dagger story of "Operation Mincemeat." Efforts
of the British to mislead the Germans about the invasion of Italy are aided
by giving a nameless corpse an officer's identity.

SENJE, SIGURD. Escape! (rd6) Harcourt, c1964. 156p. $3
A fourteen-year-old Norwegian boy and girl join with the Underground in
the rescue of a Russian prisoner from a German camp near their home in
1940. Suspense heightens as the crises occur in this novel for young people.

The symbol "rd" accompanied by the figure, in parentheses, following the
title in each entry, indicates the estimated grade level of reading difficulty
(see p. 18-19).

TOLAND, JOHN. The Flying Tigers. (rd6) Random, c1963. 170p. $1.95
The episode of the AVG, known as the "Flying Tigers," and its success in the face of great odds. A history of the American flyers who volunteered to fight with the Chinese against Japan in World War II presented in exciting style for teen-age readers. (Landmark Books)

TREGASKIS, RICHARD. John F. Kennedy and PT-109. (rd7) Random, c1962. 192p. $1.95
The experiences of John F. Kennedy as the skipper of a PT boat in the South Pacific in World War II. Included is his rescue of his crew when the boat was cut in half, showing the courage and determination of the young lieutenant who was one day to become the President of the United States. Photographs and maps make a useful addition to the story. (Landmark Books)

TRUMBULL, ROBERT. The Raft. (rd6) Holt, c1942. 205p. $2.50 (paper, Pyramid, 35c)
The true hair-raising adventures of three American Navy fliers adrift in the Pacific for thirty-four days without food or equipment.

TUNIS, JOHN R. Silence Over Dunkerque. (rd5) Morrow, c1962. 215p. $3.25
A realistic and gripping novel of the grim days when the British soldiers waited to be rescued from the terrible trap that held them on the French coast as the Battle for Britain began. One of the British soldiers left behind is searched for by his twin fifteen-year-old sons, who take part in the rescue operation.

WERSTEIN, IRVING. The Battle of Midway. (rd6) Crowell, c1961. 145p. $2.95
The thrilling true story of a great naval engagement in the Pacific theater during World War II, the attack on Midway by the Japanese. As the action unfolds, the focus alternates between the American and Japanese sides, thus describing the strategy, hopes, and fears of each.

WHITE, ROBB. Up Periscope. (rd7) Doubleday, c1956. 251p. $2.95
The adventures of a young naval officer during World War II in the Pacific on a top-secret mission. There is gripping action and suspense in this story of submarine warfare, told with accuracy and realism. Another novel by White is *Secret Sea*.

WORLD PROBLEMS

COLLINS, RUTH PHILPOTT. The Flying Cow. (rd5) Walck, c1963. 128p. $3.50
American school children send a prize dairy cow as a gift to the needy people of a small village in India. There are crises created by the American Bossy in the land of the "sacred cow." A maharajah with modern ideas and a school-age boy together help to solve the problems. A timely and interesting story.

EPSTEIN, BERYL and SAMUEL. The Story of the International Red Cross. (rd6) Nelson, c1963. 183p. $3.50
The amazing story of how the Red Cross grew from the interest of five citizens of Geneva in wounded European soldiers in 1863. It traces the development of the organization to its present services involving 87 nations and millions of people, as it helps the needy of the world every day of the year in war and in peace, in flood and fire and famine—an outstanding example of "people helping people."

FRANK, ANNE. Diary of a Young Girl. (rd5) Doubleday, c1952. 285p. $3.95. (Paper, Pocket, 35c)

The now-famous diary kept by the sensitive fifteen-year-old Dutch girl whose family hideout was finally raided by the Nazis after two years spent living in secret. Made into a successful play in 1956 by Frances Goodrich and Albert Hackett. (Random, 174p.)

GRAHAM, LORENZ. South Town. (rd7) Follett, c1958. 189p. $3.50

An account of events on a small farm near South Town during mob violence. A story of racial tensions in the contemporary South.

HÁMORI, LÁSZLÓ. Dangerous Journey. (rd5) Harcourt, c1962. 190p. $3.25

The fast-paced story of two Hungarians who escape from the Comrade Youth Warden over the border into Austria. They have many thrilling and dangerous adventures before they reach their goal. This story shows how strong is the urge to be free.

HEMMING, JAMES. Mankind Against the Killers. (rd7) McKay, c1956. 231p. $5.95

An absorbing study of world health problems, especially the three companions—malnutrition, poverty, and disease. As exciting as a detective story when it tells of the microbe hunters, and as thrilling as a war story when it shows a World Health Organization team battling a plague. A must for anyone interested in world affairs.

PIKE, ESTHER, ed. Who Is My Neighbor? (rd7) Seabury, c1960. 230p. $3.50

People around the world need help in many ways. These fourteen short articles tell of persons who have worked with alcoholics, the physically handicapped, the mentally ill, the segregated, the underprivileged, and others who need their help.

SAVAGE, KATHERINE. The Story of the United Nations. (rd5) Walck, c1962. 224p. $4.50

A clear and up-to-date story of the United Nations organization that is so important in man's struggle to achieve peace in the world. It is a useful book, often an inspiring one, and manages to be hopeful without being sentimental. There is also a helpful index and list of further readings.

SCHECHTER, BETTY. The Peaceable Revolution. (rd7) Houghton, c1963. 243p. $3.75

A book in three sections that will help young people understand the possibility for promoting justice and for developing principles through peaceful, nonviolent resistance. The use of this effective weapon is demonstrated by the work of Thoreau, of Gandhi, and, in most recent times, of Martin Luther King and the Freedom Riders.

The symbol "rd" accompanied by the figure, in parentheses, following the title in each entry, indicates the estimated grade level of reading difficulty (see p. 18-19).

SHIPPEN, KATHERINE BINNEY. The Pool of Knowledge: How the United Nations Share Their Skills. (rd8) Harper, c1954. 148p. $2.75

An interesting account of the work the United Nations organizations are doing in sixteen places in the world to help the people of those areas better their ways of living and combat the poverty, hunger, and disease that have been their lot for many generations.

SHIRER, WILLIAM L. The Rise and Fall of Adolf Hitler. (rd6) Random, c1961. 188p. $1.95

The fateful story of one man's influence on the course of recent history and all the evils which have arisen as a result of his desire to conquer the world. (World Landmark Books)

WHITE, W. L. Lost Boundaries. (rd7) Harcourt, c1948. 91p. $2.25

The stirring story of a New England Negro family that has passed as white for many years until the father's dramatic revelation and its results.

YOUNG PEOPLE HERE AND ABROAD

ANCKARSVÄRD, KARIN. Springtime for Eva. (rd9) Harcourt, c1961. 157p. $2.95

With deep understanding, the author portrays a young Swedish girl, Eva, her friends, family, and first love—and her efforts to continue a normal life after an accident in which a boy is killed.

BEIM, JERROLD. Trouble After School. (rd4) Harcourt, c1957. 128p. $3 (Paper, Scholastic Book Services, 35c)

A fast-moving and realistic story about a failing eighth grade boy who becomes a truant and gets in with a gang. Young people face a real problem when they must decide between backing out on their friends or doing what they know to be wrong.

BOTHWELL, JEAN. The Silver Mango Tree. (rd7) Harcourt, c1960. 190p. $3.25

The story of an unhappy adolescent American girl in India. Complications and problems in her life there help her mature.

BUCK, PEARL. The Big Wave. (rd5) Day, c1947. 61p. $3.50 (Paper, Scholastic Book Services, 50c)

When a Japanese boy sees his home and family wiped out in a tidal wave that destroys his village, he takes a while to regain his courage. The love and care of neighbors help him to start a new life.

CARSE, ROBERT. Great Venture. (rd6) Scribner, c1960. 239p. $2.95

A sixteen-year-old boy and his uncle go to New Caledonia and have unusual and exciting adventures.

CAVANAH, FRANCES, ed. We Came to America. (rd7) Macrae, c1954. 307p. $3.95

Firsthand accounts by twenty-four immigrants who came to this country to make new lives for themselves and to help make our nation great.

CAVANNA, BETTY. A Time for Tenderness. (rd7) Morrow, c1962. 220p. $3.25

A romance helps Peggy toward maturity as she and her family try to accustom themselves to life in Brazil. Concerns the basic problems of human relations.

CLARK, ANN NOLAN. Medicine Man's Daughter. (rd5) Farrar, c1963. 160p. $2.95

Any teen-ager whose loyalties are divided will feel with the medicine man's daughter in her decision to go to the white man's school and leave the wild beauty of her country and the customs of her people.

CRAYDER, TERESA. Cathy and Lisette. (rd4) Doubleday, c1964. 143p. $2.95

An interesting story of an exchange student from France who comes to live with an American teen-age girl and her family in a small Ohio town. (Signal Books)

DAVIS, RUSSELL G. The Choctaw Code. (rd6) McGraw, c1961. 152p. $3

A moving book about a man with deep ethical convictions. The story of a friendship between a young boy and a Choctaw Indian who has been sentenced by his tribe to die. Tom wants him to escape, but the Indian shows him why this is wrong.

DU JARDIN, ROSAMUND and JUDY. Junior Year Abroad. (rd7) Lippincott, c1960. 192p. $2.95

When two American college girls travel abroad to study, they find adventure and romance on their European journey.

DURSTINE, VIRGINIA GARDINER. Monty of Montego. (rd6) Bobbs, c1963. 123p. $3.50

The story of Monty of Jamaica and his experiences in adjusting to new ways of life in the city, learning big-city ways and making big-city friends. He proves himself a local hero and a true son of his policeman father.

FALK, ANN MARI. Who Is Erika? (rd7) Harcourt, c1963. 124p. $2.75

The story of a Swedish girl's struggle to accept her widowed mother's remarriage, her new home, and her stepfather.

FELSEN, HENRY GREGOR. Boy Gets Car. (rd6) Random, c1960. 314p. $3.50

Woody Ahern thinks owning a car that he can fix up and call his own will give him status with the high-school crowd. His sobering experiences with the car provide an interesting story of teen-age status and the youth of today.

FENTON, EDWARD. The Golden Doors. (rd5) Doubleday, c1957. 262p. $2.95

The two children of a famous movie couple are fed up with moving around the world and being gushed over. Then, when they are traveling in Florence, they meet an Italian waif who shows them the beauties of his city. Here the action and mystery begin. An exciting story for both boys and girls.

The symbol "rd" accompanied by the figure, in parentheses, following the title in each entry, indicates the estimated grade level of reading difficulty (see p. 18-19).

FITCH, FLORENCE MARY. One God; the Ways We Worship Him. (rd6) Lothrop, c1944. 144p. $3

An objective explanation of the three great religions in the United States—Judaism, Catholicism, and Protestantism. Excellent photographs highlight the rituals and customs of each faith.

FORBES, KATHRYN. Mama's Bank Account. (rd6) Harcourt, c1949. 204p. $2.50 (Textbook ed., $1.75)

Teen-age Katryn tells heartwarming tales of a Norwegian-American family—especially Mama—and their everyday life in San Francisco.

GALLANT, KATHRYN. Flute Player of Beppu. (rd3) Coward, c1960. 43p. $2.75

A shy Japanese boy dreams of being able to play the flute as well as the village flute player. How he wins a chance to make his wish come true when he finds the musician's lost instrument makes an exciting tale.

GARST, DORIS SHANNON. The Golden Bird. (rd3) Houghton, c1956. 152p. $2.25

A young Indian boy is separated from his family on his first visit to Mexico City and has many adventures with the old and the new.

GARTHWAITE, MARION. Mario, a Mexican Boy's Adventures. (rd4) Doubleday, c1960. 167p. $2.75

When a Mexican boy is forced to cross the border with wetbacks to pick cotton in California, he suffers loneliness and fear as he struggles with a new language in a strange country.

GIDAL, TIM and SONIA. My Village in Spain. (rd5) Pantheon, c1962. 83p. $3.50

The story of a Spanish boy and his village where thousands of black bulls are raised for the bullfights. The text is focused on a trip to Cordoba to see Antonio's first bullfight where he begins to understand why his father does not approve of them.

HAYES, FLORENCE S. Skid. (rd5) Houghton, c1948. 216p. $3.25

A Negro boy who loves baseball and plays a good game moves away from his Georgia home, where he was the team captain. He is not very happy at first in his new school in the North until something happens that brings him friends and a chance to play baseball again.

HEIDERSTADT, DOROTHY. Lois Says Aloha. (rd5) Nelson, c1963. 159p. $2.95

Lois Teramoto, of Polynesian, Japanese, and American ancestry, establishes her own ties with the mainland by corresponding with a girl in Washington, D.C., and is proud when Hawaii achieves statehood. The chief interest in the book lies in the appraisal of the Hawaiian attitude toward diverse ancestry.

HOLISHER, DESIDER. Growing Up in Israel. (rd6) Viking, c1963. 192p. $5

Present-day Israel is viewed through the experiences of a young Israeli brother and sister. Descriptions of the children's studies and habits and tours to Jerusalem, Haifa, and Acre are interspersed with details of Biblical history, both Jewish and Christian.

KIRCHGESSNER, MARIA. High Challenge. (rd7) Harcourt, c1962. 287p. $3.50

Four high-school girls in a Bavarian village use determination and ingenuity in earning money to rehabilitate an abandoned mountain hut as their own ski lodge. The story skillfully moves back and forth from episodes about each girl alone to episodes that concern the group.

LENSKI, LOIS. Coal Camp Girl. (rd5) Lippincott, c1959. 192p. $4.50

A true-to-life story of the daughter of a miner in a West Virginia coal mining town.

_____Shoo Fly Girl. (rd5) Lippincott, c1963. 176p. $3.95

The delightful story of an Amish family of nine children. Suzanna helps her older brother through a difficult time and enjoys the love and security of a closely knit family.

LINDQUIST, JENNIE D. Golden Name Day. (rd4) Harper, c1955. 247p. $3.50

What the Swedish-American customs mean to a young American girl is told in a beautiful and sensitive story.

LIPKIND, WILLIAM. Boy of the Islands. (rd4) Harcourt, c1955. 55p. $2.75

A bright adventure about a youth, showing the life and customs of Hawaii. Lua wanted to be a runner, but was destined instead for real leadership of his people.

NIXON, LUCILLE M. Young Ranchers at Oak Valley. (rd5) Lippincott, c1960. 64p. $2.95

Some young people live on a western ranch with horses, cattle, and cowboys and have fun with neighbors.

PARKER, RICHARD. Voyage to Tasmania. (rd5) Bobbs, c1963. 127p. $3.50

When Ray's parents are killed in an accident, he becomes bitter and hates everybody. As he travels by ship to Tasmania to live with his aunt, he becomes friendly with a Finnish boy who speaks no English. With the help of his new friend, Ray gradually learns to enjoy life again.

RITCHIE, BARBARA. Ramon Makes a Trade. (rd3) Parnassus, c1959. 48p. $3.25

The achievement of his dearest wish is the aim of the young Mexican boy, Ramon, in this charming tale. The story is told simply in both English and Spanish and may stimulate interest in languages. The illustrations are superb.

SCHARTUM-HANSEN, INGVILD. Ingvild's Diary. (rd3) Lothrop, c1954. 144p. $2.50

Six Norwegian children attend the first international children's camp in Ohio. Here are the impressions, often amusing and sometimes penetrating, of America as seen by one of them.

The symbol "rd" accompanied by the figure, in parentheses, following the title in each entry, indicates the estimated grade level of reading difficulty (see p. 18-19).

SOMMERFELT, AIMEE. The White Bungalow. (rd6) Criterion, c1964.
   128p. $3

Although this is a sequel to the popular *The Road to Agra*, it can be read
independently. Lalu is now fifteen and must decide between being a farmer
or a doctor in his native India. Because of his father's illness should he stay
home and take charge, or should he accept the scholarship he has won?

SPERRY, ARMSTRONG. Call It Courage. (rd5) Macmillan, c1940. 95p.
   $2.95

The story of a boy who was afraid. The son of a Polynesian chief goes off
alone to fight his fear of the sea and win the praise of his people for a brave
deed.

TARSHIS, ELIZABETH K. The Village That Learned to Read. (rd5)
   Houghton, c1941. 157p. $3.50

A country boy in Mexico wants to be a bullfighter, but learns that he must be
able to read.

TITUS, NANCY. A Dream of Her Own. (rd5) Lippincott, c1960. 192p.
   $2.95

A seventeen-year-old faces an important change. In spite of people around her
she feels very much alone and has, because of her need, a dream of belong-
ing to someone.

VAN RHIJN, ALEID. The Tide in the Attic. (rd6) Criterion, c1961.
   127p. $3

The story of how one Dutch farm family managed to survive the disastrous
flood which followed the storm of 1953. Marooned, finally, on the roof of
their farmhouse, the Wielemakers are rescued by helicopter. The ending is
realistic: the farm is ruined, the livestock gone, and the Wielemakers know
that they must return and start again.

WARNER, GERTRUDE CHANDLER. The Boxcar Children. (rd3) Scott,
   c1942. 156p. $1.45

The adventures of four resourceful brothers and sisters; a story filled with
action and suspense. Further events about this family appear in *Surprise
Island*.

READING TEXTS AND WORKBOOKS

ANDERSON, LORENA; DECHANT, EMERALD; GULLION, FLOYD THOMAS; and TAYLOR, STANFORD E. Listen and Read. Educational Developmental Laboratories, c1962. 30 tapes. $99

These tapes are designed to introduce students to the need for good listening in order to develop the ability to listen with greater attention, to discriminate, to organize, and to retain. An output jack is available with eight listening stations. The *Guide* and *Scripts to Accompany Tapes* come with the 30 tapes. The *Listen and Read Workbook* may be purchased for $1.80; additional *Scripts*, $1.50; and additional *Guides*, 30c.

BAILEY, MATILDA, and LEAVELL, ULLIN W. The Mastery of Reading Series. (rd7-9) American Book. (Revised and enlarged)

THE WORLD AND OUR ENGLISH HERITAGE. c1961. 732p. $5.04

THE WORLD OF AMERICA. c1961. 705p. $4.96

THE WORLD OF ENDLESS HORIZONS. c1961. 644p. $4.72

WORLDS OF ADVENTURE. c1961. 503p. $4.04

WORLDS OF PEOPLE. c1961. 506p. $4.28

WORLDS TO EXPLORE. c1961. 548p. $4.64

A series of six books with a twofold purpose: to encourage reading enjoyment, and to develop reading skills. Each chapter contains selections grouped according to theme, and develops one specific reading skill. Teachers' Guides, $1.

BREWTON, JOHN E.; LEMON, BABETTE; and ERNST, MARIE. New Horizons Through Reading and Literature. Laidlaw, c1962

Book 1. (rd7) 431p. $3.80

Book 2. (rd8) 431p. $3.80

Book 3. (rd9) 479p. $3.96

The reading appreciation selections in all three books touch such subjects as Understanding Ourselves and Others; Action—Games and Sports, Outdoor Life; Adventure—Danger, Daring, Strength, and Courage; Discovery—Nature, Science, and Invention; Heritage; etc. The new separate reading skills developmental program consists of short, interesting reading selections especially adapted to the teaching of basic reading skills (reading rate, getting the main idea, vocabulary development, outlining, etc.).

CASS, A., and others. Adult Education Reader. (rd1-3) Reader's Digest Services, Inc., Educational Division, c1954. 126p. 60c

LEVEL A: First Patrol and Other Stories

LEVEL B: Map the World and Other Stories

These are lively and entertaining selections from the *Reader's Digest* simplified to primary levels. Practical learning aids are included.

The symbol "rd" accompanied by the figure, in parentheses, following the title in each entry, indicates the estimated grade level of reading difficulty (see p. 18-19).

COLEMAN, J. H., and JUNGEBLUT, ANNE. Reading for Meaning Series. (rd4-6) Lippincott, c1962 (rev. ed.). 56p. 88c

These workbooks represent the latest revision of the Guiler and Coleman series for the intermediate grades. (Teacher's Guide, 46p. 60c).

DIXSON, R. J. Elementary Reader in English. (rd1) Regents, c1950. 120p. Paper, $1.25

Having a vocabulary range within the first thousand most commonly used words, these seventeen stories stress the oral approach and are illustrated as well. Especially helpful to the foreign-born.

GAINSBURG, JOSEPH C., and others. Advanced Skills in Reading. (rd7-9) Macmillan

Book 1. c1962. 313p. $3.24
Book 2. c1962. 328p. $3.40
Book 3. c1964. 326p. $3.60

A program of sequential instruction in advanced reading skills. These volumes give step-by-step procedures for reading various kinds of material. They recognize reading as a cluster of skills that students must master in order to be able to read well in any content area.

GATES, A. I., and PEARDON, C. C. Practice Exercises in Reading. Books III, IV, V, VI; Types A, B, C, D. (rd3-7) Teachers College, c1933. $1.85 per package of 10

A series of sixteen books containing brief reading selections followed by multiple-choice questions to test comprehension. For each grade level there is a separate booklet on each of the following types of reading: general significance, prediction of outcomes, understanding directions, and noting details.

GRAY, WILLIAM S.; MONROE, MARION; and ARTLEY, A. S. Basic Reading Skills for Junior High School Use. (rd7) Scott, c1957. 192p. $1.36

Variety of practice in basic skills for the younger high-school student, plus survey tests and a reading list.

GUILER, W. S., and COLEMAN, J. H. Reading for Meaning Series. (rd4-12) Lippincott, c1955 (rev. ed.). 56p. 88c

A series of workbooks designed to improve both speed and comprehension in reading. Workbooks provide activities for drill on the following six basic skills necessary for effective reading: word meanings, total meaning, central thought, detailed meanings, organization, and summarization. (Manual for grades 4-8, 63p. 88c; for grades 9-12, 62p. 88c).

GUYTON, M. L., and KIELTY, M. E. From Words to Stories. (rd1) Noble, c1951. 83p. $1.50

The forty-two reading units are very simply written on topics of adult interest. Here is help in learning to read and write English for everyday use.

HARDING, L. W., and BURR, J. B. Men in the Armed Forces: A Serviceman's Reader. (rd1) (Education Manual-EM 140) U.S. Armed Forces Inst. c1950. $1

A primer for and about servicemen, successor to the original *Private Pete*. This provides adult material of interest to the older high-school boys and to men in the Service or about to enter, but at a beginning level of reading. To accompany it is the practice book *Servicemen Learn to Read* (EM141). 105p. 50c.

HOVIOUS, CAROL. New Trails in Reading. (rd9) Heath, c1956. 480p. $4.20

For good readers as well as for retarded readers in senior high school, this book provides a systematic course in reading improvement, with many related language projects. Full and complete directions enable the student to proceed largely under his own power. (Teacher's Manual, 72p. 68c).

———and SHEARER, ELGA M. Wings for Reading. (rd6) Heath, c1952. 474p. $4.40

Interesting, easy-to-read short articles, ingenious practice exercises, and aids to the enrichment of word meanings make this a popular text for junior high school. (Teacher's Manual, 127p. $1).

JEWETT, A.; EDMAN, M.; SCANNELL, R.; and McKEE, P. Reading for Meaning Series. High School Level. Houghton, c1956
ADVENTURE BOUND. (rd7) 598p. $3.68
JOURNEYS INTO AMERICA. (rd8) 630p. $3.80

Anthologies containing short stories, biographies, essays, plays, and poetry, arranged by topics, such as animals, sports, science, interesting people, laughs, tall tales, the past, etc. They are accompanied by a handbook of developmental reading skills and a dictionary.

JOHNSON, ELEANOR M.; YOUNG, WILLIAM E.; LEARY, BERNICE E.; and MYERS, ELIZABETH ARNDT. New Reading Skilltext Series. (rd1-6) Merrill, c1961. 72c; net 54c

This is a developmental skills program in workbook form. The stories are human, modern, and lively, designed to fit the interests of adolescents. Diversified exercises provide for training in understanding and organizing ideas, in making judgments, and in studying words. Titles include *Pat the Pilot* (rd6), about the flying adventures of two high school classmates; *Tom Trott* (rd5), about a roving reporter and his dog; and *Uncle Ben* (rd4), about a great world traveler.

KELLEY, VICTOR H., and GREENE, HARRY A. Better Reading and Study Habits. (rd8) Harcourt, c1947. 73p. 64c

A practical workbook giving instruction in vocabulary, comprehension, preparation of assignments, and other aspects of reading and study. Instruction is followed by specific practice exercises.

KITCHIN, A. T., and ALLEN, V. F. Reader's Digest Readings: English as a Second Language. (rd1) Reader's Digest Services, Inc., Educational Division
Books I and II, c1953. 128p. 76c
Books III and IV, c1963. Paper, 75c; Glossary 20c

Contains articles and stories chosen on the basis of their world-wide popularity. Excellent for senior high school students who are not fond of reading. The separate Glossary includes answers to exercises and an alphabetical list of words used in the *Readings*, along with their definitions and a pronunciation guide.

The symbol "rd" accompanied by the figure, in parentheses, following the title in each entry, indicates the estimated grade level of reading difficulty (see p. 18-19).

KOHAN, FRANCES N., and WEIL, TRUDE T. Juan's Adventures in Mexico. (rd4-6) Noble, c1961. 183p. $3

A social studies reader about Mexico, based on the adventures of a young Tarascan Indian. Easy-to-read context for boys and girls in intermediate grades or for those in the junior and senior high school who need material with high interest and simple vocabulary. Word and map studies are included along with suggestions for class discussion and research reports.

LEAVELL, ULLIN W., and others. Reading Essentials Series. (rdPP-8) Steck. Paper, 76c

A series of worktexts giving practice, beginning with skills needed in the first two grades and continuing to higher level skills of critical and reflective thinking and interpretation.

MASTERY IN READING. (rd8) c1957. 144p.

Thorough reviews, maintenance, and extension of essential reading skills. Widely varied themes in story content encourage appreciation of our American way of life.

NEW ADVENTURES IN READING. (rd6) c1953. 128p.

Practice exercises that require thinking and interpretation. Special emphasis on phonics.

NEW AVENUES IN READING. (rd4) c1953. 128p.

Skills previously introduced are reviewed and extended. New skills introduced in practice exercises and easy-to-read stories.

NEW GOALS IN READING. (rd3-4) c1960. 112p.

High story interest, a carefully selected vocabulary, and simple sentence structure for remedial students at the middle-grade level.

NEW JOURNEYS IN READING. (rd5) c1953. 128p.

Through review, maintenance, and extension of reading skills developed in the first four grades, a strong phonetic and structural analysis program is introduced. High interest level stories.

PROGRESS IN READING. (rd7) c1957. 144p.

Major skills are reviewed, extended, and developed through interpretation, critical reading, use of dictionary, encyclopedia, and other reference tools, poetry reading, and skimming.

WORK TIME. (rd3) c1955. 112p.

Maintains all skills introduced in the first two grades and introduces new ones. Special emphasis is given to the use of phonics; easy, low vocabulary of 148 new words.

McCALL, WILLIAM A., and CRABBS, LELAH MAE. Standard Test Lessons in Reading. Books A, B, C, D, and E. (rd2-12) Teachers College, c1961. 78p. 45c per booklet, including Pupil Record Blank

A series of booklets to test reading speed and comprehension in grades 2 through 12 inclusive. Each lesson consists of a paragraph followed by multiple-choice questions. The number of questions answered correctly is translated into a G-score.

McCRORY, M., and WALLS, P. Phonics Skilltext. Books A, B, C, and D. (rd4-6) Merrill, c1955. 64p. 44c each

Series of four workbooks, popular in junior and senior high school, for development of phonic skills. Book A includes grades 1 and 2; Book B, grades 2 and 3; Book C, grades 3 and 4; Book D, grades 4 and 5.

McKEE, PAUL; HARRISON, L.; McCOWEN, A.; and LEHR, E. Reading for Meaning Series. Reading for Enjoyment Basal Books. Intermediate Level. (rd4-6) Houghton
BRIGHT PEAKS. (rd6) c1957. 340p. $2.44
HIGH ROADS. (rd4) c1952. 304p. $2.32
SKY LINES. (rd5) c1953. 336p. $2.44
Three attractive storybooks at the intermediate level designed to develop various reading skills. Excellent practice books accompany each volume.

THE MACMILLAN READING SPECTRUM. (rd4-6) Macmillan, c1964. $44-$72
Booklets that build skills of word analysis, vocabulary development, and comprehension. Six self-directing, self-correcting booklets in each area build skills step by step through thirty carefully selected children's books, including old favorites, modern best sellers, and new books on each intermediate grade level.

MASON, J. D., and O'BRIEN, G. E. Practical First Reader for Adults. (rd3) Heath, c1946. 217p. $2.76
Short, easy units of essential information about everyday living. Inviting practice exercises.

MEIGHAN, MARY; PRATT, MARJORIE; and HALVORSEN, MABEL. Phonics We Use. Lyons, c1957. 64p.
BOOK A. (rd Readiness) 52c   BOOK D. (rd3) 60c
BOOK B. (rd1) 52c   BOOK E. (rd4) 68c
BOOK C. (rd2) 60c   BOOK F. (rd5up) 72c
Easy to teach yet comprehensive and thorough. Provides sound training in all types of word recognition aids. Teacher's edition of each book available at student book price.

MONROE, MARION; HORSMAN, GWEN; and GRAY, WILLIAM S. Basic Reading Skills for High School Use. (rd9) Scott, c1948. 160p. $1
A great variety of reading material and unusual exercises including some excellent ones in word recognition skills.

MURPHY, GEORGE, and others. Let's Read. (Third Series) Holt, c1962
BOOK 1. (rd7) 302p. $3.36 Teacher's Manual, 80c
BOOK 2. (rd8) 325p. $3.44 Teacher's Manual, 80c
The latest revised editions of the original four-book Let's Read series. Stories and articles of high interest level designed for use with high-school readers.

The symbol "rd" accompanied by the figure, in parentheses, following the title in each entry, indicates the estimated grade level of reading difficulty (see p. 18-19).

READING TEXTS AND WORKBOOKS 139

MY WEEKLY READER, EDITORS OF. Reading Adventures. Merrill, c1950.
128p. 49c each
BOOK A—Grades 1 and 2
BOOK B—Grades 3 and 4
BOOK C—Grades 5 and 6
Graded materials in science and social science aimed at developing reading
skills in these areas.

NILES, OLIVE STAFFORD; BRACKEN, DOROTHY KENDALL; DOUGHERTY,
MILDRED A.; and KINDER, ROBERT FARRAR. Tactics in Reading.
(rd9) Scott, c1961. $56
Includes 102 exercises plus a diagnostic and an evaluation test, printed on
fifty durable, reusable cards, with thirty-five copies of each card for distribu-
tion to students as needed. Cards are tabbed and labeled for easy re-filing.
Designed to parallel the text *Vanguard*, in the Galaxy Program, for less able
readers in the ninth grade. Teacher's Guidebook with answer key included in
the kit box.

PARKER, DON H. The SRA Reading Laboratory. (rd1-12) Science Re-
search Associates, c1957. $39.50
A multilevel developmental reading program for use in upper elementary,
junior, and senior high schools, and college. It is built around carefully graded
reading selections with comprehension, word study, and vocabulary exercises.
The student corrects his exercises and charts his own progress in the Student
Record Book (48c each).
————SRA Pilot Library. Science Research Associates, c1963. 3 levels:
11a (rd2-7); 11c (rd4-9); 11b (rd5-12) $49.50 each
Carefully graded and coded by reading level, these three Pilot Libraries of-
fer a sequential and easily-controlled enrichment program. Each contains 72
selections in separate booklets, ranging from 24 to 32 pages. A Teacher's
Handbook, Student Record Book, and Key Booklets are also available.
————SRA Reading for Understanding Laboratory (RFU). Science
Research Associates, c1960. $29.50 each
GENERAL EDITION. (rd5-12)
JUNIOR EDITION. (rd3-8)
The flexible RFU Program covers eighty lessons during the school year—no
more than twenty minutes per lesson, two or three times a week. Both kits include 400 practice lessons on 100 graduated levels of comprehension; one
placement test to determine correct RFU starting level for each student
(package of 40, $2.10); one student record book (1-99 at 27c each); 40
answer key booklets; and one Teacher's Handbook describing the program
clearly and concisely with complete instructions.

POOLEY, ROBERT C., and others. Vanguard. (rd9) Scott, c1961. 608p.
$4.36
An anthology and handbook of reading in the Galaxy Program. A reading
skills text for poor readers in junior-senior high school which contains short,
interesting selections with discussion and word study. The latter part of the
book is devoted to exercises in picture interpretation, word attack, library
skills, comprehension, etc. See also Niles, O. S., above.

POTELL, HERBERT, and others. Adventures in Literature, Track 2. Harcourt

ADVENTURES FOR AMERICANS. (rd6-9) c1956. 718p. $4.16

ADVENTURES FOR TODAY. (rd4-7) c1955. 623p. $3.76

ADVENTURES IN LIVING. (rd5-8) c1955. 626p. $3.76

ADVENTURES IN MODERN LITERATURE. (rd7-10) c1956 (4th ed.). 690p. $4.12

A reading improvement program for the reluctant reader from grades nine through twelve. (Readability of selections from two to five years below grade level.) The texts include stories, articles, plays, and poems that provide steady growth in reading skills and power. The literature program includes teaching and learning aids and pictorial material. Reading workbooks (96c each. 154p.), tests, and teachers' manuals accompany each of the texts.

READER'S DIGEST SERVICES. Help Yourself to Improve Your Reading. Reader's Digest Services, Inc., Educational Division, c1963. 160p. $1 each

PART I. (rd7)

PART II. (rd8)

Especially interesting *Digest* articles appear in these two books along with improvement practice material and a progress chart.

————Reader's Digest Adult Reader. Reader's Digest Services, Inc., Educational Division, c1964. 32p. 20c each for 10 or more copies

A series of twelve books of adult interest. Inviting stories on a wide range of topics will attract older readers who would normally find the material too hard. There are four books in each of three "steps": Step I for reading levels 1-2; Step II for reading levels 2-3; and Step III for reading levels 3-4. Titles in Step I are *Workers in the Sky, Send for Red!, Second Chance,* and *Mystery of the Mountains.*

————Reader's Digest Advanced Reading Skill Builder. (rd7-8) Reader's Digest Services, Inc., Educational Division, c1958. 160p. 80c each

BOOKS 1 and 2. (rd7)

BOOKS 3 and 4. (rd8)

These selected articles have special appeal for the high-school student who is a retarded reader.

————Reader's Digest Reading Skill Builder. (rd1-6) Reader's Digest Services, Inc., Educational Division, c1959

(rd1) books. 64p. 56c

(rd2-3) books. 128p. 80c each

(rd4-6) books. 144p. 80c each

A series of seventeen *Reading Skill Builders,* two books for grade one, and three books each for grade levels two through six. They contain articles covering a wide range of interests and a variety of exercises testing speed and comprehension.

The symbol "rd" accompanied by the figure, in parentheses, following the title in each entry, indicates the estimated grade level of reading difficulty (see p. 18-19).

RICHARDS, I. A., and GIBSON, C. M. A First Workbook of English. (rd1) English Language Research, Inc., c1946. 80p. 60c each (2 vols.)

Volume I covers pages 1-112, and Volume II, pages 113 to the end of *English Through Pictures*. Fully illustrated.

————Learning the English Language. Houghton, c1943. 44c each (3 vols.). Teacher's Guide, $1.12. Vol. I, unp.; Vol. II, 35p.; Vol. III, 31p.

A graded direct-method text for classroom use, proceeding from zero knowledge of English to the use of some five hundred words of high utility. Workbooks (56c each) to accompany these volumes give systematic exercises for each step.

————Words on Paper. (rd1) Houghton, c1943. 42p. 40c

A reading primer, using very simple sentence structure with material of adult interest level.

ROBERTSON, M. S. Veteran's Reader. (rd1) Steck, c1949. 127p. Paper, 88c

Seventy reading units at beginning reading level on topics of adult interest.

ROCHESTER OCCUPATIONAL READING SERIES. (rd6-10) Science Research Associates, c1954

The vocational content is of interest to adolescent readers, and the three levels of difficulty present the same content for unified class work with a group of varying reading ability. Included at each level are suggested social experiences and enrichment exercises. Titles include: *Bakeries, Supermarkets, Truck Farming* ($1.20 each; six or more copies, 96c each); *Gas Stations*, and *Restaurants and Cafeterias* (90c each; six or more copies, 72c each).

SCHOOLFIELD, LUCILLE D., and TIMBERLANE, JOSEPHINE B. The Phonovisual Method. (rdPP-3) Phonovisual, c1960. (7th ptg., 1963) 79p. $9.25

This Method Book contains special instruction for remedial procedures. The Phonovisual Method Book, Vowel Chart, and Consonant Chart comprise the basic unit for the above price. There are practice sheets, workbooks, and a game book for use in the remedial program.

SIMPSON, ELIZABETH A. SRA Better Reading Books. Science Research Associates, c1962 (rev. ed.). 90p. each. $2.50 each

BOOK 1 (rd5.0-6.9)   BOOK 3 (rd9.0-10.9)
BOOK 2 (rd7.0-8.9)   Book 4 (rd11.0-12.9)

A series of reading improvement materials, high in interest, at four successive levels of reading difficulty. Each book contains twenty suggestions for improving rate and comprehension, twenty articles for measuring reading rate, and twenty tests for measuring reading comprehension.

SMITH, NILA BANTON. Be a Better Reader. Books I, II, III, IV, V, and VI. Grades 7-12. Prentice, c1958. $1.76 each

A series of six books for high school which develop skills in reading literature, history, science, and mathematics. Various approaches to reading and studying in the content fields are given. Selections in the four subject areas closely approximate the content of junior-senior high-school texts.

SPENCER, P. R.; FRITSCHLER, L. D.; and HORST, HELEN W. Exploring
New Trails. (rd5) Lyons, c1953. 454p. $2.40
———Finding New Trails. (rd4) Lyons, c1954. 440p. $2.40
———Traveling New Trails. (rd6) Lyons, c1954. 528p. $2.40
Practice books that feature stories and tell how to make and do things, how
to read arithmetic problems, and how to read correctly.

SPENCER, P. R.; JOHNSON, W. H.; and ROBINSON, T. E. Driving the
Reading Road. (rd7) Lyons, c1953. 526p. $2.40
———Progress on Reading Roads. (rd8) Lyons, c1953. 552p. $2.40
These texts offer practice in locating information and organizing material; in
special types of reading, such as interpreting maps, tables, graphs, charts, and
the like; in how to read arithmetic problems, history, and other subjects.

STONE, CLARENCE. The Eye and Ear Fun Series. (rd Readiness-4)
McGraw, 64p. each. Paper
Books 1-3. c1946 (rev. ed.). 80c
Book 4. c1946 (rev. ed.). 96c
Let's See. (rd Readiness) c1949. 72c
These books give help in developing independence in word recognition.

STRANG, RUTH, and others. Study Type of Reading Exercises. Teachers College, c1956 (rev. ed., high school). 112p. 55c (Manual,
54c; specimen set, 80c)
Unique in that it gives practice in a study type of reading at the same time
that it gives information about the reading process. It tests comprehension by
written summaries and outlines as well as by multiple-choice questions.
———Study Type of Reading Exercises, College Level.
For college students and superior high-school students.

TURNER, RICHARD H. The Turner-Livingston Reading Series. (rd5-6)
New York University Press, c1962. 60c each plus postage, to
schools
Consists of the following six workbooks: *The Person You Are, The Money
You Spend, The Family You Belong To, The Job You Get, The Friends You
Make,* and *The Town You Live In.* Each book relates a story which deals
with the everyday problems teen-agers face, and presents a unit of work in
English, social studies, citizenship, and arithmetic. The reading skills required
by these workbooks are at fifth and sixth grade level, but the interest of the
subject matter is geared to the thirteen- to seventeen-year-old student and
some adults. Especially useful for disadvantaged groups, not for college pre-
paratory groups.

The symbol "rd" accompanied by the figure, in parentheses, following the
title in each entry, indicates the estimated grade level of reading difficulty
(see p. 18-19).

WITTY, PAUL. How to Become a Better Reader. (rd7-adult) Science Research Associates, c1962 (rev. ed.). 324p. $4.90 (Paper, $3.50)

A combination of workbook and text designed to increase reading ability. Contains a variety of interesting stories and selections, covering such fields as health, science, history, humor, adventure, and creative writing. The book has four parts: twenty practical reading lessons, twenty general reading exercises, the reading progress folder, and a list of suggested books to read. (SRA Reading Progress Folder, package of 20, $2.75).

_____How to Improve Your Reading. (rd6-9) Science Research Associates, c1956. 380p. $4.95

An illustrated reading-training textbook containing twenty practical lessons designed to help the student improve basic reading skills. Included in the book are interesting, relatively easy-to-read fiction and nonfiction, and tests to measure progress in rate, comprehension, vocabulary, and other essential reading abilities. (The SRA Reading Progress Folder can also be used with this text.)

_____and others. Reading Roundup Series. (rd7-9) Heath, c1958. 502p. $2.25 (3 vols.)

A developmental series in anthology style. The material is arranged by topics and includes a variety of appealing stories and poems.

BOOKS IN SERIES

ABOUT BOOKS. (rd3-5) Melmont. 24-36p. $2.50

Interesting information on many topics, including conservation, science, nature, the community and its workers.

AIR-AGE BOOKS. (rd2-3) Benefic. 96p. $1.92

Science fiction tales for those interested in space exploration. Realistic stories about spacemen and how they will live. Titles by Hazel W. Corson include:

Peter and the Big Balloon (rd2)
Peter and the Moon Trip (rd3)
Peter and the Rocket Ship (rd3)
Peter and the Two-Hour Moon (rd3)
Peter and the Unlucky Rocket (rd2)

ALLABOUT BOOKS. (rd4-6) Random. $1.95

A series of books on different kinds of science, written simply by experts in their fields. See publisher's catalog for complete list. Some titles of special interest are:

ANDREWS, R. C. All About Dinosaurs
_____All About Strange Beasts of the Past
_____All About Whales
*COMMINS, D. B. All About the Symphony Orchestra
*DIETZ, D. All About Great Medical Discoveries
EPSTEIN, S. and B. All About the Desert
FREEMAN, I. and M. All About Electricity
*_____All About Sound and Ultra-Sonics
_____All About the Atom
_____All About the Wonders of Chemistry
*GOODWIN, H. L. All About Rockets and Space Flights
GOULD, J. All About Radio and Television
LANE, F. C. All About the Insect World
_____All About the Sea
LEMON, R. S. All About Strange Beasts of the Present
McCLUNG, R. M. All About Animals and Their Young
POUGH, F. H. All About Volcanoes and Earthquakes
PRATT, F. All About Famous Inventions and Their Inventors

The symbol "rd" accompanied by the figure, in parentheses, following the title in each entry, indicates the estimated grade level of reading difficulty (see p. 18-19).

*Titles marked with an asterisk are annotated in the main text of this book.

SPERRY, A. All About the Arctic and Antarctic
TANNEHILL, I. R. All About the Weather
WHITE, A. T. All About Archeology
———All About Great Rivers of the World
———All About the Stars

ALL-STAR SPORTS BOOKS. (rd4-6) Follett. $1.50
Information about various sports and helpful tips for playing. Titles include:
ARCHIBALD. Bowling for Boys and Girls
BEDARD. Gymnastics for Boys
DIGBY and McCLELLAND. Baseball for Boys
JORDAN and McCLELLAND. Track and Field for Boys
KUHARICH and McCLELLAND. Football for Boys
L'HEUREUX. Hockey for Boys
McNALLY. Fishing for Boys
———Hunting for Boys
MOHAN and MOHAN. Horseback Riding for Boys and Girls
OSBORN and McCLELLAND. Basketball for Boys

AMERICAN ADVENTURE SERIES. (rd2-6) Harper. $2.20
Interesting and exciting stories about people and events in America's development, told simply and with wide appeal. Some titles are:
ANDERSON. Friday, the Arapaho Indian (rd2)
———Fur Trappers of the Old West (rd6)
———Squanto and the Pilgrims (rd2)
———Wild Bill Hickok (rd5)
BEALS. Buffalo Bill (rd5)
———Chief Black Hawk (rd3)
———Davy Crockett (rd5)
———Kit Carson (rd4)
———The Rush for Gold (rd6)
BROWN. John Paul Jones (rd6)
GARST. Cowboys and Cattle Trails (rd4)
McGUIRE. Daniel Boone (rd6)
TUCKER. Dan Morgan, Rifleman (rd4)
Also: Alec Majors (rd3), Grant Marsh, Steamboat Captain (rd4),
    Pilot Jack Knight (rd3), Portugee Phillips and the Fighting
    Sioux (rd2), and Sabre Jet Ace (rd5)

AMERICAN HERITAGE JUNIOR LIBRARY SERIES. (rd4-5) Harper. 150p.
Here is America's past living again in story. Some titles include:
BERGER. Discoveries of the New World $3.95
BLACKBURN. The Bells of Carmel (California) $3.75
DERLETH. Empire of Fur (Lake Superior region) $3.75

FRANKLIN. Back of Beyond (Colorado frontier) $3.75
JONES. Trappers and Mountain Men. $3.95
LaFARGE. Cochise of Arizona. $3.75
LANE. Greatest Adventure (Jack London) $3.75
———The Magnificent Mariner (John Paul Jones) $3.75
MARKEY. The Little Giant of Schenectady (Charles Steinmetz)
     $3.75
See publisher's catalog for complete list.

AVIATION READERS. (rd1-6) Macmillan. $2.75
A graded series all about flying. Old favorites:
Airplanes at Work
Aviation Science for Boys and Girls
Men Who Gave Us Wings
Planes for Bob and Andy
Straight Down
Straight Up

BASIC SCIENCE EDUCATION SERIES. (rd2-6) Harper. 56c
This series includes more than seventy-five titles in the physical and biological sciences of interest to all ages. Some titles are:

Animals and Their Young   Garden Indoors
Beyond the Solar System   Keeping Well
Birds in the Big Woods   Saving Our Wild Life
Community Health   You as a Machine
Fire, Friend and Foe

BASIC VOCABULARY SERIES. (rd2) Garrard. $2.75
These books are a popular mixture of true stories, folklore, and Indian tales. They are based on the Dolch list of sight words and commonest nouns. Titles include:

Animal Stories   Lion and Tiger Stories
Bear Stories   Lodge Stories
Circus Stories   Navaho Stories
Dog Stories   Pueblo Stories
Elephant Stories   Tepee Stories
Folk Stories   Why Stories
Horse Stories   Wigwam Stories
Irish Stories

The symbol "rd" accompanied by the figure, in parentheses, following the title in each entry, indicates the estimated grade level of reading difficulty (see p. 18-19).

BEGINNER BOOKS. (rd1-2) Random. $1.95
A series of books for beginning readers, all written by experienced authors.
Titles include:
*CERF. Animal Riddles
*_____Book of Laughs
*_____Book of Riddles
*_____More Riddles
ELKIN. The King's Wish
FREEMAN. You Will Go to the Moon
*SEUSS. The Cat in the Hat
_____The Cat in the Hat Comes Back
*_____Green Eggs and Ham
_____Hop on Pop

BEGINNING SCIENCE BOOKS. (rd2) Follett. $1.60
There are several titles covering many areas of science—plants, insects, birds, animals, machines, the earth and space. See publisher's catalog for complete list. Titles include:

BROUILLETTE. Butterflies	TELLANDER. Space
_____Insects	VICTOR. Friction
DILLON. Salmon	_____Machines
FOLLETT. Your Wonderful Body	_____Magnets
JOHN. Hummingbirds	_____Molecules and Atoms
MEEKS. Snakes	WASSON. Birds
NEAL. Sound	WOOD. Beavers
PAGE. Rocks and Minerals	_____Plants With Seeds
SCHOENKNECHT. Ants	
_____Frogs and Toads	

BEGINNING-TO-READ BOOKS. (rd1-3) Follett. $2
A variety of stories, some of which will appeal to older readers. All are attractively illustrated and some are humorous. Those with special appeal are:
Christopher Columbus
The Four Friends
*Too Many Dogs

BIG TREASURE BOOKS. (rd2-4) Grosset. $2.78
Realistic illustrations in color with brief and simple text make this series interesting. See publisher's catalog for complete list. Titles include:
Big Treasure Book of Cowboys
Big Treasure Book of Dogs
Big Treasure Book of Horses
Big Treasure Book of Real Boats and Ships
Big Treasure Book of Real Helicopters
Big Treasure Book of Real Trucks
Big Treasure Book of Space

*Titles marked with an asterisk are annotated in the main text of this book.

BREAKTHROUGH BOOKS. (rd5) Harper. $2.95

Each volume tells of a development that led the way to achievements that were previously considered impossible or out of man's reach. Some titles are:

LORD, W. Peary to the Pole

*PUTNAM. The Triumph of the Seeing Eye

BUTTON FAMILY ADVENTURE SERIES. (rdPP-3) Benefic. $1.52 to $1.96

The fun-loving Button family have many adventures. Amusing illustrations add to the attractiveness of the books.

Bucky Button (rdPP)

The Buttons and Mr. Pete (rd1)

The Buttons and the Boy Scouts (rd2)

The Buttons and the Little League (rd3)

The Buttons and the Pet Parade (rdP)

The Buttons and the Whirlybird (rdP)

The Buttons at the Farm (rd1)

The Buttons at the Soap Box Derby (rd3)

The Buttons at the Zoo (rdPP)

The Buttons Go Camping (rd2)

The Buttons See Things That Go (rdPP)

The Buttons Take a Boat Ride (rdP)

CAPITOL ADVENTURE BOOKS. (rd5) Capitol. $3.95

These will interest older pupils, although they are not hard to read, because the topics are for those with mature interests. Typical titles are:

*BURGDORF, O. P. Adventure Book of Human Biology

*EVANS, E. K. Adventure Book of Archaeology

*GOLDBERG, L. Adventure Book of Chemistry

*MILLER, DR. J. Adventure Book of the Human Mind

Other topics include forest wonders, nature craft, underwater life, arts, needlework, birds, money, etc.

CHILDHOOD OF FAMOUS AMERICANS SERIES. (rd3-5) Bobbs. $2.25

People who contributed to the growth of America in many ways are pictured in their childhood. Their adult life and achievement are summarized at the end. There is plenty of action and dialogue. Some titles are:

HAMMONTREE. Albert Einstein, Boy Mathematician

HOWE. Amelia Earhart, Kansas Girl

MYERS, and BURNETT. Carl Ben Eielson, Young Alaskan Pilot

STEVENSON. Francis Scott Key: Boy With a Song

VAN RIPER. Babe Ruth

_____Knute Rockne

WAGONER. Louisa Alcott

WILSON. Ernie Pyle

See publisher's catalog for the complete list of more than 140 titles.

The symbol "rd" accompanied by the figure, in parentheses, following the title in each entry, indicates the estimated grade level of reading difficulty (see p. 18-19).

*Titles marked with an asterisk are annotated in the main text of this book.

CHILDREN OF EARLY AMERICA SERIES. (rd4) Benefic. 192p. $2.20
These are lively stories of real young people and their adventures during important periods in pioneer and colonial life.
Children of the Colonies
Children of the Mayflower
Flatboats and Wagon Wheels
Prairie Schooners West

COWBOY SAM SERIES. (rdPP-3) Benefic. $1.52 to $1.96
The humorous and action-packed adventures of Cowboy Sam and his ranch hands. They capture the flavor of the West today, and are very popular with young people.
Cowboy Sam (rdP) 64p. $1.60
Cowboy Sam and Big Bill (rdPP) 48p. $1.52
Cowboy Sam and Dandy (rdPP) 48p. $1.52
Cowboy Sam and Flop (rd1) 64p. $1.68
Cowboy Sam and Freckles (rdPP) 48p. $1.52
Cowboy Sam and Freddy (rd1) 64p. $1.68
Cowboy Sam and Miss Lilly (rdP) 64p. $1.60
Cowboy Sam and Porky (rdP) 64p. $1.60
Cowboy Sam and Sally (rd2) 96p. $1.80
Cowboy Sam and Shorty (rd1) 64p. $1.68
Cowboy Sam and the Airplane (rd3) 128p. $1.96
Cowboy Sam and the Fair (rd2) 96p. $1.80
Cowboy Sam and the Indians (rd3) 128p. $1.96
Cowboy Sam and the Rodeo (rd2) 96p. $1.80
Cowboy Sam and the Rustlers (rd3) 128p. $1.96

DAN FRONTIER SERIES. (rdPP-4) Benefic. $1.80 to $2.48
Exciting adventures of a mature young frontiersman by William J. Hurley. The vigorous adult action of this popular series appeals to all ages.
*Dan Frontier (rdPP) 48p. $1.80
 Dan Frontier and the Big Cat (rdP) 64p. $1.96
 Dan Frontier and the New House (rdPP) 48p. $1.80
*Dan Frontier and the Wagon Train (rd 2) 128p. $2.32
 Dan Frontier Goes Exploring (rd3) 128p. $2.32
*Dan Frontier Goes Hunting (rdP) 64p. $1.96
*Dan Frontier Goes to Congress (rd4) 160p. $2.48
 Dan Frontier Scouts With the Army (rd2) 128p. $2.32
 Dan Frontier, Sheriff (rd3) 128p. $2.32
 Dan Frontier, Trapper (rd1) 96p. $2.20
 Dan Frontier With the Indians (rd1) 96p. $2.20

---

*Titles marked with an asterisk are annotated in the main text of this book.

DEEP-SEA ADVENTURE SERIES. (rd1-6) Harr Wagner
  Exciting, informative, and very popular series, with excellent illustrations and
  adult appeal. Titles, by Coleman and others, include:
  *Danger Below (rd4) 104p. $2.12
  Frogmen in Action (rd3) 96p. $2
  The Pearl Divers (rd2) 80p. $1.92
  Rocket Divers (rd5) 104p. $2.12
  The Sea Hunt (rd1) 72p. $1.84
  Submarine Rescue (rd2) 80p. $1.92
  Treasure Under the Sea (rd2) 80p. $1.92
  Whale Hunt (rd4) 104p. $2.12

DISCOVERY BOOKS. (rd3) Garrard. 80p. $2.50
  Fast-moving, exciting biographies of famous people. Over thirty books in the
  series. See publisher's catalog for complete list. Some titles are:
  BISHOP, C. H. Lafayette: French-American Hero
  CAMPION, N. R. Kit Carson: Pathfinder of the West
  CARMER, C. Henry Hudson: Captain of the Ice-bound Seas
  COLVER, A. Abraham Lincoln: For the People
  _____Florence Nightingale: War Nurse
  _____Thomas Jefferson: Author of Independence
  *DeLEEUW, A. Richard E. Byrd: Adventurer to the Poles
  EPSTEIN, S. and B. George Washington Carver: Negro Scientist
  FABER, D. Luther Burbank: Partner of Nature
  GRAFF, S. George Washington: Father of Freedom
  GRAVES, C. P. Benjamin Franklin: Man of Ideas
  _____Robert E. Lee: Hero of the South
  KAUFMAN, M. Thomas Alva Edison: Miracle Maker
  MONTGOMERY, E. R. Alexander Graham Bell: Man of Sound
  *PATTERSON, L. Booker T. Washington: Leader of His People
  REEDER, R. Ulysses S. Grant: Horseman and Fighter
  ROSE, M. C. Clara Barton: Soldier of Mercy
  WILKIE, K. E. William Penn: Friend to All

EASY-TO-READ BOOKS. (rd3-5) Random. $1.95
  This attractive series captures interest through the understandable explana-
  tions and many illustrations covering a great variety of topics from ancient
  times to modern. Titles include:
  *ANDREWS, R. C. In the Days of the Dinosaurs (rd4)
  *ASIMOV, I. Satellites in Outer Space (rd3)

  The symbol "rd" accompanied by the figure, in parentheses, following the
title in each entry, indicates the estimated grade level of reading difficulty
(see p. 18-19).

  *Titles marked with an asterisk are annotated in the main text of this book.

*FREEMAN, M. and I. The Story of Electricity (rd5)
*_____The Story of the Atom (rd5)
*HITTE, K. Hurricanes, Tornadoes and Blizzards (rd4)
*LAUBER, P. The Story of Numbers (rd4)
*POOLE, L. and G. Danger! Icebergs Ahead (rd4)

ENCHANTMENT OF AMERICA SERIES. (rd6) Childrens. 96p. $3.50
Different regions of the United States are illustrated and the history of each area and its people is given in this attractive series.

EVERYGIRLS LIBRARY. (rd6-8) Lantern. $2.95
Short story collections on various topics such as horses, careers, romance, mystery, and adventure.

FIRST BOOKS. (rd2-6) Watts. $2.50
There are many titles in this series planned to answer the first questions about many things. Topics include nature, science, American history, crafts, hobbies, humor, travel, transportation, people, the world's work, and the arts. Titles include:
BENDICK. The First Book of Automobiles
_____The First Book of Space
_____The First Book of Space Travel
*_____and BERK. The First Book of How to Fix It
BERK. The First Book of Stage Costume and Make-up
BOTHWELL. The First Book of Roads
BREWSTER. The First Book of Cowboys
_____The First Book of Eskimos
_____The First Book of Firemen
_____The First Book of Indians
CHRYSTIE. The First Book of Jokes and Funny Things
COMMAGER. The First Book of American History
CORMACK. The First Book of Stones
_____The First Book of Trees
DICKINSON. The First Book of Plants
EPSTEIN, S. and B. The First Book of Electricity
_____The First Book of Italy
_____The First Book of Mexico
_____The First Book of Printing
_____The First Book of Words
HAHN. The First Book of India
HAMILTON, E. The First Book of Caves
HAMILTON, R. The First Book of Trains
HOKE, H. The First Book of Dolls
_____The First Book of Tropical Mammals
HOKE, J. The First Book of Photography
_____The First Book of Snakes

---

*Titles marked with an asterisk are annotated in the main text of this book.

HUGHES. The First Book of Jazz
_____The First Book of Negroes
_____The First Book of Rhythms
_____The First Book of the West Indies
ICENHOWER. The First Book of Submarines
_____The First Book of the Antarctic
JAGENDORF. The First Book of Puppets
KIRKUS. The First Book of Gardening
KUBIE. The First Book of Archaeology
_____The First Book of Israel
LEEMING. The First Book of Chess
LINEAWEAVER. The First Book of Canada
LOBSENZ. The First Book of West Germany
MARKUN. The First Book of the Panama Canal
MEARS. The First Book of Japan
NORMAN. The First Book of Music
PETERSON. The First Book of Poetry
PEET. The First Book of Bridges
RECK. The First Book of Festivals Around the World
ROBINSON. The First Book of Ancient Rome
ROGERS. The First Book of Cotton
SCHIFFER. The First Book of Basketball
_____The First Book of Football
SMITH. The First Book of Conservation
STODDARD. The First Book of Magic
_____The First Book of Television
STREATFEILD. The First Book of Ballet
_____The First Book of England
TABER. The First Book of Cats
_____The First Book of Dogs
WILLIAMSON. The First Book of Mammals
WYLER. The First Book of Science Experiments

FIRST READING BOOKS. (rd1) Garrard. 64p. $2.25
These attractive books by Edward and Marguerite Dolch are about all kinds
of animals and give folk tales as well as facts about them. Titles include:

Dog Pals	Once There Was a Bear
Friendly Birds	Once There Was a Cat
*I Like Cats	Once There Was a Monkey
In the Woods	Once There Was an Elephant
Monkey Friends	

The symbol "rd" accompanied by the figure, in parentheses, following the
title in each entry, indicates the estimated grade level of reading difficulty
(see p. 18-19).

*Titles marked with an asterisk are annotated in the main text of this book.

FOLKLORE OF THE WORLD BOOKS. (rd3) Garrard. 176p. $3
Appealing stories retelling myths and legends from around the world. These tales help bring understanding of people in strange countries by showing their customs and native culture. Titles include:

Stories From Old China

Stories From Old Egypt

Stories From Old Russia

Other places represented include Alaska, France, Hawaii, India, Italy, Japan, Mexico, and Spain.

FRONTIERS OF AMERICA BOOKS. (rd3) Childrens. $2.50
Several fast-moving stories about people who participated in the development of America. Titles, all by Edith McCall, include:

Cumberland Gap and Trails West

*Explorers in a New World

Heroes of the Western Outposts

Log Fort Adventures

Mail Riders

Men on Iron Horses

Settlers on a Strange Shore

Steamboats to the West

Wagons Over the Mountains

FUN WITH _____ BOOKS. (rd4-5) Random, c1957. 64p. $1.95
How to have fun with a variety of activities and hobbies, including astronomy, ballet, chemistry, mathematics, and many others. Some titles, all by Freeman, are:

*Fun and Experiments With Light

Fun With Ballet

*Fun With Chemistry (Paper, Scholastic Book Services, 25c)

Fun With Figures

Fun With Science

Fun With Your Camera

FUN WITH _____ SERIES. (rd5) Lippincott, $3-$4.50
These craft and hobby books by Joseph Leeming have easy directions and diagrams, with excellent ideas for collections, for puzzles, and for making things of all sorts. See publisher's catalog for complete list. Titles include:

Fun for Young Collectors	Fun With Leather
Fun With Artificial Flowers	Fun With Magic
Fun With Clay	Fun With Paper
Fun With Fabrics	Fun With Pencil
*Fun With Greeting Cards	Fun With Wood

FUNTIME BOOKS. (rd3-4) Childrens. $2.50
These books give easy-to-follow instructions on leisure-time activities, such as puppets, crafts, and magic.

---

*Titles marked with an asterisk are annotated in the main text of this book.

GETTING TO KNOW SERIES. (rd5) Coward. $2.50

An unusual series which concentrates less on factual information about cities and industries and more on the people—their history, their customs, their life today. Titles included are:

AYER. Getting to Know Thailand
CRAZ. Getting to Know Liberia
DAVIS. Getting to Know Turkey
JAKEMAN. Getting to Know Japan
OLDEN. Getting to Know Nigeria
TOR. Getting to Know Korea
_____Getting to Know Puerto Rico

GOLDEN BOOK SERIES. (rd5) Golden. $3.95 and up

A popular and attractive illustrated series on many topics. Titles include:

PARKER. The Golden Book of Science
_____The Golden Treasury of Natural History
PETER. McCall's Giant Golden Make-It Book
WYLER and AMES. The Golden Book of Astronomy
See publisher's catalog for complete list.

GOLDEN NATURE GUIDE SERIES. (rd5) Golden. $3.85 (Paper, $1)

Fine books to tuck in your pocket on a nature hike. Titles include:

Birds	Reptiles and Amphibians
Fishes	Seashores
Flowers	Stars
Fossils	Trees
Insects	Weather
Mammals	

GUIDANCE SERIES BOOKLETS FOR HIGH SCHOOL STUDENTS. (rd6-8) Science Research Associates. 48p. 50c

Easy-to-read booklets designed to help young people with everyday problems. Topics cover school, personality, family and friends, health, vocations, leisure, and the world today.

HORIZON CARAVEL BOOKS. (rd6-7) Harper. 156p. $3.95

Excellent illustrations add to the exciting stories of major events and great men in world history. Some titles are:

*ANDRIST, R. K. Heroes of Polar Exploration
DONOVAN, F. R. The Vikings
ISENBERG, I. The Age of Caesar
*MERCER, C. Alexander the Great
WARNER, O. Captain Cook and the South Pacific
_____Nelson and the Age of Fighting Sail
*WILLIAMS, J. Knights of the Crusades

The symbol "rd" accompanied by the figure, in parentheses, following the title in each entry, indicates the estimated grade level of reading difficulty (see p. 18-19).

*Titles marked with an asterisk are annotated in the main text of this book.

HOW AND WHY WONDER BOOKS. (rd4-5) Grosset. 48p. $2.78 (Deluxe
    ed., $1; Paper, 50c)
These books answer clearly and simply, with many illustrations, questions
most often asked about science, nature, and history. There are about thirty
titles, some of which are:

Atomic Energy	Human Body
Ballet	Microscope
Chemistry	Primitive Man
*Dinosaurs	Rockets and Missiles
Electricity	*Science Experiments
Horses	Wild Animals

I-CAN-READ BOOKS. (rd2) Harper, c1963. 64p. $1.95
A series of easy-to-read books on a variety of topics, some fact, some fiction.
Among the more popular titles enjoyed by junior high school readers are:
    HOFF. Danny and the Dinosaur
    *WYLER and AMES. Prove It!
    *ZION. Harry and the Lady Next Door
    _____Harry the Dirty Dog

I WANT TO BE BOOKS. (rd1-3) Childrens. $2
Easy-to-read vocational material is presented for all sorts of careers from
fisherman to cowboy, from telephone operator to zoo keeper, from carpenter
to dairy farmer. See publisher's catalog for complete list. Some titles are.
I Want to Be a Bus Driver
I Want to Be a Dentist
I Want to Be a Fireman
I Want to Be a Mechanic
I Want to Be a Musician
I Want to Be a Restaurant Owner
I Want to Be a Storekeeper
I Want to Be an Airplane Hostess

ILLUSTRATED BOOKS. (rd5) Grosset. $2.95-$5.95
Fascinating pictures and facts about the different countries on five continents.
This is an armchair tour. Titles include:
    APPEL. The Illustrated Book About South America
    *BOTKIN and WITHERS. The Illustrated Book of American Folklore
    REUSSWIG, ed. The Illustrated Book About the Far East (rev. ed.)
    SUTTON. The Illustrated Book About Africa
    _____The Illustrated Book About Europe

INTERESTING READING SERIES. (rd2-3) Penns Valley. $2. Also pub-
    lished by Follett at $1.56
A variety of stories, fact and fiction, including adventures on land, at sea, in
space. Exciting moments in sports and in history are also presented.
    *ALLEN. Ten Great Moments in Sports (rd3-low) 64p.
    *BULETTE. An Adventure in Space (rd3-low) 64p.

---

*Titles marked with an asterisk are annotated in the main text of this book.

*CLARK. First Men in Space (rd3-low) 64p. (rev.)

*EISNER. Buried Gold (rd2-high) 64p.

*＿＿＿Mystery of Broken Wheel Ranch (rd2-high) 64p.

KENDRICK. The Indian Fighters (rd3-low) 48p.

*PARKER. Great Moments in American History (rd3-high) 48p.

*RIFKIN. First Adventure at Sea (rd3-low) 48p.

SEYLAR. Mary Elizabeth and Mr. Lincoln (rd3-high) 64p.

JIM FOREST READERS. (rd1-3) Harr Wagner. $2-$2.20
Fast-paced adventures filled with suspense and humor as Jim and his forest ranger uncle climb mountains, fight flood and fire, and chase bandits.
Jim Forest and Dead Man's Peak (rd2) 96p. $2.20
Jim Forest and Lone Wolf Gulch (rd3) 96p. $2.20
Jim Forest and Ranger Don (rd1) 64p. $2
Jim Forest and the Bandits (rd1) 80p. $2.12
Jim Forest and the Flood (rd2) 96p. $2.20
Jim Forest and the Mystery Hunter (rd2) 96p. $2.20

JUNIOR GUIDANCE SERIES. (rd5-7) Science Research Associates. 48p. 50c
Booklets designed to help younger adolescents with problems related to health, school, and personality; to getting along with people and planning for the future.

JUNIOR RESEARCH BOOKS. (rd4-6) Prentice. $2.95
Books that supply answers not usually found in science, mathematics, and social studies texts. See publisher's catalog for complete list. Some titles are:
ALEXANDER, A. The Hidden You
CARONA, P. B. Magic Mixtures: Alloys and Plastics
＿＿＿Things That Measure
DAVID, E. Television and How It Works
KOHN, B. Computers at Your Service
＿＿＿Our Tiny Servants: Molds and Yeasts
＿＿＿The Peaceful Atom
LERNER, M. Who Do You Think You Are
McCARTHY, A. Creatures of the Deep
＿＿＿Giant Animals of Long Ago
SANDER, L. Animals That Work for Man
*VERRAL, C. S. Go! The Story of Outer Space
＿＿＿Robert Goddard: Father of the Space Age

The symbol "rd" accompanied by the figure, in parentheses, following the title in each entry, indicates the estimated grade level of reading difficulty (see p. 18-19).

*Titles marked with an asterisk are annotated in the main text of this book.

JUNIOR SCIENCE BOOKS. (rd3) Garrard. $1.87

Physical science and natural science are presented in attractive and easy-to-read form. Some topics duplicate those in other series; some are different. Among the titles are:

Bacteria	Light
Beavers	Magnets
Big Cats	Penguins
Elephants	Rain, Hail, Sleet, and Snow
Icebergs and Glaciers	*Weather Experiments

KEYS TO THE CITIES SERIES. (rd4-6) Lippincott. 128p. $2.95

Each volume gives a complete picture of one of the world's important cities, including its geography, history, culture, landmarks, and present conditions. Maps and pictures are helpful. Among the cities are Paris, New York, San Francisco, Chicago, Philadelphia, Tokyo, Rome, London, Washington, Boston, Vienna and *Moscow.

KEYSTONE BOOKS IN MUSIC. (rd7) Lippincott. $2.75-$3.50 (Some titles in paper, $1.25 to $1.95)

Different authorities in the world of music give help in selecting records. Each book is on one or more composers or period or style of music. Composers include Bach, Haydn, Chopin, and Schumann. Other titles are:

BRIGGS, J. The Collector's Beethoven. c1962. 160p. $3.50

*COHN, A. The Collector's Twentieth Century Music in the Western Hemisphere. c1961. 256p. $1.95 (paper only)

DeSCHAUENSEE, M. The Collector's Verdi and Puccini. c1962. 160p. $3.50 (Paper, $1.75)

WILSON, J. S. The Collector's Jazz: Modern. c1959. 320p. $3.50 (Paper, $1.65)

_____The Collector's Jazz: Traditional and Swing. c1958. 320p. $3

LANDMARK BOOKS. (rd5) Random. 192p. $1.95

This famous and popular series makes history exciting and vivid as it tells about people, places, and events that are landmarks in American history from the period of exploration to the present. Some titles are:

ADAMS. The Erie Canal

BLIVEN. The Story of D-Day

BROWN. Ethan Allen and the Green Mountain Boys

*DOLSON. William Penn

HILL. The Doctors Who Conquered Yellow Fever

HOLBROOK. Wyatt Earp

JACKSON. The Witchcraft of Salem Village

JANEWAY. The Vikings

KANTOR. Lee and Grant at Appomattox

KUHN. Commodore Perry and the Opening of Japan

LAWSON. Thirty Seconds Over Tokyo

---

*Titles marked with an asterisk are annotated in the main text of this book.

*LOOMIS. Great American Fighter Pilots of World War II
McNEER. The Alaska Gold Rush
MARRIOTT. Sequoyah: Leader of the Cherokees
MOODY. Kit Carson and the Wild Frontier
NORTH. Abe Lincoln: Log Cabin to White House
_____George Washington: Frontier Colonel
OWEN. The Conquest of the North and South Poles
PINKERTON. The First Overland Mail
*PLACE. The Copper Kings of Montana
*RACHLIS. The Story of the U. S. Coast Guard
ROSS. Heroines of the Early West
STEWART. To California by Covered Wagon
Other titles include:
America's First World War: General Pershing and the Yanks
Andrew Carnegie and the Age of Steel
The Barbary Pirates
The Battle for the Atlantic
Clipper Ship Days
The Coming of the Mormons
The Early Days of Automobiles
The F.B.I.
The Pirate Lafitte and the Battle of New Orleans
Prehistoric America
Robert Fulton and the Steamboat
The Santa Fe Trail
The Story of San Francisco
The Story of the Naval Academy
The Story of the Paratroops
*The Story of the Secret Service
The Story of the U. S. Air Force
The Story of the U. S. Marines
The Swamp Fox of the Revolution
The Texas Rangers
Thomas Jefferson, Father of Democracy
The West Point Story
The Winter at Valley Forge
The Wright Brothers
See publisher's catalog for complete list.

The symbol "rd" accompanied by the figure, in parentheses, following the title in each entry, indicates the estimated grade level of reading difficulty (see p. 18-19).

*Titles marked with an asterisk are annotated in the main text of this book.

LANDS AND PEOPLES SERIES. (rd6) Macmillan. $2

Brief, interesting presentations of the land and people of many countries that are not so well known. Some areas treated are Arab Lands, Australia, Brazil, Egypt, India, Iran, Japan, Mexico and Inca Lands, Oceania, Palestine, Scandinavia, South Africa, Turkey, and Yugoslavia, as well as the more usual British Isles, France, Germany, Italy, the Low Countries, *Central America, and *Chile.

LEGACY BOOKS. (rd4-5) Random. $1.95

Great myths, legends, and folk tales are retold by well-known present-day storytellers. Some titles include:

BENCHLEY. Sinbad the Sailor

CLARK. The Song of Roland

DOLBIER. Paul Bunyan

FADIMAN. The Adventures of Hercules

——The Story of Young King Arthur

*GUNTHER. Jason and the Golden Fleece (Paper, Scholastic Book Services, 25c)

SCHERMAN. William Tell

LET'S GO BOOKS. (rd4-5) Putnam. $1.95

Several titles are offered, each describing one of the workers found in almost every community.

LET'S READ AND FIND OUT SERIES. (rd1-2) Crowell. 40p. $2.75

These are attractive introductions to science, with full illustrations, diagrams, and only a little text. Titles included are:

BRANLEY. The Big Dipper

——Rockets and Satellites

BULLA. A Tree Is a Plant

HURD. Sandpipers

JORDAN. How a Seed Grows

LIFE IN AMERICA SERIES. (rd5) Fideler. $3.88-$4.88

There are two parts to this series. One concentrates on the geography of a region, and the other on its history. Well illustrated, with easy-to-read and accurate information that is useful to adults who do not read easily. In the geography series are:

BANTA. The South

FERGUSON. Hawaii

TOMPKINS. Alaska

In the history series are:

ADAMS. Pioneer Days

CAIN. Transportation

LIFE IN EUROPE SERIES. (rd5) Fideler. $3.88

Visit European countries through the large, vivid photographs and easy-to-read maps, along with the dramatic story of each. Countries included are Austria, British Isles, France, Germany, Italy, the Netherlands, Norway, Spain, Sweden, and Switzerland.

---

*Titles marked with an asterisk are annotated in the main text of this book.

LIFE IN OTHER LANDS SERIES. (rd5) Fideler. $3.88 and $4.88
Large, clear photographs with simple, interesting text promote understanding of different areas and countries and their achievements. Volumes include Africa, Australia, Brazil, Canada, China, India, Japan, Mexico, South America, and the Soviet Union. They are constantly revised and brought up to date.

LOOK! READ! AND LEARN SERIES. (rd1-3) Melmont. $2.50
These books cover a great variety of topics, including science, industry, animals, Indians, community, etc. Attractive and easy, the books vary in interest according to the topic. Some titles are:
ALLEN. About Vegetables on Your Plate
FOSTER. Seeds Are Wonderful
GREEN. About Apples From Orchard to Market
REDLAUER. Atomic Power for People
———Four Seasons and Five Senses
REES. Our Flag
SHANNON. Caves
SIMPSON. News and How It Travels

MADE IN ——— SERIES. (rd4-6) Knopf. $2.75-$4
These books present the arts and crafts of different countries. They are beautiful and especially valuable because they present less well-known places. Titles include:
GOLDEN. Made in Iceland
ROSS. Made in Mexico
SPENCER. Made in India
TOOR. Made in Italy

MAXTON BOOKS FOR YOUNG PEOPLE. (rd6-7) Maxton. $1.50 (cloth-bound, 69c)
Very beautiful but brief books on a great variety of subjects. Titles include Alaska, Space Travel, Ballet, Wild Birds, Prehistoric Animals, Coins and Currency, Mankind, Music Makers. See publisher's catalog for complete list.

MORGAN BAY MYSTERIES. (rd2-3) Harr Wagner, c1962. 96p. $2.20
These are good stories for those who like suspense and mystery along with humor. The characters are believable and the plots well developed. Illustrations are attractive. Titles, all by John and Nancy Rambeau, are:
*The Mystery of Morgan Castle (rd2)
The Mystery of the Marble Angel (rd2)
The Mystery of the Midnight Visitor (rd3)
The Mystery of the Missing Marlin (rd3)

The symbol "rd" accompanied by the figure, in parentheses, following the title in each entry, indicates the estimated grade level of reading difficulty (see p. 18-19).

*Titles marked with an asterisk are annotated in the main text of this book.

MY HOBBY IS _____ SERIES. (rd6) Childrens $3.95
All kinds of things to do and make in spare time are included in this series.
My Hobby Is Birdwatching
My Hobby Is Collecting Rocks and Minerals
My Hobby Is Collecting Sea Shells and Coral
My Hobby Is Collecting Stamps
My Hobby Is Photography

OUTDOOR ADVENTURE SERIES. (rd4-5) Benefic. 160p. $2.20
Two teen-age boys have action-packed adventures on vacation trips and
learn about sea life and animal characteristics.
Adventures Fishing (rd4)
Adventures Hunting (rd5)

PICTURE STORY SERIES. (rd5-6) McKay. $4.50
Attractive picture books about many lands around the world, including
Alaska, Denmark, Hawaii, Norway, Sweden, and others.

PIONEER SERIES. (rd4) Benefic. 160p. $2.60
Stories of the hardy pioneers who moved into new lands or new industries,
showing their family life as well as the adventures they had. Titles, all by
Irene Estep, are:
Pioneer Buckaroo   Pioneer Sodbuster
Pioneer Engineer   Pioneer Tenderfoot
Pioneer Pilgrim

PIPER BOOKS. (rd5) Houghton. $1.95 (Paper, $1.32)
Biographies of men and women who have influenced American history and
development in many ways. There are some titles about people who do not
often appear in life stories, as well as several books about those who do. Typi-
cal titles are:
*EDWARDS, C. P. Horace Mann: Sower of Learning. c1960
_____King Philip: Loyal Indian. c1962
*GILBERT, M. Henry Ford: Maker of the Model T. c1962
JONES, W. Patrick Henry: Voice of Liberty. c1960
KELLY, R. Z. Abigail Adams: The President's Lady. c1962
*_____Henry Clay: Statesman and Patriot. c1960
*_____Paul Revere: Colonial Craftsman. c1963
OLGIN, J. Sam Houston: Friend of the Indians. c1958
_____Thomas Jefferson: Champion of the People. c1960
*SEIBERT, J. Dan Beard: Boy Scout Pioneer. c1963
SNOW, D. J. Henry Hudson: Explorer of the North. c1962
TOTTLE, J. Benjamin Franklin: First Great American. c1959
*WILKIE, K. E. Robert Louis Stevenson: Storyteller and Adven-
turer. c1961

---

*Titles marked with an asterisk are annotated in the main text of this book.

PORTRAITS OF THE NATIONS SERIES. (rd5-7) Lippincott. 128p. $2.95
Interesting profiles, in travelogue style, of the history, geography, culture, and life of nations around the world. Maps and photographs add to their value. They are revised regularly to keep them up to date. Some of the countries are Holland, Finland, Canada, Peru, Scotland, Tanganyika, Mexico, *Ghana, Indonesia, and thirty-two others.

PUFFIN PICTURE BOOKS. (rd6-8) Penguin. Various prices
Paperback picture stories of different occupations, industries, and common objects. Drawings, diagrams, and pictures add to their value. British terms and objects may make them harder for American readers.

READING-MOTIVATED SERIES. (rd4) Harr Wagner. $2.60
A popular series of adventure stories by Helen Heffernan and others, they are of special appeal to junior high school students.
Desert Treasure. 309p. (Fast-paced Western)
The Mysterious Swamp Rider. 314p. (Dramatic mystery)
The Secret of Lonesome Valley. 314p. (Suspense and adventure on a Texas cattle ranch)

REAL BOOKS. (rd3) Doubleday. $1.95
Easy, inexpensive series on many subjects. Some titles are:
BONNER. The Real Book About Crime Detection
COY. The Real Book About Gold
EPSTEIN. The Real Book About the Sea
GOSSETT. The Real Book of Jokes
HARRINGTON. The Real Book About Canada
KNIGHT. The Real Book About Our Armed Forces
LEEMING. The Real Book of Games
LONG. The Real Book About Our National Capital
Other titles on airplanes, electronics, horses, Indians, magic, crafts, science experiments, snakes, space travel, submarines, and stars. See publisher's catalog for complete list.

REAL PEOPLE SERIES. (rd3-4) Harper. 8 sets of 6 titles each. $3.16 per set or 64c each
These attractive, simply written, brief biographies are about famous people, including Jane Addams, Alfred the Great, Daniel Boone, Christopher Columbus, Benjamin Franklin, John Paul Jones, Leonardo da Vinci, and many others.

REGIONS OF AMERICA BOOKS. (rd5-6) Harper. $5.95 and $6.95
The history and people of various sections of America are covered in this series, including areas of Alaska, California, New England, Southern Highlands, the Great Plains, and others.

The symbol "rd" accompanied by the figure, in parentheses, following the title in each entry, indicates the estimated grade level of reading difficulty (see p. 18-19).

RIVERS OF THE WORLD. (rd5) Garrard. 96p. $2.75
Dramatic stories that give vivid pictures of important rivers around the world, and tell how early explorers braved dangers to map these great waterways, how men have used them to live by, and how these highways have influenced the lives of men and the events of history. They are well illustrated with maps and beautiful pictures. Titles include:

CARMER, C. and E. The Susquehanna: From New York to the Chesapeake
CROSBY, A. The Colorado: Mover of Mountains
LAUBER, P. The Congo: River into Central Africa
————The Mississippi: Giant at Work
McNEER, M. The Hudson: River of History
*SPENCER, C. The Yangtze: China's River Highway
SPERRY, A. The Amazon: River Sea of Brazil
WEINGARTEN, V. The Nile: Lifeline of Egypt
WHITE, A. T. The St. Lawrence: Seaway of North America
WILSON, H. The Seine: River of Paris

SAILOR JACK SERIES. (rdPP-3) Benefic
Ten true-to-life stories of sea voyages, told with humor and fast-moving action. Exciting things happen when Sailor Jack and his jolly parrot Bluebell go to sea. Teacher's Guide, $1.
*Sailor Jack (rdPP) 48p. $1.60
Sailor Jack and Bluebell (rdP) 64p. $1.68
Sailor Jack and Bluebell's Dive (rdP) 64p. $1.68
Sailor Jack and Eddy (rdPP) 48p. $1.60
Sailor Jack and Homer Potts (rdPP) 48p. $1.60
Sailor Jack and the Ball Game (rd1) 64p. $1.68
*Sailor Jack and the Jet Plane (rdP) 64p. $1.68
*Sailor Jack and the Target Ship (rd2) 96p. $1.88
Sailor Jack Goes North (rd3) 96p. $1.88
Sailor Jack's New Friend (rd1) 64p. $1.68

SIGNAL BOOKS. (rd4) Doubleday. $2.95
These short novels, many based on the lives of real people, are action-packed and realistic. They cover many types of fiction: adventure, mystery, career tales, historical stories, and sports. Some titles are:
*BOWEN. Dirt Track Danger
*BRENNAN. Hot Rod Thunder
*DOHERTY. The Mystery of Hidden Harbor
*FINLAYSON. Runaway Teen
*FORBES-ROBERTSON. Footlights for Jean
*FRANKEL. Adventure in Alaska
————Rodeo Roundup
*GELMAN. Baseball Bonus Fun

---

*Titles marked with an asterisk are annotated in the main text of this book.

LAKLAN. Nancy Kimball, Nurse's Aide
*MORSE. Judy North, Drum Majorette
PARKER. Carol Heiss: Olympic Queen
PEARSON. Pony for the Sioux
*PHILLIPS. Lightning on Ice
*SEE. The Jungle Secret
*SENSENEY. Austin of the Air Force
*_____Scanlon of the Sub Service
SIMON. North Pole
*TOWNSEND. Dinny and Dreamdust
*WYKOFF. Kendall of the Coast Guard

SIGNATURE BOOKS. (rd3-4) Grosset. $1.95
Lively stories of well-known men and women whose adventures have shaped history. Good for those who do not read well, for the biographies are easy, dramatic, and realistic. Titles include:
BECKHARD, A. J. Dwight D. Eisenhower
HICKOK, L. Franklin D. Roosevelt
*_____Helen Keller (Paper, Scholastic Book Services, 50c)
HOWARD, J. John J. Audubon
_____Robert Louis Stevenson
KAUFMAN, H. L. Beethoven
_____Mozart
MALKUS, A. S. Good Queen Bess
_____Winston Churchill
MEADOWCROFT, E. L. Crazy Horse
NOLAN, J. C. Joan of Arc
*THORNE, A. Madame Curie (Paper, Scholastic Book Services, 50c)
WEBB, R. N. Dan Beard
WILSON, H. Mad Anthony Wayne

SPORTS ILLUSTRATED LIBRARY. (rd5-6) Lippincott. 90p. $2.95
These books are concerned with both team and individual sports, giving instructions under the advice of successful athletes. Subjects include baseball, basketball, boating, diving, fencing, football, horseback riding, skiing, small-boat sailing, swimming, tennis, wet-fly fishing, and dog training.

TERRIFIC TRIPLE TITLE SERIES. (rd5-6) Watts. $2.95
Collections of short stories on various topics. Titles include:
FENNER. Cowboys, Cowboys, Cowboys
_____Dogs, Dogs, Dogs
_____Fun, Fun, Fun
_____Heroes, Heroes, Heroes

The symbol "rd" accompanied by the figure, in parentheses, following the title in each entry, indicates the estimated grade level of reading difficulty (see p. 18-19).

*Titles marked with an asterisk are annotated in the main text of this book.

———Indians, Indians, Indians
———Pirates, Pirates, Pirates
———Speed, Speed, Speed
FERRIS. Girls, Girls, Girls
HOKE. Jokes, Jokes, Jokes
LEEMING. Riddles, Riddles, Riddles
PRATT. Sport, Sport, Sport (Paper, Pratt, 50c)
SLOANE. Space, Space, Space

THIS IS ——— SERIES. (rd3) Macmillan. $3
Beautiful and informative books on several interesting cities around the world.
Titles, all by Miroslav Sasek, include:

*This Is Edinburgh   This Is Paris
This Is London   This Is Rome
This Is Munich   This Is San Francisco
This Is New York   This Is Venice

TRUE BOOK SERIES. (rdP-3) Childrens. $2
For fact-hungry young minds, here are books about all kinds of things—space.
fun, nature, pets, science, people.
CLARK. True Book of Dinosaurs (rd2)
HARMER. True Book of the Circus (rd2)
LEAVITT. True Book of Tools for Building (rd2)
LEWELLEN. True Book of Airports and Airplanes (rd2)
———True Book of Knights (rdP)
MINER. True Book of Policemen and Firemen (rd1)
PODENDORF. True Book of Animals of Sea and Shore (rd2)
———True Book of Space (rd2)
———True Book of Weeds and Wildflowers (rd2)
PURCELL. True Book of African Animals (rd3)
———True Book of Holidays (rd3)

UNITED STATES BOOKS. (rd4) Whitman. 32p. $1.50
There is one book for each of the fifty states. The picture-story combination
makes a good guide to the states.

WALT DISNEY SERIES. (rd6) Golden. Various prices
Those interested in science will enjoy the beautiful pictures and the accurate
text in these books based on the films. They include, among others:
HABER. Walt Disney's Our Friend the Atom
PLATT. Walt Disney's Secrets of Life

WE-WERE-THERE BOOKS. (rd4-5) Grosset. $1.95
Highlights in history are presented as true-to-life stories in the manner of
news reporting. Titles include:
APPEL. We Were There at the Battle for Bataan
———We Were There With the Klondike Gold Rush
HOLT. We Were There With the California Forty-Niners

---

*Titles marked with an asterisk are annotated in the main text of this book.

KJELGAARD. We Were There at the Oklahoma Land Run
KNIGHT. We Were There at the Normandy Invasion
MALKUS. We Were There at the Battle of Gettysburg
MIERS. We Were There When Washington Won at Yorktown
MUNVES. We Were There at the Opening of the Atomic Era
ORBAAN. We Were There at the Driving of the Golden Spike
STEELE. We Were There on the Oregon Trail
_____We Were There With the Pony Express
STRONG. We Were There With Byrd at the South Pole
SUTTON. We Were There at Pearl Harbor
_____We Were There at the Battles of Lexington and Concord
_____We Were There at the First Airplane Flight
WEBB. We Were There at the Boston Tea Party
*_____We Were There on the Nautilus
_____We Were There With Caesar's Legions
_____We Were There With Richard the Lionhearted in the Crusades.

WHAT IS IT SERIES. (rd1-6) Benefic. 48p. $1.80
There are twelve books at the easiest levels (1-3), the other twenty-six being a little more difficult (4-6). They cover many areas of science, giving basic facts along with interesting, accurate, and colorful illustrations. Very useful for those with reading problems and for adult beginners. Some titles are:

What Is a Bird (rd2)
What Is a Cow (rd3)
What Is a Dinosaur (rd4-6)
What Is a Rodent (rd4-6)
What Is a Season (rd1)
What Is a Simple Machine (rd1)
What Is a Solar System (rd4-6)
What Is a Tree (rd3)
What Is an Atom (rd4-6)
What Is Electronic Communication (rd4-6)
What Is Energy (rd4-6)
What Is Light (rd4-6)
What Is Matter (rd4-6)
What Is the Earth (rd2)

See publisher's catalog for complete list.

WINSTON ADVENTURE BOOKS. (rd6-7) Holt. $1.75-$2.25
A dozen books of dramatized fiction based on facts in American history. Titles include:
*ASHLEY, R. P. The Stolen Train: A Story of the Andrews Raiders (Paper, Scholastic Book Services, 35c)
*BAKER, N. B. Nellie Bly, Reporter (Paper, Scholastic Book Services, 35c)
*FRAZEE, S. Year of the Big Snow

The symbol "rd" accompanied by the figure, in parentheses, following the title in each entry, indicates the estimated grade level of reading difficulty (see p. 18-19).

*Titles marked with an asterisk are annotated in the main text of this book.

WINSTON SCIENCE FICTION SERIES. (rd6-7) Holt. $2.95-$3.50
Stories of science fiction that are dramatic and exciting. Included among the titles are:
*CLARKE, A. C. Dolphin Island (rd7)
*SILVERBERG, R. The Time of the Great Freeze (rd6)

WORLD EXPLORER BOOKS. (rd4) Garrard. 96p. $2.75
Easy-to-read biographies of world-famous people who sought adventure and new horizons. Colorful maps and striking illustrations add to their appeal. Titles include:
DeLEEUW, A. A World Explorer: James Cook
———A World Explorer: Sir Walter Raleigh
GRAVES, C. P. A World Explorer: John Smith
*———A World Explorer: Marco Polo
GROH, L. A World Explorer: Ferdinand Magellan
KAUFMAN, M. D. A World Explorer: Christopher Columbus
MONTGOMERY, E. R. A World Explorer: Hernando De Soto

WORLD LANDMARK BOOKS. (rd4-6) Random. 192p. $1.95
Inviting books, full of adventure, this series tells of events and people who have influenced world history. Some titles are:
*BUCK. The Man Who Changed China
DANIEL. The Story of Albert Schweitzer
DAUGHERTY. The Magna Charta
DAVENPORT. Garibaldi, the Father of Modern Italy
*FERMI. The Story of Atomic Energy
FOSDICK. Martin Luther
GUNTHER. Alexander the Great
HAHN. Leonardo da Vinci
———Mary, Queen of Scots
HORNBLOW. Cleopatra of Egypt
*HUME. Great Men of Medicine
*LECKIE. The War in Korea
NEUBERGER. Royal Canadian Mounted Police
REYNOLDS. The Life of St. Patrick
ROBINSON. King Arthur and His Knights
ROSS. Joan of Arc
*SHIRER. The Rise and Fall of Adolf Hitler
*WHITE. The First Men in the World (Paper, Scholastic Book Services, 35c)
WINWAR. Napoleon and the Battle of Waterloo
Other titles include:
The Battle of Britain
The French Foreign Legion
The Story of Scotland Yard
Will Shakespeare and the Globe Theatre

---

*Titles marked with an asterisk are annotated in the main text of this book.

WORLD OF ADVENTURE SERIES. (rd2-5) Benefic. 72p. $2
An exciting series of modern adventures of great variety. Titles, all by Bamman and Whitehead, include:
City Beneath the Sea (rd4)
Fire on the Mountain (rd3)
Hunting Grizzly Bears (rd3)
*Lost Uranium Mine (rd2)
Sacred Well of Sacrifice (rd5)
Search for Piranha (rd4)

YOU AND _____ SERIES. (rd5) Childrens. $2
Topics of interest to high school pupils appear in these books about atomic energy, space travel, the United Nations, the earth. Typical titles are:
You and Space Neighbors
You and the Constitution of the United States
You and Your Amazing Mind

YOUNG HEROES LIBRARY. (rd6-8) Lantern. Various prices.
These novels for young people include mystery stories, Indian stories, sports stories, and others.

YOUNG READERS BOOKSHELF. (rd4-5) Lantern. $2.75
A series with a variety of short stories on animals, sports, mystery, pioneering. Typical titles are:
Young Readers Baseball Stories
Young Readers Detective Stories
Young Readers Horse Stories
Young Readers Pioneer Stories
Young Readers Sports Treasury

YOUNG SPORTSMAN'S LIBRARY. (rd6) Nelson. 96p. $2.75
A popular series about all kinds of sports, both team and individual, all well illustrated. Typical titles are:
*Anderson. The Young Sportsman's Guide to Baseball
ELLMAN. The Young Sportsman's Guide to Scuba Diving
*GARDNER. The Young Sportsman's Guide to Wrestling
*WEBER and WHITE. The Young Sportsman's Guide to Bowling
Other sports in the series include archery, basketball, camping, canoeing, fly fishing, game birds, golf, ice hockey, ice skating, sailing, skiing, sports car racing, swimming, tennis, and water skiing.

ZIM SCIENCE BOOKS. (rd5-6) Morrow. 64p. $2.50
Beautifully illustrated books with short, simple text on a great variety of science facts.

The symbol "rd" accompanied by the figure, in parentheses, following the title in each entry, indicates the estimated grade level of reading difficulty (see p. 18-19).

*Titles marked with an asterisk are annotated in the main text of this book.

ADAPTED OR SIMPLIFIED EDITIONS

EASY READING SERIES. (rd4-6) (Scott) Whitman.
  These simplified versions preserve much of the interest, plot, excitement, and style of the originals. Some titles in the series are:
  COOPER. The Last of the Mohicans. $2.68
  DEFOE. Robinson Crusoe. $2.68
  DICKENS. David Copperfield. $3.08
  ELIOT. Silas Marner. $2.68
  KIPLING. Captains Courageous. $2.60
  LONDON. Call of the Wild. $2.40
  MELVILLE. Moby Dick. $2.68
  STEVENSON. Treasure Island. $2.76
  TWAIN. Huckleberry Finn. $2.64
  _____The Prince and the Pauper. $2.68
  _____Tom Sawyer. $2.64
  VERNE. Around the World in Eighty Days. $2.76
  _____Twenty Thousand Leagues Under the Sea. $2.76

EVERYREADER LIBRARY (adapted by William Kottmeyer and others). (rd4) McGraw. $1.96 (Paper, 88c)
  Some of the best of the classics put into easy and abridged forms. Illustrations capture the mood and drama of the stories.
  DICKENS, CHARLES. A Tale of Two Cities. 151p.
  DOYLE, SIR ARTHUR CONAN. Cases of Sherlock Holmes. 118p.
  DUMAS, ALEXANDRE. The Count of Monte Cristo. 119p.
  JOHNSTON, MARY. To Have and to Hold. 170p.
  POE, EDGAR ALLAN. The Gold Bug and Other Stories. 119p.
  PYLE, HOWARD. Men of Iron. 136p.
  SCOTT, SIR WALTER. Ivanhoe. 133p.
  WALLACE, LEW. Ben Hur. 138p.

GLOBE READABLE CLASSICS. Globe. $2.80
  Over sixty titles are listed in these adaptations of famous stories, retaining much of the original style. Among the titles are:
  AUSTEN. Pride and Prejudice. (rd6)
  BLACKMORE. Lorna Doone. (rd6)
  BRONTË, C. Jane Eyre. (rd5)
  BRONTË, E. Wuthering Heights. (rd6)
  DEFOE. Robinson Crusoe. (rd5)
  DICKENS. David Copperfield. (rd6)
  _____Great Expectations. (rd6)
  _____Nicholas Nickleby. (rd5)
  _____Oliver Twist. (rd6)

DICKENS. A Tale of Two Cities.† (rd6)
DOYLE. Sherlock Holmes. (rd6)
DUMAS. The Three Musketeers. (rd6)
ELIOT. The Mill on the Floss. (rd6)
————Silas Marner. (rd5)
HAWTHORNE. The House of the Seven Gables. (rd7)
HOMER. The Odyssey. (rd5)
HUGO. Les Misérables. (rd5)
MELVILLE. Moby Dick.† (rd6)
SCOTT. Ivanhoe.† (rd5)
————Kenilworth. (rd6)
STEVENSON. The Black Arrow. (rd6)
————Kidnapped. (rd5)
————Treasure Island.† (rd5)
TWAIN. Connecticut Yankee. (rd6)
VERNE. Twenty Thousand Leagues Under the Sea. (rd4)
† Available from Globe in paperback edition at 99c class price.

HARCOURT, BRACE AND WORLD
Abridged editions of Dickens that retain the suspense, emotion, and reality of the original. Included are:
David Copperfield. (rd7) $2.60
Great Expectations. (rd7) 306p. $2.40
A Tale of Two Cities. (rd7) 239p. $2.40

JUNIOR EVERYREADER LIBRARY (adapted by William Kottmeyer and others). (rd3) McGraw, c1952. (Paper, 88c)
Like the slightly more difficult Everyreader Library, this presents some of the best-loved stories in easy form.

Bob, Son of Battle
Call of the Wild
Greek and Roman Myths
Indian Paint
Jungle Trails

King Arthur and His Knights
Old Testament Stories
Robin Hood Stories
The Trojan War
Wild Animals I Have Known

MODEROW, GERTRUDE, and others. Six Great Stories. (rd4) (Scott) Whitman. $3.28
Adapted versions of six favorite classics with much of the flavor and attraction of the originals:

As You Like It
Gareth and Lynette
The Golden Touch

The Legend of Sleepy Hollow
Rip Van Winkle
Treasure Island

The symbol "rd" accompanied by the figure, in parentheses, following the title in each entry, indicates the estimated grade level of reading difficulty (see p. 18-19).

PLEASURE READING BOOKS. (rd4) Garrard. 176p. $2.75

These books, adapted by Dolch, retell famous stories in easy, interesting fashion. Some of the titles in the series that appeal to junior and senior high school students are:

Bible Stories (from the Old Testament, from Adam and Eve to Daniel)

Famous Stories (from *The Arabian Nights*)

Far East Stories (from Japan to India)

Gospel Stories (from the New Testament)

Greek Stories (Hercules, Jason, Ulysses, and other Greek heroes)

Ivanhoe (adventure and chivalry)

Old World Stories (favorites from western Europe)

Robin Hood Stories (famous outlaw of Sherwood Forest)

Robinson Crusoe (shipwreck and survival favorite)

SANDRUS, MARY Y., and others. Eight Treasured Stories. (rd4-5) (Scott) Whitman. $2.68 (text ed.)

Adapted versions of eight favorite tales with much of the appeal of the originals:

A Christmas Carol	The Legend of Sleepy Hollow
The Golden Touch	The Necklace
The Jumping Frog	Rip Van Winkle
The Lady or the Tiger	Ulysses and the Cyclops

MAGAZINES AND NEWSPAPERS

AMERICAN GIRL. Girl Scouts of the U.S.A., 830 Third Ave., New York 10022. Subscription price, $3 per year
A magazine which includes adventure, mystery, and boarding school stories; also articles on etiquette, athletics, and vocations.

ARIZONA HIGHWAYS. Arizona Highway Dept., 2039 W. Lewis Ave., Phoenix, Ariz. 85009. Subscription price, $4 per year
A travel magazine with superb color photographs and with articles about Indian tribes and reservations, points of scenic interest, etc.

BOYS' LIFE. Boy Scouts of America, New Brunswick, N.J. 08903. Subscription price, $3 per year
The official magazine for all Boy Scouts. Contains stories and miscellaneous articles interesting to high school boys.

CALLING ALL GIRLS. Calling All Girls, 80 New Bridge Rd., Bergenfield, N.J. 07621. Subscription price, $5 for 10 issues
Contains interesting fiction and cartoons. Young adolescent girls (11-14) like it, learn by it, and live by it.

CURRENT BIOGRAPHY. H. W. Wilson Co., 950 University Ave., Bronx, New York 10452. Subscription price, $6 per year
Supplies biographical information about prominent people in every field of contemporary life.

CURRENT EVENTS. (rd6-8) American Education Publications, Education Center, Columbus, Ohio 43216. Subscription price, $1.40 per year (Weekly)
Brings top news at home and abroad in a colorful and varied writing style with a balanced blend of news and features.

CURRENT SCIENCE. (rd7-9) American Education Publications, Education Center, Columbus, Ohio 43216. Subscription price, $1.40 per year (Weekly)
This newspaper brings science texts up to date, relates basic principles to everyday problems, keeps classes in step with each new advance in the march of science.

EBONY. Johnson Publishing Company, 1820 S. Michigan Ave., Chicago 60616. Subscription price, $5 per year
Deals with Negro life. Although it is largely pictorial, it also contains some articles and biographical material.

The symbol "rd" accompanied by the figure, in parentheses, following the title in each entry, indicates the estimated grade level of reading difficulty (see p. 18-19).

ELIZABETHAN. Periodical Publications, Ltd., Rolls House, Breams Buildings, London E.C. 4. Subscription price, $4 per year
The magazine for boys and girls. Contents: fiction, articles, quizzes, book reviews, questions and answers, news of Young Elizabethan Club, information on choosing a career, pages for boys only and for girls only, etc.

EVERY WEEK. American Education Publications, Education Center, Columbus, Ohio 43216. Subscription price, $1.20 per year. Grades 9-10 (Weekly)
Designed for use in world history, civics, and geography classes. Special articles relate text material to current history. Timely features on community civics in the news.

FIELD AND STREAM. Holt, Rinehart & Winston, Inc., 383 Madison Ave., New York 10017. Subscription price, $4 per year
Good coverage of hunting, fishing, camping, and boating through the accounts of personal experiences of sportsmen. Articles on conservation, reports on fish and game laws, and advice on equipment and techniques.

FLYING. Ziff-Davis Publishing Co., 1 Park Ave., New York 10016. Subscription price, $5 per year (Monthly, 60c)
Emphasizes the dramatic and personal aspects of flying with a sprinkling of technical articles. Easy and interesting reading for aviation enthusiasts.

GLAMOUR. Condé-Nast Publications, Inc., 420 Lexington Ave., New York 10017. Subscription price, $5 per year
Contains articles on fashions, beauty aids, brides, jobs, etc. Profusely illustrated.

HOLIDAY. Curtis Publishing Co., Independence Square, Philadelphia 19105. Subscription price, $5.95 per year (Monthly, 60c)
A travel magazine combining beautiful photography with descriptions of cities, regions, and countries. Discussions of fine arts, sports, and other leisure-time pursuits.

HOT ROD MAGAZINE. Petersen Publishing Co., 5959 Hollywood Blvd., Los Angeles 90028. Subscription price, $5 per year
World's most complete hot rod coverage. Information and illustrations on sports and racing cars for the hot rod enthusiast.

JUNIOR NATURAL HISTORY MAGAZINE. American Museum of Natural History, Central Park West at 79th St., New York 10024. Subscription price, $1.50 per year
Simple and attractive. Reading level about third grade. Illustrated with excellent photographs.

LADIES' HOME JOURNAL. Curtis Publishing Co., Independence Square, Philadelphia 19105. Subscription price, $3 per year (Monthly, 35c)
Many of the light novels so useful with girls who want stories simple in style but mature in content appear in women's magazines like this. Also appeals through articles on home care, manners, cooking, sewing, etc.

LIFE. Time, Inc., Time & Life Bldg., Rockefeller Center, New York 10020. Subscription price, $7.75 per year
One of several magazines appealing to reluctant readers largely through pictures.

MECHANIX ILLUSTRATED. Fawcett Publications, Inc., Subscription Dept., Fawcett Bldg., Greenwich, Conn. 06830. Subscription price, $3 per year (25c per copy)
Short articles and illustrations in the fields of mechanics, science, and outdoor life. Contents also include money-making ideas, new ideas for the home and shop, gadgets, etc. The how-to-do magazine that makes leisure hours more profitable and more fun.

METRONOME. Metronome Corp., 276 W. 43d St., New York 10036. Subscription price, $3.50 per year
Covers the field of modern music. Reviews films, radio programs, new records, and musical events.

MISSILES AND ROCKETS. Circulation Fulfillment Manager, Missiles and Rockets, 1001 Vermont Ave., N.W., Washington, D.C. 20005. Subscription price, $5 per year
The weekly of space systems engineering. Discussions of space electronics, space medicine, and names in the space news.

MODEL AIRPLANE NEWS. Air Age, Inc., 551 Fifth Ave., New York 10017. Subscription price, $5 per year
Many diagrams. Directions not too technical.

MOTOR TREND MAGAZINE. Petersen Publishing Co., 5959 Hollywood Blvd., Los Angeles 90028. Subscription price, $5 per year
One of the winners of the National Safety Council's Public Interest awards. A magazine which emphasizes safety in the design, manufacture, and use of motor vehicles. Efforts to make cars, drivers, highways, and traffic codes safer for all motorists, passengers, and pedestrians.

MY WEEKLY READER. American Education Publications, Education Center, Columbus, Ohio 43216. Subscription price, $1 per year
This little weekly newspaper is issued on six levels of reading difficulty (rd1-6). Even the lower levels often contain articles of interest to adolescents. It makes an excellent transition to adult newspapers.

NATIONAL GEOGRAPHIC MAGAZINE. National Geographic Society, 17th and M Sts., N.W., Washington, D.C. 20036. Subscription price, $8 per year
The color pictures attract all boys and girls. Some read the articles, which are closely related to the topics of the school curriculum.

The symbol "rd" accompanied by the figure, in parentheses, following the title in each entry, indicates the estimated grade level of reading difficulty (see p. 18-19).

NATURAL HISTORY. American Museum of Natural History, Central Park West at 79th St., New York 10024. Subscription price, $5 per year
A magazine primarily for adults, but often read by young naturalists of high school age. Many articles and illustrations pertaining to nature. It now includes the former *Nature Magazine*.

NEWSWEEK. Newsweek, Inc., 444 Madison Ave., New York 10022. Subscription price, $8 per year
Easier reading than *Time*. Useful in both junior and senior high schools.

OUR DUMB ANIMALS. Massachusetts Society for the Prevention of Cruelty to Animals, 180 Longwood Ave., Boston 02115. Subscription price, $2 per year; for clubs of 5 or more, $1.50
A monthly magazine containing interesting, easy-to-read articles about animals, and, in addition, poetry and photographs. An attractive feature is poetry and other material contributed by young readers.

OUR TIMES. American Education Publications, Education Center, Columbus, Ohio 43216. Subscription price, $1.20 per year. Grades 11-12 (Weekly) ($1 per year for 10 or more)
A mature paper for high school students of American history, economics, advanced civics, and senior problems courses. The news in brief, current personalities, etc.

OUTDOOR LIFE. Popular Science Publishing Co., Inc., 355 Lexington Ave., New York 10017. Subscription price, $4 per year
Accounts of sportsmen's experiences in hunting, big-game expeditions, and fishing. Color photography. Popular with junior high school boys for personal reading.

PLAYS: THE DRAMA MAGAZINE FOR YOUNG PEOPLE. Plays, Inc., 8 Arlington St., Boston 02116. Subscription price, $6 per school year
A magazine for young people of all ages, bringing each month twelve royalty-free plays that can be used to celebrate holidays and special occasions, to entertain, to instruct, and to improve reading skill.

POPULAR ELECTRONICS. Ziff-Davis Publishing Co., 1 Park Ave., New York 10016. Subscription price, $4 per year
Extremely popular magazine that keeps you up to date on electronic developments and hi-fi. Includes experiments and do-it-yourself projects. Easy-to-follow plans and articles for the electronics tinkerer, experimenter, and hobbyist.

POPULAR MECHANICS. Popular Mechanics Co., 575 Lexington Ave., New York 10022. Subscription price, $4 per year
Very well liked. Eagerly awaited by boys from the sixth grade through senior high school. Contains up-to-the-minute news from the areas of mechanics, science, and inventions. Easy-to-follow directions for making practical articles.

POPULAR SCIENCE MONTHLY. Popular Science Publishing Co., 355 Lexington Ave., New York 10017 (Subscription Dept., P.O. Box 1083, Boulder, Colo. 80313). Subscription price, $4 per year (35c per copy)
Much miscellaneous information. Many illustrations. Tips on cars, homes, workbench projects. Space-age features. Almost as well liked as *Popular Mechanics*.

READ MAGAZINE. American Education Publications, Education Center, Columbus, Ohio 43216. Subscription price, $1.75 per school year; $1 per school year for 10 or more copies. Grades 6-9 (Semimonthly)
Designed to suit the interests and the reading range of older boys and girls. Balanced variety of the best in current reading for English and social studies. Helpful in vocabulary development.

READER'S DIGEST. Reader's Digest Association, Inc., Pleasantville, N.Y. 10570. Subscription price, $2.97 per year
Condensed articles from current magazines. Used by good readers as well as slow ones. Approximately sixth-grade level of difficulty.

THE RING. Nat S. Fleischer, Madison Square Garden, 307 W. 49th St., New York 10019. Subscription price, $4 per year
Articles, photographs, and scores for boxing, amateur and professional, all over the country.

ROAD AND TRACK. Western Outdoor Publishing Corp., 325 N. Newport Blvd., Newport Beach, Calif. 92663. Subscription price, $5 per year
"The motor enthusiast's magazine." Contents include information about foreign cars and sports cars, racing news, articles, photographs, etc.

SCHOLASTIC MAGAZINES. Scholastic Magazines, Inc., 904 Sylvan Ave., Englewood Cliffs, N.J. 07632
Junior Scholastic. (rd6-8) Classroom subscription price, $1.25 per year
Literary Cavalcade. (rd10-12) Classroom subscription price, $1.25 per year
News Explorer. (rd4) Classroom subscription price, 50c per year
News Trails. (rd3) Classroom subscription price, 50c per year
Newstime. (rd5-6) Classroom subscription price, 80c per year
Practical English. (rd9-12) Classroom subscription price, $1.50 per year

---

The symbol "rd" accompanied by the figure, in parentheses, following the title in each entry, indicates the estimated grade level of reading difficulty (see p. 18-19).

Science World. (rd7-12)
   Edition I for General Science Classes. Classroom subscription
      price, $1.25 per year
   Edition II for Senior High School Classes in Biology, Chem-
      istry, Physics, Earth, and Space Science. Classroom sub-
      scription price, $1.50 per year
Senior Scholastic. (rd10-12) Classroom subscription price, $1.50
   per year
World Week. (rd8-10) Classroom subscription price, $1.50 per
   year

Classroom periodicals offering a variety of current materials to supplement
courses in reading and social studies, current affairs, English, homemaking,
and science. Lesson plans included to aid teaching. Lively writing with many
illustrations.

SEVENTEEN. Seventeen, Subscription Dept., Radnor, Pa. 19088. Subscription price, $6 per year

A "slick" for teen-age girls, with articles on hygiene, current affairs, manners,
clothes, food, etc. Stories are sometimes a bit difficult, but the articles are both
straightforward in style and sound in matter. The numerous advertisements of
clothes attract all girls, and most of them read parts of the articles.

SKIN DIVER. Petersen Publishing Co., 5959 Hollywood Blvd., Los Angeles 90028. Subscription price, $4 per year

For underwater enthusiasts. Gives information on skin diving and underwater
spearfishing. News of fishing, diving equipment and apparatus.

SPORT. Macfadden-Bartell Corp., 205 E. 42d St., New York 10017.
   Subscription price, $4 per year

Magazine for sports spectators which has articles on games and players in
baseball, basketball, boxing, tennis, ice hockey, golf, and dog racing.

SPORTS ILLUSTRATED. Time, Inc., Time & Life Bldg., Rockefeller Center, New York 10020. Subscription price, $7.50 per year

Coverage of the various sports: football, baseball, basketball, track, golf, horse
shows, motor sports, the Olympics. etc. News of prominent people in the sports
world. Many illustrations and color photographs.

TODAY'S HEALTH. American Medical Association, 535 N. Dearborn
   St., Chicago 60610. Subscription price, $4 per year

Information about common diseases and treatment, medical discoveries, nutrition, and child care. Cartoons, articles, and brief columns of advice. Very
readable style.

SIMPLIFIED DICTIONARIES

COURTIS, STUART A., and WATTERS, GARNETTE. The Courtis-Watters Illustrated Dictionary for Young Readers. (rd4) Golden, c1956 (rev. ed.). 544p. $4.95

An inviting book, aimed at capturing interest in words and helping the growth of the independent reader.

MOORE, LILIAN. The Golden Picture Dictionary. (rd3) Golden, c1954 (rev. ed.). 80p. $1.50

A combination of familiar and new vocabulary gives first aid in reading and spelling while also supplying new ideas and new meanings.

REED, MARY, and OSSWALD, EDITH. My First Little Golden Dictionary. (rd1-3) Golden, c1957 (rev. ed.). Unp. $1.99

A good first dictionary and helpful to the beginning reader.

RICHARDS, I. A., and GIBSON, C. M. English Through Pictures. (rd1) Washington Square, c1959. 286p. (2 vols.) Paper, 45c

A self-learning text in two volumes, designed to help the reader when teacher aid is not available. Simple drawings illustrate the basic English words and phrases. Especially helpful to the beginner for whom English is a second language.

THORNDIKE, E. L., and BARNHART, CLARENCE L. Thorndike-Barnhart Beginning Dictionary. (rd3) Scott, c1962 (rev. ed.). 720p. $4
_____Thorndike-Barnhart Junior Dictionary. (rd5) Scott, c1962 (rev. ed.). 784p. $4.50

Simplified definitions illustrated in sentences and pictures arranged in a way that is planned to aid the learner. Also helpful with spelling.

WALPOLE, ELLEN W., ed. The Golden Dictionary. (rd2) Golden, c1944. 96p. $2.95

A picture dictionary helpful in increasing skill in understanding meanings.

WERNER, ELSA JANE. The Golden Picture Book of Words. (rd2-3) Golden, c1954. Unp. $1.50

This is especially helpful in building a good vocabulary.

WRIGHT, WENDELL W. Rainbow Dictionary. (rd3) World, c1959 (rev. ed.). 433p. $4.95

The 2,300 words are based on frequency counts in eight word lists for children, and are taught in context.

The symbol "rd" accompanied by the figure, in parentheses, following the title in each entry, indicates the estimated grade level of reading difficulty (see p. 18-19).

DIRECTORY OF PUBLISHERS
AND DISTRIBUTORS

Abelard. Abelard-Schuman, Ltd., 6 W. 57th St., New York 10019
Abingdon. Abingdon Press, 201 Eighth Ave. S., Nashville, Tenn. 37203
Abrams. Harry N. Abrams, Inc., 6 W. 57th St., New York 10019
Affiliated. Affiliated Publishers, 630 Fifth Ave., New York 10020
American Book. American Book Company, 55 Fifth Ave., New York 10003
Ariel. Ariel Books. See Farrar
Association. Association Press, 291 Broadway, New York 10007
Atheneum. Atheneum Publishers, 162 E. 38th St., New York 10016
Avon. Avon Books (Div. of Hearst Corp.), 959 Eighth Ave., New York 10019

Bantam. Bantam Books, Inc., 271 Madison Ave., New York 10016
Barnes. A. S. Barnes-Thomas Yoseloff, Box 421, Cranbury, N.J. 08512
Basic. Basic Books, Inc., Publishers, 404 Park Ave. S., New York 10016
Beckley. Beckley-Cardy Company, 1900 N. Narragansett, Chicago 60639
Benefic. Benefic Press. See Beckley
Bennett. Charles A. Bennett Co., Inc., 237 N.E. Monroe St., Peoria, Ill. 61602
Berkley. Berkley Publishing Corporation, 15 E. 26th St., New York 10010
Binfords. Binfords & Mort, 2505 S.E. 11th Ave., Portland, Ore. 97242
Bobbs. The Bobbs-Merrill Co., Inc., 4300 W. 62d St., Indianapolis, Ind. 46206

Capitol. Capitol Publishing Co., Inc., 850 Third Ave., New York 10020
Caxton. The Caxton Printers, Ltd., Caldwell, Idaho 83605
Childrens. Childrens Press, Inc., 1224 W. Van Buren St., Chicago 60612
Chilton. Chilton Books, Trade Book Division, 227 S. 6th St., Philadelphia 19106
Coward. Coward-McCann, Inc., 200 Madison Ave., New York 10016
Criterion. Criterion Books, Inc., 6 W. 57th St., New York 10019
Crowell. Thomas Y. Crowell Company, 201 Park Ave. S., New York 10003

Day. The John Day Company, 62 W. 45th St., New York 10036
Dell. Dell Publishing Co., Inc., 750 Third Ave., New York 10017
Dodd. Dodd, Mead & Co., 432 Park Ave. S., New York 10016
Donohue. M. A. Donohue & Co., 711 S. Dearborn St., Chicago 60605
Doubleday. Doubleday & Company, Inc., 501 Franklin Ave., Garden City, N.Y. 11530
Duell. Duell, Sloan & Pearce, 60 E. 42d St., New York 10017
Dutton. E. P. Dutton & Co., Inc., 201 Park Ave. S., New York 10003

E.D.L. See Educational Development Laboratories, Inc.
Educational Development Laboratories, Inc., 284 Pulaski Rd., Huntington, N.Y. 11744
English Language Research, Inc., 13 Kirkland St., Cambridge, Mass. 02138

Farrar. Farrar, Straus & Giroux, Inc., 19 Union Square W., New York 10003
Fawcett. Fawcett Publications, Inc., Fawcett Pl., Greenwich, Conn. 06830
Fideler. The Fideler Company, 31 Ottawa Ave., N.W., Grand Rapids, Mich.
     49502
Follett. Follett Publishing Company, 1010 W. Washington Blvd., Chicago
     60607
Friendship. Friendship Press, 475 Riverside Dr., New York 10027
Funk. Funk & Wagnalls Co., Inc., 360 Lexington Ave., New York 10017

Garrard. Garrard Publishing Co., 862 Scarsdale Ave., Scarsdale, N.Y. 10583
Globe. Globe Book Company, Inc., 175 Fifth Ave., New York 10010
Golden. Golden Press, Inc., 850 Third Ave., New York 10023
Grosset. Grosset & Dunlap, Inc., 51 Madison Ave., New York 10010

Harcourt. Harcourt, Brace & World, Inc., 757 Third Ave., New York 10017
Harper. Harper & Row, Publishers, 49 E. 33d St., New York 10016
Harr Wagner. Harr Wagner Publishing Co., 609 Mission St., San Francisco
     94105
Hastings. Hastings House, Publishers, Inc., 151 E. 50th St., New York 10022
Hawthorn. Hawthorn Books, Inc., 70 Fifth Ave., New York 10011
Heath. D. C. Heath & Company, 285 Columbus Ave., Boston 02116
Hill. Hill & Wang, Inc., 141 Fifth Ave., New York 10010
Holiday. Holiday House, Inc., 8 W. 13th St., New York 10011
Holt. Holt, Rinehart & Winston, Inc., 383 Madison Ave., New York 10017
Houghton. Houghton Mifflin Company, 2 Park St., Boston 02107

Knopf. Alfred A. Knopf, Inc., 501 Madison Ave., New York 10022
Knox. John Knox Press, Box 1176, Richmond, Va. 23209

Laidlaw. Laidlaw Brothers, Thatcher and Madison Sts., River Forest, Ill.
     60305
Lantern. Lantern Press, Inc., 257 Park Ave S., New York 10010
Lippincott. J. B. Lippincott Co., E. Washington Square, Philadelphia 19105
Little. Little, Brown and Company, 34 Beacon St., Boston 02106
Longmans. Longmans, Green & Co., Inc. See McKay
Lothrop. Lothrop, Lee & Shepard Co., 419 Park Ave. S., New York 10016
Lyons. Lyons & Carnahan, 407 E. 25th St., Chicago 60616

McGraw. McGraw-Hill Book Company, Inc., 330 W. 42d St., New York 10036
McKay. David McKay Co., Inc., 750 Third Ave., New York 10017
Macmillan. The Macmillan Company, 60 Fifth Ave., New York 10011
Maco. Maco Magazine Corporation, 1012 W. Washington Blvd., Chicago
     60607
Macrae. Macrae Smith Co., 225 S. 15th St., Philadelphia 19102
Maxton. Maxton Publishing Corporation, 1012 W. Washington Blvd., Chicago
     60607
Melmont. Melmont Publishers, Inc. See Childrens
Mentor. Mentor Books. See New American Library
Meredith. Meredith Press, 1716 Locust St., Des Moines, Iowa 50303
Merrill. Charles E. Merrill Books, Inc., 1300 Alum Creek Dr., Columbus,
     Ohio 43216
Messner. Julian Messner, 8 W. 40th St., New York 10018

Military Publishing Institute. See Stackpole
Modern Library, Inc., 457 Madison Ave., New York 10022
Morrow. William Morrow & Co., Inc., 425 Park Ave. S., New York 10016

Nelson. Thomas Nelson & Sons, 18 E. 41st St., New York 10017 (Write to Nelson-National, Copewood and Davis Sts., Camden, N.J. 08103)
New American Library. New American Library of World Literature, Inc., 1301 Ave. of the Americas, New York 10019 (For hard-cover editions, see World Publishing Company.)
New York University Press, 32 Washington Pl., New York 10003
Noble. Noble & Noble, Publishers, Inc., 67 Irving Pl., New York 10003
Norton. W. W. Norton & Company, Inc., 55 Fifth Ave., New York 10003

Obolensky. Ivan Obolensky, Inc., 1114 First Ave., New York 10021 (Send orders to World Publishing Company.)
Oxford. Oxford University Press, Inc., 417 Fifth Ave., New York 10016

Pantheon. Pantheon Books, Inc., 22 E. 51st St., New York 10022
Parnassus. Parnassus Press, 2422 Ashby Ave., Berkeley, Calif. 94705
Pauper. Peter Pauper Press, 629 N. McQuesten Pkwy., Mount Vernon, N.Y. 10552
Penguin. Penguin Books, Inc., 3300 Clipper Mill Rd., Baltimore, Md. 21211
Penns Valley. Penns Valley Publishers, Inc., 102 S. Allen St., State College, Pa. 16801
Permabook. Permabooks (Pocket Books, Inc.). See Affiliated
Phonovisual. Phonovisual Products, Inc., 4708 Wisconsin Ave. N.W., Washington, D.C. 20016
Platt. Platt & Munk, Inc., 200 Fifth Ave., New York 10010
Plays, Inc., 8 Arlington St., Boston 02116
Pocket. Pocket Books, Inc. (Order from Affiliated Publishers.)
Pratt. J. Lowell Pratt & Co., Inc., Publishers, 15 E. 48th St., New York 10017
Prentice. Prentice-Hall, Inc., Englewood Cliffs, N.J. 07632
Puffin. See Penguin
Putnam. G. P. Putnam's Sons, 200 Madison Ave., New York 10016
Pyramid. Pyramid Publications, Inc., 444 Madison Ave., New York 10022

Rand McNally. Rand McNally & Co., Box 7600, Chicago 60680
Random. Random House, Inc., 457 Madison Ave., New York 10022
Reader's Digest Services, Inc., Educational Division, Pleasantville, N.Y. 10570
Regents. Regents Publishing Co., Inc., 200 Park Ave. S., New York 10003
Reilly. The Reilly & Lee Co., 114 W. Illinois St., Chicago 60610
Ridge. The Ridge Press, Inc., 17 E. 45th St., New York 10017
Riverside. Riverside Literature Series. See Houghton

S.R.A. See Science Research Associates
St. Martin. St. Martin's Press, Inc., 175 Fifth Ave., New York 10010
Scholastic Book Services, 904 Sylvan Ave., Englewood Cliffs, N.J. 07632
Science Research Associates, Inc., 259 E. Erie St., Chicago 60611
Scott. Scott, Foresman & Company, 433 E. Erie St., Chicago 60611
Scott, W. R. William R. Scott, Inc., 333 Ave. of the Americas, New York 10014
Scribner. Charles Scribner's Sons, 597 Fifth Ave., New York 10017 (Order from Vreeland Ave., Boro of Totowa, Paterson, N.J. 07512)

Seabury. The Seabury Press, Inc., 815 Second Ave., New York 10017
Simon & Schuster. Simon and Schuster, Inc., 630 Fifth Ave., New York 10020
Stackpole. The Stackpole Co., Telegraph Press Bldg., Cameron and Kelker
   Sts., Harrisburg, Pa. 17105
Steck. Steck-Vaughn Company, Box 2028, Austin, Tex. 78767
Stein. Stein & Day Publishers, 7 E. 48th St., New York 10017
Sterling. Sterling Publishing Co., Inc., 419 Park Ave. S., New York 10016

Teachers College. Teachers College, Bureau of Publications, Columbia Uni-
   versity, 525 W. 120th St., New York 10027
Transatlantic. Transatlantic Arts, Inc., Hollywood-by-the-Sea, Fla. 33020
Tuttle. Charles E. Tuttle Co., Inc., 28 S. Main St., Rutland, Vt. 05701

U.S. Armed Forces Inst. United States Armed Forces Institute, Madison, Wis.
   53703

Vanguard. Vanguard Press, Inc., 424 Madison Ave., New York 10017
Van Nostrand. D. Van Nostrand Co., Inc., 120 Alexander St., Princeton, N.J.
   08540
Viking. The Viking Press, Inc., 628 Madison Ave., New York 10022

Walck. Henry Z. Walck, Inc., 19 Union Square, New York 10003
Washburn. Ives Washburn, Inc., 750 Third Ave., New York 10018
Washington Square. Washington Square Press, Inc. See Pocket
Watts. Franklin Watts, Inc., 575 Lexington Ave., New York 10022
Webster. Webster Publishing. See McGraw
Westminster. The Westminster Press, Witherspoon Bldg., Philadelphia 19107
Whiteside, Inc. See Morrow
Whitman. Albert Whitman & Co., 560 W. Lake St., Chicago 60606
Winston. John C. Winston Company. See Holt
World. The World Book Company. See Harcourt
World Publishing Company, 2231 W. 110th St., Cleveland, Ohio 44102

AUTHOR INDEX*

* Authors of Books in Series, listed on p. 144-168, are not included in this index. Authors of Reading Texts and Workbooks series, listed on p. 134-143, are included.

TITLE INDEX*

* This index contains all titles in all sections, including the series titles listed on p. 144-168 and the individual titles of books in those series.

INDEX TO GRADE LEVEL OF READING DIFFICULTY*

* The symbol "rd" accompanied by the figure indicates the grade level of reading difficulty (see p. 18-19).

rd4

rd6